PRACTICAL MATH
FOR BUSINESS

ALAN R. CURTIS

Quinsigamond Community College
Worcester, Massachusetts

PRACTICAL MATH
FOR BUSINESS

SECOND EDITION

HOUGHTON MIFFLIN COMPANY • BOSTON
Dallas   Geneva, Illinois   Hopewell, New Jersey   Palo Alto   London

Cartoons by Jack Reilly.

Library of Congress Catalog Card Number: 77-073944

ISBN: 0-395-25431-0

CONTENTS

INVENTORY

MATH BOOKS

PREFACE

Practical Math for Business offers a new, more stimulating way of learning a traditional business subject. It surveys basic fundamentals of math step-by-step, always applying them to actual business situations and problems. This shows the student how to reach practical solutions to mathematical problems that arise daily in the various areas of a business career.

Every chapter begins with a summary of key points covered in the chapter. Then a short minicase, accompanied by a student-oriented illustration, depicts the topics covered in the chapter. Each chapter has several sections containing one or more projects in which the student may gain valuable practice by working with the mathematical skills just learned. The text proceeds from easy to more difficult material, starting with a substantial review of arithmetic. A chapter on the basics of algebra is also included for those who may need it. Applications of business math as used in accounting, finance, management, consumer economics, and the rapidly growing field of retailing round out the text.

The second edition of the student text features all new project pages, minicases, and problems. Two additional homework projects have been included, while other projects have been revised to help the student learn the material more effectively. A section on the metric system has been added to Chapter 4, Basic Math: Part Two.

My thanks go to the many faculty members who helped to make this book successful, especially Russell K. Davis, III, of the University of Akron.

Finally, I cannot thank enough my wife, Merlene Curtis, for typing the manuscript and for her patience and cooperation throughout the writing period of both editions. Donald, Deborah, and Linda—our children—also deserve our thanks for their patience.

A.R.C.

PRACTICAL MATH FOR BUSINESS

UNIT PRICE?

1 BASIC MATH: PART ONE

KEY POINTS TO LEARN FROM THIS CHAPTER

1. **How to do basic arithmetic more accurately and quickly**

2. **How to check your arithmetic**

3. **How to handle common and decimal fractions**

4. **How to use aliquot parts as short cuts in arithmetic**

MINICASE

Let's listen in on the first day of the semester at Your Community College in a mathematics of business class.

"Do we have to study arithmetic again?"

"I have had arithmetic for the past twelve years. I don't want it anymore!"

The instructor, Patricia Luitjens, is trying to explain why a quick review even at this level would be helpful in improving accuracy and increasing speed—two points regarded as basic requirements for most positions in the business world. "We are not trying to reteach the same old arithmetic, but rather increase your speed and accuracy. Furthermore, a recent study funded by the U.S. Department of Health, Education, and Welfare has found that both teenagers and adults are very deficient in the skills necessary to perform the day-to-day purchasing and financial problems they face. Let's look at some of the statistics from this study:

Test	Accuracy (approximate)
Unit price of a box of rice	Males (43%); females (31%)
Unit price of canned tuna	Males (49%); females (38%)
Cost of financing a new car	17-year-olds (56%); adults (68%)
Door-to-door sales representative's commission	17-year-olds (37%); adults (57%)
Cooking time for a turkey	17-year-olds (35%); adults (42%)

"In addition, they couldn't calculate a taxi fare, balance a checkbook, or judge the best food buy. So let's get on with our important review of arithmetic."

1

A. FOUR BASIC ARITHMETIC PROCESSES

Addition is the process of combining numbers of the same kind. Measures like dollars and miles cannot be added because they are two different things.

ADDITION

To improve accuracy and speed in addition, remember to:

1. *Use clear, neat writing.* Line up the digits of each number one directly under the other, units under units, tens under tens, and so on.

```
  1
 37
245
 89
  6
```

2. *Combine numbers that total 10.* (Tens are easier to add.) Train yourself to spot these combinations in any column of numbers you are adding.

$$
\left.\begin{matrix}6\\5\\2\\3\end{matrix}\right\} \rightarrow 10
$$
$$
\left.\begin{matrix}9\\1\end{matrix}\right\} \rightarrow 10
$$
$$
\left.\begin{matrix}8\\2\end{matrix}\right\} \rightarrow 10
$$
$$
\overline{36}
$$

3. *Leave out unnecessary words as you combine numbers in your mind.* Don't name the number to be added every time; name only the sum. In the example above, don't say $6 + 10 = 16$ plus $10 = 26$ plus $10 = 36$. Instead, say 16, 26, 36.

4. *Add in pairs.* Train yourself to add two figures at a time, and add their sum to the previous total as you go down the column.

$$
\left.\begin{matrix}5\\4\end{matrix}\right\} \longrightarrow 9
$$
$$
\left.\begin{matrix}7\\3\end{matrix}\right\} \xrightarrow{(10)} 19
$$
$$
\left.\begin{matrix}8\\6\end{matrix}\right\} \xrightarrow{(14)} 33
$$
$$
\left.\begin{matrix}1\\2\end{matrix}\right\} \xrightarrow{(3)} 36
$$
$$
\overline{36}
$$

5. *Use multiplication when a number is repeated many times.* In the example below, 7 occurs four times and 6 three times in the hundreds column.

```
724    The sum of the hundreds column may be found as
785    follows:
773        carry      4
748        4 × 7     28
696        3 × 6     18
687                  50
679
5,092
```

6. *Record addition by columns.* This method saves time. Add each column separately, setting the sum one place farther to the left each time. After the last column has been added, add the individual sums in regular order (from right to left).

```
 4,572
 3,986
 2,173
 5,911
 2,765
 4,937
    24
    32
    40
    20
24,344
```

7. *Check your work carefully.* Ways of doing this will be discussed in Section B.

SUBTRACTION

Subtraction is the process of finding the difference between two like numbers by taking one (the *subtrahend*) from the other (the *minuend*). The answer is the *remainder*. Many errors in subtraction occur in "borrowing." Borrowing from the next higher order must be remembered. For example,

```
 7,436     To 6 add 10, then subtract 9:              1
-3,569                                             7,436
 3,867                                            -3,569
                                                       7
```

```
                                                       1
            Next reduce the 3 by 1 (to 2), add 10 and sub-    2
            tract 6:                              7,436
                                                 -3,569
                                                      67
```

```
                                                       1
            Now reduce 4 by 1 (to 3), add 10, and sub-    3
            tract 5:                             7,436
                                                -3,569
                                                    867
```

```
            Finally, reduce the 7 by 1 (to 6), and subtract    6
            3:                                    7,436
                                                 -3,569
                                                   3,867
```

Addition and subtraction are closely related. In fact, cashiers make change (a form of subtraction) by adding. If Jones gives Smith, the druggist, three $1 bills for a purchase of $2.54, Smith will place the bills on the shelf of the cash register and begin to count: $2.54 (purchase price), $2.55 (one penny), $2.75 (two dimes), $3.00 (one quarter). As he counts, he takes the 46¢ from the register, and gives them to Jones. He has added to the purchase price until he arrived at the $3.00 Jones gave him.

MULTIPLICATION

Multiplication is the process of adding one number (the *multiplicand*) to itself as many times as there are units in another number (the *multiplier*). The answer is called the *product*.

You can improve your speed and accuracy in multiplication if you remember the following suggestions:

1. *To multiply by 10, 100, or 1,000*: Add the number of zeros in the multiplier to the multiplicand.

$$628 \times 10 = 6,280$$
$$628 \times 100 = 62,800$$
$$628 \times 1,000 = 628,000$$

2. *To multiply by other numbers that end in zero*: When multiplying other numbers that end in zero, first multiply by the numbers preceding the zeros (disregard all end-of-number zeros); then add those end-of-number zeros to the product.

```
  3,400
 ×380
  272
102
1,292 + 3 zeros = 1,292,000
```

3. *To multiply by 25*: Add two zeros to the multiplicand, and then divide by 4. (This is really multiplying by 100 and then dividing by 4; $100 \div 4 = 25$.)

$$7,562 \times 25$$

```
    189,050
 4)756,200
```

4. *To multiply by 15*: Add a zero to the multiplicand; divide that figure by 2; then add these two numbers together (10, plus half of 10, or 5, equals 15).

$$8,435 \times 15$$

```
  84,350
 +42,175
 126,525
```

DIVISION

Division is the process of finding how many times one number (the *divisor*) is contained in another number (the *dividend*). The result is the *quotient*.

The work of division can be made easier by using multiplication, especially when dividing by 25 or 50. To divide 2,300 by 25, divide the dividend by 100 (thus dropping two zeros), and multiply the result by 4. If the divisor is 50, divide the dividend by 100 and multiply by 2.

Projects 1 and 2 may be done now.

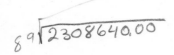

PROJECT 1   ADDITION

Find the sum of each example. Problems 22 and 23 should be added both horizontally and vertically. Work as quickly as you can, using the suggestions given in the chapter.

1.		2.		3.		4.		5.	
	463		557		834		8,649		1,836
	384		648		175		7,580		2,954
	299		300		934		9,750		7,038
	302		419		746		7,379		8,694
	237		568		865		2,597		4,985
	48		299		239		7,672		7,672
	_1733_		_2791_		_3793_		_43627_		_33179_

6.		7.		8.		9.	
	67,179		47,125		967,981		678,675
	40,251		16,501		500,100		594,389
	89,908		17,921		616,668		519,005
	15,516		34,548		839,378		845,652
	61,902		78,924		391,200		838,440
	20,660		77,329		344,546		571,918
	66,509		11,239		934,216		950,006
	91,673		83,291		361,459		821,002
	23,129		45,803		782,226		314,849
	65,423		78,106		237,780		772,681
	_542150_		_490787_		_5975554_		_6906617_

10.		11.		12.		13.	
	28,401		58,711		47,518		39,826
	74,472		92,195		54,258		48,768
	11,121		76,665		87,503		87,986
	47,284		45,237		18,920		24,379
	92,587		89,281		27,171		65,478
	34,135		50,401		12,131		24,329
	21,199		35,542		58,409		69,487
	66,287		55,667		47,284		74,538
	91,675		20,096		31,834		29,356
	48,462		16,165		77,145		86,749
	_515623_		_539960_		_462173_		_550896_

7

14.	$ 31.48	15.	$ 98.23	16.	$ 75.50	17.	$ 38.65
	89.02		75.02		86.75		8.42
	77.97		80.12		93.29		78.98
	60.83		73.61		47.99		98.90
	37.48		20.01		24.89		87.24
	44.17		60.99		6.79		23.17
	8.69		88.53		98.17		29.56
	84.11		32.55		35.76		94.38
	98.96		2.98		12.75		47.93
	57.62		44.36		42.01		98.75
	590.33		*576.40*		*523.90*		*605.98*

18.	4,268	19.	4,122	20.	4,790	21.	4,238
	3,576		3,219		3,548		7,284
	4,386		8,217		2,459		8,372
	3,878		6,984		6,245		7,889
	5,482		2,732		6,723		5,867
	7,342		1,297		7,825		9,210
	9,297		7,986		8,642		8,757
	3,621		1,578		3,887		6,981
	5,428		1,226		6,825		2,867
	2,135		6,125		9,837		9,829
	6,421		8,368		4,218		8,761
	3,768		2,178		9,765		5,680
	59602		*54032*		*74764*		*85735*

22.

$$39 + 57 + 45 + 63 = 204$$
$$83 + 37 + 29 + 34 = 183$$
$$28 + 21 + 32 + 28 = 109$$
$$150 \quad 115 \quad 106 \quad 135 \quad 496$$

23.

$$345 + 254 + 829 = 1428$$
$$698 + 736 + 847 = 2281$$
$$378 + 574 + 925 = 1877$$
$$694 + 692 + 381 = 1767$$
$$2115 \quad 2256 \quad 2982 \quad 7353$$

PROJECT 2 SUBTRACTION; MULTIPLICATION; DIVISION

Perform the indicated operations as quickly as you can. Follow the suggestions given earlier for speed and accuracy.

min.
sub.
Rem

1. $\begin{array}{r} 32,145 \\ -30,646 \\ \hline 1,499 \end{array}$	2. $\begin{array}{r} 19,854 \\ -10,975 \\ \hline 8879 \end{array}$	3. $\begin{array}{r} 300,000 \\ -198,459 \\ \hline 101,541 \end{array}$	4. $\begin{array}{r} 350,000 \\ -296,028 \\ \hline 53972 \end{array}$
5. $\begin{array}{r} 56,275 \\ -43,289 \\ \hline 12,986 \end{array}$	6. $\begin{array}{r} 38,950 \\ -21,845 \\ \hline 17,105 \end{array}$	7. $\begin{array}{r} 549,241 \\ -127,887 \\ \hline 421354 \end{array}$	8. $\begin{array}{r} 975,662 \\ -678,558 \\ \hline 297104 \end{array}$
9. $\begin{array}{r} 67,457 \\ -31,579 \\ \hline 35878 \end{array}$	10. $\begin{array}{r} 36,373 \\ -21,819 \\ \hline 33554 \end{array}$	11. $\begin{array}{r} 554,055 \\ -324,706 \\ \hline 229349 \end{array}$	12. $\begin{array}{r} 564,663 \\ -230,507 \\ \hline 334156 \end{array}$
13. $\begin{array}{r} 24,454 \\ -13,907 \\ \hline 10547 \end{array}$	14. $\begin{array}{r} 68,457 \\ -34,138 \\ \hline 34319 \end{array}$	15. $\begin{array}{r} 754,345 \\ -224,596 \\ \hline 529749 \end{array}$	16. $\begin{array}{r} 597,138 \\ -348,379 \\ \hline 248759 \end{array}$
17. $\begin{array}{r} 73,654 \\ -24,347 \\ \hline 49307 \end{array}$	18. $\begin{array}{r} 89,838 \\ -32,329 \\ \hline 57509 \end{array}$	19. $\begin{array}{r} 985,430 \\ -565,466 \\ \hline 419964 \end{array}$	20. $\begin{array}{r} 567,451 \\ -324,763 \\ \hline 242688 \end{array}$
21. $\begin{array}{r} 80,742 \\ -73,656 \\ \hline 7086 \end{array}$	22. $\begin{array}{r} 67,067 \\ -45,408 \\ \hline 21659 \end{array}$	23. $\begin{array}{r} 329,300 \\ -102,507 \\ \hline 226793 \end{array}$	24. $\begin{array}{r} 504,548 \\ -388,796 \\ \hline 115752 \end{array}$

9

In the problems below, where necessary rearrange the numbers to follow suggestions given for short cuts. Carry all quotients to three decimal places, then round off to two places.

25. $\begin{array}{r} 6,432 \\ \times 554 \end{array}$ 26. $\begin{array}{r} 3,829 \\ \times 413 \end{array}$ 27. $\begin{array}{r} 0.0563 \\ \times 3.74 \end{array}$ 28. $\begin{array}{r} 509 \\ \times 407 \end{array}$

3563328   *1,581,3.77*   *.210562*   *207163*

29. $\begin{array}{r} 72,080 \\ \times 6,000 \end{array}$ 30. $\begin{array}{r} 65,007 \\ \times 4,900 \end{array}$ 31. $\begin{array}{r} 8,759 \\ \times 57 \end{array}$ 32. $\begin{array}{r} 5,972 \\ \times 28 \end{array}$

43,248000   *61,106,580*   *499263*   *167216*

33. $18,000 \div 50$ 34. $4,475 \div 25$ 35. $37\overline{)135,124}$

360   *179*   *3652*

36. $89\overline{)2,308,640.000}$ 37. $0.057\overline{)0.0004731}$

2,5939,775.28   *0.01*

38. $35.89\overline{)947.496}$ 39. $33.165 \div 50$ 40. $0.972 \div 25$

264   *.6633*   *0.03888*

.664

B. HOW TO CHECK YOUR WORK

It helps to know how to do these basic operations easily, accurately, and speedily, and also to know how to check your answers quickly. Checking insures accuracy, but it should take a minimum of time, because it cuts down your productivity as an employee.

ADDITION

Checking addition is done by adding each column in reverse order. A good habit is always to add in one direction (either always up or always down), and then to check in the opposite direction. For example, add all the columns *up*, and check by adding *down*; or add down and check by adding up.

SUBTRACTION

A simple and effective way to check subtraction is to add the answer (remainder) to the subtrahend; the sum should be equal to the minuend.

Subtract:

```
  568,432   minuend
 −390,681   subtrahend
  177,751   remainder
```

Check:

```
  390,681   subtrahend
 +177,751   remainder
  568,432   minuend
```

MULTIPLICATION

Either of two methods may be used to check multiplication.

1. Interchange multiplicand and multiplier.

Multiply:

```
  673   multiplicand
  ×52   multiplier
 1346
 3365
34,996   product
```

Check:

```
   52   multiplier
 ×673   multiplicand
  156
  364
  312
34,996   product
```

2. Divide the product by one of the factors.

The multiplicand and multiplier are also called *factors* of the product. Dividing the product by one of these factors yields a quotient that must be equal to the other factor. The product obtained above may be checked as follows:

```
        673  (multiplicand
   52)34,996   in example)
      31 2
        379
        364
        156
        156
```

or

```
         52  (multiplier
   673)34,996   in example)
       33 65
        1346
        1346
```

DIVISION

Division is the reverse of multiplication. Therefore, the best way to check division is to multiply (remember that one way to check multiplication is to divide). Find the product of the divisor and the quotient, and add the remainder if there is one. The result must be equal to the dividend.

Divide:

```
      15   (quotient)
23)356    (dividend)
  23
 ─────
 126
 115
 ─────
   11   (remainder)
```

Check:

```
   23   (divisor)
  ×15   (quotient)
 ─────
  115
   23
 ─────
  345   (product)
  +11   (remainder)
 ─────
  356   (dividend)
```

ESTIMATING: QUICK-CHECK

The preceding methods given above are useful for checking the accuracy of an answer as carefully as possible. Sometimes you must find out quickly if an answer is at least close to the correct one. This is very helpful in deciding whether decimal points are placed correctly. Estimate the correct answer by rounding off the numbers involved to simple numbers that can be handled in your head. For example: $673 \times 52 = 34,996$. By estimation, $700 \times 50 = 35,000$.

Projects 3, 4, and 5 may be done now.

PROJECT 3 CHECKING BASIC ARITHMETIC OPERATIONS

Perform the indicated operation, then check the example in the space provided. Work as quickly as possible.

1.	2.	3.	4.
314	635	482	4,743
726	438	543	854
392	663	447	1,294
517	456	287	9,395
513	370	418	2,234
886	295	38	7,246
548	71	745	8,623
437	253	846	3,329
142	783	928	4,611
+251	+112	+351	+6,162
_4726_ Ans.	_4076_ Ans.	_3085_ Ans.	_48491_ Ans.
_4726_ Check	_4076_ Check	_5085_ Check	_48491_ Check

5.	6.	7.
$ 8.08	$ 48.32	$ 25.09
0.73	16.91	42.63
9.19	43.65	71.34
1.51	90.08	96.15
0.09	88.16	55.76
7.01	35.95	47.38
1.37	43.72	65.80
9.81	17.07	40.05
7.49	19.46	16.41
+2.41	+88.25	+63.52
_4769_ Ans.	_491.57_ Ans.	_524.13_ Ans.
_4764_ Check	_491.57_ Check	_524.13_ Check

8.	9.	10.
$32.85	$34.68	38,019
44.63	23.95	25,903
72.25	50.32	3,387
1.81	67.18	96,281
12.69	88.44	29,023
38.07	91.67	7,798
51.73	16.61	44,819
2.63	5.16	9,281
43.36	20.09	82,638
+75.93	+88.93	+55,991
_375.95_ Ans.	_487.03_ Ans.	_393140_ Ans.
_375.95_ Check	_487.03_ Check	_393140_ Check

13

11. 739 + 390 + 207 = *1336*   12. 426 + 798 + 372 = *15*
     193 + 772 + 922 = *1887*   892 + 205 + 889 = *98*
     325 + 826 + 239 = *1390*   422 + 788 + 283 = *14*
     893 + 540 + 783 = *2216*   152 + 239 + 642 = *10*

2150   2528   3151   6829   *1892   2030   2186   6*

13. 739,549
     −490,168

     249381 Ans.
     739549 Check

14. 4,028,141
     −643,239

     3384902 Ans.
     4028141 Check

15. 80,238,063
     −65,372,199

     14865864 Ans.
     80238063 Check

16. 31.4
     −4.934

     26.466 Ans.
     31.4 Check

17. 1,982
     −539.605

     1442.395 Ans.
     1982 Check

18. 89.427
     −0.8446

     88.5824 Ans.
     89.427 Check

19.   7,659
          ×890

     6816510

     Check: *890)6816510 7659*

20.   5,103
          ×283

     1444149

     Check: *283)1444149 5103*

PROJECT 4   CHECKING BASIC ARITHMETIC OPERATIONS

A.   Perform the indicated operation, then check each example in the space provided. Work as quickly as possible. Express remainders as fractions.

1. $72.3\overline{)3.316548}$ *Check:*

2. $315\overline{)7,560}$ *Check:*

3. $364\overline{)332.332}$ *Check:*

4. $36,248 \div 0.8202$ *Check:*

15

B. Fill in the totals needed to complete the following report.

Monthly expense summary, October 1977

Sales rep	Meals	Hotel	Gas and Oil	Misc. Expenses	Total
Alden	$184.30	$ 235.00	$ 71.30	$ 12.50	*503.10*
Bean	141.22	338.50	78.93	13.10	*571.75*
Curtin	197.80	228.25	81.58	17.83	*525.46*
Eyster	88.65	305.00	87.15	26.36	*567.16*
Moses	173.45	315.75	45.35	22.69	*557.24*
Thomas	155.10	222.00	53.62	32.75	*463.47*
Totals	*940.52*	*1644.50*	*417.93*	*125.23*	*3128.18*

C. The sales for Henry's Appliance Company for the three-month period ending June 30, 1977 are recorded below. Add horizontally, then check by adding vertically.

	April	May	June	Totals
Color TV's	$ 5,735	$ 4,695	$ 6,135	*16565*
Dryers	4,878	3,910	3,257	*12045*
Vacuum cleaners	2,200	2,895	3,353	*8448*
Fry pans	1,787	2,240	2,672	*6699*
Toaster ovens	1,890	2,369	2,583	*6842*
Portable radios	695	899	1,239	*2833*
Totals	*17185*	*17008*	*19239*	*53432*

PROJECT 5   ADDITION AND SUBTRACTION

1. Complete the following sales report by adding horizontally and vertically.

CLARA'S CLOTHES CORPORATION

COMPARATIVE SALES REPORT FOR 1976–1977

Month	1976	1977	Increase	Decrease
January	$ 2,549	$ 2,937	$ 388	
February	3,721	3,684		37
March	4,696	4,602		94
April	3,411	4,096	685	
May	5,489	4,233		1256
June	2,894	3,711	817	
July	4,678	4,083		595
August	3,934	3,005		929
September	4,901	4,699		202
October	4,811	4,619		192
November	3,362	3,117		245
December	2,870	3,095	225	
Totals	47316	45881	$ 2115	3550

Netdecrease 1435

17

2. Complete the following monthly profit-and-loss summary statement of sales and cost figures. (Sales — cost of goods sold = gross profit. Gross profit — expenses = net profit.)

MORRIS ENVELOPE COMPANY

1977 REPORT

Month	Sales	Cost of Goods Sold	Gross Profit	Expenses	Net Profit
January	$ 38,250	$ 24,979	*13271*	$ 3,942	*9329*
February	50,092	37,014	*13078*	3,011	*10067*
March	66,484	47,700	*18784*	6,735	*12049*
April	56,160	40,484	*15676*	5,211	*10465*
May	81,789	63,482	*18307*	6,267	*12040*
June	68,979	51,490	*17489*	4,479	*13010*
July	67,049	44,490	*22559*	5,077	*17482*
August	61,959	45,354	*16605*	4,399	*12206*
September	55,361	39,928	*15433*	4,441	*10992*
October	49,315	33,522	*15793*	3,878	*11915*
November	47,483	30,277	*17206*	3,654	*13552*
December	28,364	20,556	*7808*	3,448	*4360*
Totals	*671285*	*479276*	*192009*	*34542*	*137467*

[Handwritten annotations:]

Gross Profit Net Sales less Goods Sold

Left 465,276 2,000 Subtract as right

Gross Sales — 675,285
Less sales returns + allowances — -3,000
—1,000
671,285

Net Sales

Cost of Goods Sold

Beginning Inventory — 30,000
ADD Purchases — 465,276
Purchase discounts — 2,000
463,276
Net Purchases — 499,276
Goods Available for sale — 90,000
Less Ending Inventory
Cost of Goods Sold — 479,276

Gross Profit — 192,009

C. COMMON FRACTIONS

A fraction is a portion of the whole; it signifies division. The top number is called the *numerator* (same as the dividend), and the bottom number is called the *denominator* (same as the divisor). The line between the numbers is the division sign.

$\frac{5}{6}$ numerator (or dividend)   For convenience, this is
denominator (or divisor)   often written 5/6.

A *proper* fraction has a numerator that is smaller than the denominator, as in 3/4 or 2/3. An *improper fraction* has a numerator that is equal to or larger than the denominator, as in 6/6 or 7/6. An improper fraction can be converted to a whole number ($6/6 = 1$) or to a mixed number ($7/6 = 1\ 1/6$) by dividing the denominator into the numerator. A *mixed number* contains both a whole number and a fraction (1 1/6).

A *complex* fraction has one or more fractions in either the numerator or the denominator, or both. A complex fraction may be converted to a simple fraction by dividing the numerator by the denominator (remember the line in a fraction is a division sign). To divide by a fraction, invert the denominator fraction (divisor) and multiply:

$$\frac{\frac{3}{8}}{14} = \frac{3}{8} \div 14 = \frac{3}{8} \times \frac{1}{14} = \frac{3}{112}$$

$$\frac{7}{\frac{2}{5}} = 7 \div \frac{2}{5} = 7 \times \frac{5}{2} = \frac{35}{2}, \text{ or } 17\frac{1}{2}$$

$$\frac{\frac{2}{3}}{\frac{15}{21}} = \frac{2}{3} \div \frac{15}{21} = \frac{2}{\overset{1}{3}} \times \frac{\overset{7}{21}}{15} = \frac{14}{15}$$

The answer to any example or problem should not be left as an improper or complex fraction. It should be converted to a proper fraction or a mixed number, then reduced to *lowest terms*.

REDUCTION OF FRACTIONS

The process of converting a fraction to lower terms *without changing the value* of the fraction is called reduction. This is done by dividing both the numerator and the denominator by the *same number* (other than zero). Such conversion does not affect the quotient. When the numerator and denominator no longer have a common divisor (or factor), the fraction has been reduced to its lowest terms, or its simplest form.

$$\frac{64}{256} = \frac{8}{32} = \frac{1}{4} \quad \text{or} \quad \frac{64}{256} = \frac{1}{4}$$
$$(\div 8)\ (\div 8) \qquad\qquad (\div 64)$$

Of course, some fractions do not have a common divisor to begin with. Such a fraction is already expressed in lowest terms.

A fraction may also be converted to higher terms. This is useful in adding fractions, as shown below. To convert to higher terms, multiply both the numerator and the denominator by the *same number* (other than zero). Consider the following example:

$$\frac{1}{4} = \frac{8}{32} = \frac{64}{256}$$
$$(\times 8) \ (\times 8)$$

ADDITION OF FRACTIONS

1. To add fractions with same denominator, add the numerators.

$$\frac{2}{5} + \frac{2}{5} = \frac{2+2}{5} = \frac{4}{5}$$

2. To add fractions with different denominators, select a common denominator into which all the denominators will divide evenly. The smallest number into which all denominators divide evenly is called the *least* (or *lowest*) *common denominator* (L.C.D.). Before you can add, the original fractions must be converted into fractions whose denominators are all the same as the least common denominator. The new numerator results from dividing the L.C.D. by the old denominator and then multiplying that answer by the old numerator.* Suppose you want to find the sum of 5/8 + 3/5 + 7/20. Begin by determining the L.C.D. of 8, 5, and 20, which, as shown in the footnote below, is 40. Then

$$\frac{5}{8} = \frac{5 \times (40 \div 8)}{40} = \frac{5 \times 5}{40} = \frac{25}{40}$$

$$\frac{3}{5} = \frac{3 \times (40 \div 5)}{40} = \frac{3 \times 8}{40} = \frac{24}{40}$$

$$+\frac{7}{20} = \frac{7 \times (40 \div 20)}{40} = \frac{7 \times 2}{40} = \frac{14}{40}$$

$$\frac{63}{40} = 1\frac{23}{40}$$

3. To add mixed numbers, add the whole numbers and fractions separately (converting if necessary), then combine the results.

$$5\frac{5}{6} = 5\frac{25}{30}$$

$$+8\frac{4}{5} = 8\frac{24}{30}$$

$$13\frac{49}{30} = 13 + 1\frac{19}{30} = 14\frac{19}{30}$$

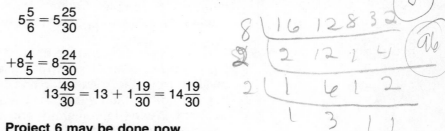

Project 6 may be done now.

*If you cannot find the L.C.D. right away, spread out all the denominators in a short-division box. Divide the denominators by a prime number (a number divisible only by itself and by 1) or a multiple of a prime number that goes into at least two of the denominators. When a denominator cannot be divided by the divisor (prime number), it is brought down into the quotient. Repeat the process until no two parts of the quotient are divisible by the same prime number. Then multiply all divisors and all parts of the quotient together. The result is the L.C.D.

To find the L.C.D. of $\frac{1}{8}$, $\frac{1}{5}$, and $\frac{1}{20}$:

$$\begin{array}{r} 5) \underline{8 \quad 5 \quad 20} \\ 4) \underline{8 \quad 1 \quad 4} \\ 2 \quad 1 \quad 1 \end{array}$$

$$5 \times 4 \times 2 \times 1 \times 1 = 40$$

PROJECT 6   FRACTIONS

A.   Reduce the following fractions to lowest terms.

1. $\dfrac{20}{32} =$ 2. $\dfrac{14}{49} =$ 3. $\dfrac{35}{15} =$ 4. $\dfrac{56}{104} =$

5. $\dfrac{130}{145} =$ 6. $\dfrac{90}{126} =$ 7. $\dfrac{2,016}{3,696} =$ 8. $\dfrac{1,240}{1,636} =$

B.   Change to mixed numbers.

9. $\dfrac{28}{6} =$ 10. $\dfrac{72}{15} =$ 11. $\dfrac{137}{64} =$ 12. $\dfrac{427}{63} =$

13. $\dfrac{53}{16} =$ 14. $\dfrac{657}{19} =$ 15. $\dfrac{329}{24} =$ 16. $\dfrac{169}{48} =$

C.   Change to improper fractions.

17. $5\dfrac{5}{6} =$ 18. $9\dfrac{2}{11} =$ 19. $14\dfrac{3}{4} =$ 20. $6\dfrac{1}{5} =$

21. $39\dfrac{3}{4} =$ 22. $13\dfrac{11}{16} =$ 23. $140\dfrac{3}{7} =$ 24. $13\dfrac{5}{17} =$

D.   In each problem, convert the fractions to equivalent fractions with the lowest common denominator.

25. $\dfrac{5}{6}, \dfrac{7}{8}, \dfrac{5}{9}$ 26. $\dfrac{1}{2}, \dfrac{1}{3}, \dfrac{7}{9}$ 27. $\dfrac{2}{3}, \dfrac{1}{4}, \dfrac{5}{8}$

28. $\dfrac{8}{15}, \dfrac{9}{16}, \dfrac{13}{20}$ 29. $\dfrac{9}{16}, \dfrac{7}{12}, \dfrac{5}{8}, \dfrac{11}{32}$ 30. $\dfrac{5}{12}, \dfrac{15}{32}, \dfrac{11}{48}$

21

E.   Add the fractions and reduce answers to lowest terms.

31.
$$\frac{7}{12} = \frac{14}{24}$$
$$\frac{5}{8} = \frac{15}{24}$$
$$\frac{5}{24} = \frac{5}{24}$$
$$+\frac{1}{6} = \frac{4}{24}$$
$$\frac{38}{24} = 1\frac{14}{24} = 1\frac{7}{12}$$

32.
$$\frac{3}{4} = \frac{36}{48}$$
$$\frac{5}{8} = \frac{30}{48}$$
$$\frac{7}{16} = \frac{21}{48}$$
$$+\frac{5}{12} = \frac{20}{48}$$
$$\frac{107}{48} \quad 2\frac{11}{48}$$

33.
$$3\frac{1}{4} = 3\frac{6}{24}$$
$$5\frac{2}{3} = 5\frac{16}{24}$$
$$+7\frac{3}{8} = 7\frac{9}{24}$$
$$15\frac{31}{24}$$
$$15\frac{7}{8}$$

34.
$$9\frac{1}{8} = 9\frac{3}{24}$$
$$8\frac{3}{4} = 8\frac{18}{24}$$
$$+12\frac{5}{6} = 12\frac{20}{24}$$
$$30\frac{17}{24}$$

35.
$$19\frac{7}{8} = 19\frac{21}{24}$$
$$35\frac{3}{4} = 35\frac{18}{24}$$
$$17\frac{5}{12} = 17\frac{10}{24}$$
$$+6\frac{2}{3} = 6\frac{16}{24}$$
$$77\frac{39}{24}$$
$$78\frac{17}{24} \quad 78\frac{5}{8}$$

36.
$$7\frac{1}{3} = 7\frac{105}{315}$$
$$12\frac{4}{5} = 12\frac{252}{315}$$
$$16\frac{5}{9} = 16\frac{175}{315}$$
$$+2\frac{3}{7} = 2\frac{135}{315}$$
$$37\frac{667}{315} = 39\frac{37}{315}$$

37.
$$9\frac{2}{3} = 9\frac{20}{30}$$
$$4\frac{1}{5} = 4\frac{6}{30}$$
$$+6\frac{1}{2} = 6\frac{15}{30}$$
$$19\frac{41}{30}$$
$$20\frac{11}{30}$$

38.
$$13\frac{2}{3} = 13\frac{48}{72}$$
$$24\frac{1}{9} = 24\frac{8}{72}$$
$$+15\frac{1}{8} = 15\frac{9}{72}$$
$$52\frac{65}{72}$$

SUBTRACTION OF FRACTIONS

1. To subtract fractions that have the same denominator, simply subtract the numerators.

$$\frac{15}{17} - \frac{4}{17} = \frac{15 - 4}{17} = \frac{11}{17}$$

2. To subtract fractions with different denominators, select the least common denominator, convert the fractions, and proceed with the operation.

$$\frac{27}{50} - \frac{3}{10} = \frac{27 - 15}{50} = \frac{12}{50} = \frac{6}{25}$$

3. Subtraction of mixed numbers uses the same method as step 2 above. Sometimes the numerator of the subtrahend is larger than the numerator of the minuend. For example, 195 1/8 less 34 3/4 involves subtraction of 3/4 (or 6/8) from the smaller fraction, 1/8. This is done by "borrowing" 1, or 8/8, from 195 and adding it to 1/8, making it 194 9/8. Then you can subtract: 194 9/8 − 34 6/8 = 160 3/8.

$$195\frac{1}{8} = 194\frac{9}{8} \quad \text{(minuend)}$$
$$-34\frac{3}{4} = 34\frac{6}{8} \quad \text{(subtrahend)}$$
$$\overline{\phantom{-34\frac{3}{4} =\ } 160\frac{3}{8}}$$

MULTIPLICATION OF FRACTIONS

1. There are three steps in multiplying fractions: (a) Multiply the numerators. (b) Multiply the denominators. (c) Reduce to lowest terms.

$$\frac{3}{7} \times \frac{5}{9} = \frac{3 \times 5}{7 \times 9} = \frac{15}{63} = \frac{5}{21}$$

2. "Canceling" saves time and work. In the above example:

$$\frac{\overset{1}{\cancel{3}}}{7} \times \frac{5}{\underset{3}{\cancel{9}}} = \frac{5}{7 \times 3} = \frac{5}{21}$$

3. When multiplying by a whole number, think of the whole number as a fraction with a denominator of 1.

$$16 \times \frac{3}{4} = \frac{\overset{4}{\cancel{16}}}{1} \times \frac{3}{\underset{1}{\cancel{4}}} = 12$$

4. When multiplying mixed numbers, convert mixed numbers to improper fractions, then continue as before.

$$5\frac{5}{8} \times 3\frac{3}{5} = \frac{(8 \times 5) + 5}{8} \times \frac{(5 \times 3) + 3}{5}$$

$$\frac{\overset{9}{\cancel{45}}}{\underset{4}{\cancel{8}}} \times \frac{\overset{9}{\cancel{18}}}{\underset{1}{\cancel{5}}} = \frac{81}{4} = 20\frac{1}{4}$$

DIVISION OF FRACTIONS

1. To divide fractions, invert the divisor, as explained earlier, and multiply. An *inverted fraction* is a fraction with the numerator and denominator interchanged.

$$\frac{5}{8} \div \frac{3}{4}$$

$$\frac{5}{\underset{2}{\cancel{8}}} \times \frac{\overset{1}{\cancel{4}}}{3} = \frac{5}{6}$$

2. When division involves a mixed number, convert all mixed numbers to improper fractions. Then invert the divisor and multiply.

$$6\frac{3}{7} \div 4\frac{1}{8}$$

$$\frac{45}{7} \div \frac{33}{8} = \frac{45}{7} \times \frac{8}{\underset{11}{\overset{15}{\cancel{33}}}} = \frac{120}{77} = 1\frac{43}{77}$$

Projects 7 and 8 may be done now.

PROJECT 7   FRACTIONS

Perform the indicated operations. Reduce answers to lowest terms where necessary.

1. $12\dfrac{2}{9} =$

   $-9\dfrac{5}{7} =$

2. $7\dfrac{1}{8} =$

   $-3\dfrac{3}{4} =$

3. $3\dfrac{1}{3} =$

   $-2\dfrac{4}{5} =$

4. $19\dfrac{3}{4} =$

   $-7\dfrac{2}{3} =$

5. $16\dfrac{4}{5} =$

   $-9\dfrac{7}{8} =$

6. $75\dfrac{1}{12} =$

   $-32\dfrac{7}{10} =$

7. $\dfrac{3}{8} \times 264 =$

8. $\dfrac{5}{6} \times \dfrac{16}{1} \times \dfrac{6}{8} =$

9. $\dfrac{15}{32} \times \dfrac{16}{18} \times \dfrac{12}{9} =$

10. $\dfrac{13}{15} \times \dfrac{5}{12} \times \dfrac{8}{9} \times \dfrac{3}{4} =$

11. $28\frac{11}{12} \times 15\frac{5}{6} =$

$\frac{347}{12} \times \frac{95}{6} = \frac{32965}{72}$

$457\frac{61}{72}$

12. $14\frac{2}{7} \times 16\frac{3}{5} =$

$\frac{100}{7} \times \frac{83}{5} \quad \frac{1660}{7} =$

$237\frac{1}{7}$

13. $17\frac{1}{2} \times 19\frac{1}{5} =$

$\frac{35}{2} \times \frac{96}{5} \quad \frac{336}{1} =$

336

14. $216\frac{5}{8} \times 12\frac{6}{7} =$

$\frac{1733}{8} \times \frac{90}{7} \quad \frac{77985}{28}$

$2785\frac{5}{28}$

15. $16\frac{2}{3} \div 12\frac{1}{2} =$

$\frac{50}{3} \times \frac{2}{25} \quad \frac{4}{3}$

$1\frac{1}{3}$

16. $33\frac{1}{3} \div 14\frac{2}{7} =$

$\frac{100}{3} \times \frac{7}{100} \quad \frac{7}{3} = 2\frac{1}{3}$

17. $20\frac{1}{2} \div 16\frac{2}{3} =$

$\frac{41}{2} \times \frac{3}{50} = \frac{123}{100}$

$1\frac{23}{100}$

18. $25\frac{4}{5} \div 27\frac{1}{2} =$

$\frac{129}{5} \times \frac{2}{55} \quad \frac{258}{275}$

19. $22\frac{3}{8} \div 17\frac{1}{8} =$

$\frac{179}{8} \times \frac{8}{137} = \frac{179}{137} =$

$1\frac{43}{137}$

20. $24\frac{19}{25} \div 16\frac{47}{75} =$

$\frac{619}{25} \times \frac{75}{1241} = \frac{1857}{1241}$

$1\frac{610}{1247}$

Extend the totals (across) and compute the total goods returned.

DEBIT MEMORANDUM

Crow Hardware Co.
29 East Main St.
Seattle, Washington 98105

June 5, 1977

Walker Hardware Distributors
100 Kings Highway
Las Vegas, Nevada 89109

We are returning the following items to you for credit:

Quantity	Unit	Stock no.	Item	Price	Unit	Total
$9\frac{1}{2}$	doz.	88798	Elec. drills	44.90	doz.	426.55
$3\frac{1}{4}$	doz.	73775	Hammers	17.10	doz.	55.58
$4\frac{3}{4}$	doz.	55874	Files	8.95	doz.	42.51
$1\frac{1}{2}$	doz.	44398	Screw-drivers	15.75	doz.	23.63
$\frac{3}{4}$	doz.	99437	Brushes	12.05	doz.	9.03 3/4 / 9.04

PROJECT 8   FRACTIONS

1. Complete the following stock report of the Inchworm Dry Goods Company. (a) Add each line across to find the total yards of braid of each color. (b) Add each column down to find the total yards in all colors of the same width. (c) Find the grand total and verify it.

Color	$\frac{1}{2}''$ wide	$\frac{3}{4}''$ wide	1" wide	$1\frac{1}{2}''$ wide	$1\frac{3}{4}''$ wide	2" wide	Totals
Black	$94\frac{1}{4}$	$105\frac{3}{8}$	$86\frac{3}{4}$	$59\frac{1}{2}$	$121\frac{1}{2}$	$49\frac{7}{8}$	
Blue	$112\frac{1}{8}$	73	$34\frac{1}{8}$	$95\frac{1}{4}$	$45\frac{1}{2}$	$72\frac{3}{4}$	
Brown	63	$26\frac{1}{8}$	$84\frac{1}{4}$	92	$50\frac{1}{4}$	$31\frac{5}{8}$	
Gray	$74\frac{3}{8}$	$34\frac{5}{8}$	$63\frac{1}{4}$	$123\frac{7}{8}$	$62\frac{3}{8}$	$36\frac{1}{2}$	
Green	$61\frac{1}{2}$	$83\frac{5}{8}$	71	$43\frac{7}{8}$	$70\frac{1}{4}$	$62\frac{1}{8}$	
Navy	$74\frac{1}{8}$	$26\frac{1}{2}$	$75\frac{1}{4}$	$44\frac{3}{8}$	60	63	
Orange	20	$21\frac{3}{8}$	$21\frac{1}{2}$	19	$19\frac{3}{4}$	$14\frac{1}{2}$	
Pink	$44\frac{7}{8}$	$73\frac{5}{8}$	54	$27\frac{1}{2}$	$32\frac{1}{4}$	$91\frac{5}{8}$	
Red	$65\frac{1}{2}$	$34\frac{1}{4}$	$84\frac{5}{8}$	$34\frac{1}{4}$	$53\frac{7}{8}$	72	
Yellow	71	$43\frac{1}{4}$	$70\frac{7}{8}$	$93\frac{1}{4}$	$63\frac{7}{8}$	$52\frac{3}{8}$	
Totals							

29

2. Compute the total hours worked by each employee and on each day, and verify the totals.

	Mon.	Tues.	Wed.	Thurs.	Fri.	Sat.	Totals
Acton, Tim	$7\frac{1}{2}$	$8\frac{3}{4}$	$7\frac{3}{4}$	$5\frac{1}{2}$	4	$2\frac{1}{4}$	$35\frac{3}{4}$
Banks, Roy	$6\frac{3}{4}$	$9\frac{1}{2}$	8	$6\frac{3}{4}$	$6\frac{1}{4}$	—	$37\frac{1}{4}$
Dawes, Joan	$8\frac{1}{2}$	$7\frac{1}{4}$	7	$10\frac{1}{4}$	$7\frac{1}{2}$	$2\frac{3}{4}$	$43\frac{1}{4}$
Frank, Ray	9	$6\frac{1}{2}$	$5\frac{1}{2}$	10	$7\frac{3}{4}$	$3\frac{1}{2}$	$42\frac{1}{4}$
Jackson, Tim	7	$7\frac{1}{2}$	$8\frac{1}{4}$	9	$4\frac{1}{4}$	$2\frac{1}{2}$	$38\frac{3}{4}\frac{1}{2}$
Nestor, Alice	$4\frac{1}{2}$	$9\frac{1}{4}$	$6\frac{1}{2}$	—	8	$2\frac{3}{4}$	31
Singer, Linda	—	8	8	$10\frac{1}{4}$	$7\frac{1}{2}$	$3\frac{1}{4}$	37
Thompson, Pete	$6\frac{1}{4}$	$7\frac{1}{2}$	$10\frac{1}{4}$	—	10	—	34
Walker, Tom	$7\frac{1}{2}$	$9\frac{1}{2}$	8	$7\frac{1}{4}$	$8\frac{1}{2}$	$2\frac{3}{4}$	$43\frac{3}{4}\frac{1}{2}$
Totals	57	$73\frac{3}{4}$	$69\frac{1}{4}$	59	$63\frac{3}{4}$	$19\frac{3}{4}$	

$342\frac{2}{4}\frac{1}{2}$

D. DECIMALS   Decimals, sometimes called decimal fractions, are fractions with denominators of 10, 100, 1,000, 10,000, etc. Examples of common fractions with their decimal equivalents are:

$$\frac{3}{10} = 0.3 \qquad \frac{27}{100} = 0.27 \qquad \frac{61}{1,000} = 0.061$$

The sign of the decimal is the decimal point. Since "deci" means ten, a decimal is one or more tenths, hundredths, thousandths, etc., of one unit. In other words, a decimal is a special kind of fraction. If there is only one digit to the right of the decimal, it is read tenths (0.3 = three tenths); two digits to the right of the decimal, hundredths (0.27 = twenty-seven hundredths); etc.

millions | hundred thousands | ten thousands | thousands | hundreds | tens | decimal point | tenths | hundredths | thousandths | ten thousandths | hundred thousandths | millionths

Dividing the denominator into the numerator converts a common fraction into a *decimal* fraction. Notice in our third example below it is necessary to place a zero to the left of the six because 1,000 cannot be divided into 610.

$$\begin{array}{r} .3 \\ 10\overline{)3.0} \\ \underline{3\,0} \end{array} \qquad \begin{array}{r} .27 \\ 100\overline{)27.00} \\ \underline{20\,0} \\ 700 \\ \underline{700} \end{array} \qquad \begin{array}{r} .061 \\ 1,000\overline{)61.000} \\ \underline{6000} \\ 1000 \\ \underline{1000} \end{array}$$

To convert a decimal to a common fraction, take the digits in the decimal as the numerator of a fraction whose denominator is 1 plus as many zeros as there are decimal places in the decimal fraction. *Or* just write the common fraction as you read the decimal.

0.83 is read 83 hundredths; therefore $\frac{83}{100}$

ADDITION OF DECIMAL NUMBERS   The important thing to remember when adding decimals is to arrange the numbers to be added in a vertical column *with the decimals directly under each other.* To prevent errors, zeros may be added so that all numbers have the same number of decimal places to be added.

$$\begin{array}{r} 3.6 \\ 45.897 \\ \underline{393.27} \end{array} \quad \text{may be written} \quad \begin{array}{r} \downarrow \\ 3.600 \\ 45.897 \\ \underline{393.270} \\ 442.767 \end{array}$$

SUBTRACTION OF DECIMAL NUMBERS

Subtraction of decimals should be handled in the same way as addition of decimals. Keep the decimals vertically lined up one under the other, and add zeros so that all numbers have the same number of decimal places.

$$
\begin{array}{r}
369.2 \\
-86.356 \\
\end{array}
\quad \text{may be written} \quad
\begin{array}{r}
\downarrow \\
369.200 \\
-86.356 \\
\hline
282.844 \\
\end{array}
$$

Project 9 may be done now.

PROJECT 9   DECIMALS

A. Write each of the following decimals in figures.

1. five thousand twenty and thirty-three hundredths   *5020.33*
2. three hundred forty-five thousandths   *.345*
3. four thousand seven hundred twenty-five millionths   *.004725*
4. two hundred one and seven tenths   *201.7*
5. three hundred three and three hundredths   *303.03*

B. Convert the following common fractions to decimals, rounding to three decimal places if necessary.

6. $\dfrac{683}{10,000} =$ *.0683*   7. $\dfrac{1}{8} =$ *.125*

8. $\dfrac{13}{27} =$ *.481*   9. $\dfrac{29}{34} =$ *.853*

10. $\dfrac{5}{48} =$ *.104*   11. $\dfrac{14}{15} =$ *.933*

12. $\dfrac{7}{11} =$ *.636*   13. $\dfrac{390}{1,300} =$ *.300*

33

C. Perform the indicated operations.

14. $245.7 + 64.65 + 22.9845 =$ *333.3345*

15. $105.0164 + 15.106 + 0.0007 =$ *120.1231*

16. $401.3 + 65.001 + 33.85 =$ *566.151*

17. $46.4 + 0.0403 + 0.35 + 47.891 + 0.2 =$ *94.8813*

18. $0.43 + 30.29 + 43.021 + 4.6752 =$ *78.4162*

19. $309.6 - 0.7394 =$ *308.8606*

20. $29.776 - 13.8 =$ *15.976*

21. $5.58435 - 0.5943 =$ *4.99005*

22. $130 - 0.3045 =$ *129.6955*

MULTIPLICATION OF DECIMAL NUMBERS

There is no difference between multiplying decimals and multiplying whole numbers except that care must be taken in placing the decimal point in the answer. The decimal point in the answer should have as many places to its right as the *total* number of places to the right of the decimal point in the multiplier and the multiplicand. It may be necessary to place zeros to the left of the other digits in order to have the proper number of digits to the right of the decimal point.

Examples

1.

$$
\begin{array}{r}
\$6.69 \\
\times 8.2 \\
\hline
1338 \\
5352 \\
\hline
\$54.858
\end{array}
$$

2 places to the right of decimal point
1 place to right of decimal point

3 places to right of decimal point

[*Note:* all answers involving money should be rounded to the nearest cent, so the answer should be $54.86. If the third digit to the right of the decimal point is 4 or less, drop it off; if it is 5 or more, add one cent.]

2.

$$
\begin{array}{r}
0.1132 \\
\times 0.26 \\
\hline
6792 \\
2264 \\
\hline
0.029432
\end{array}
$$

4 decimal places
2 decimal places

6 decimal places

DIVISION OF DECIMAL NUMBERS

When the divisor is a whole number, the decimal point in the quotient is placed directly over the decimal point in the dividend.

$4.80 \div 24$

$$
\begin{array}{r}
\$0.20 \\
24\overline{)\$4.80}
\end{array}
$$

When the divisor contains decimal places, the decimal point in the divisor is moved to the right to make it a whole number, and the decimal point in the dividend is moved the same number of places to the right. Sometimes zeros must be added to the right of the dividend in order to get the proper number of places.

Examples

1. $5400 \div 0.27$

$$
\begin{array}{r}
20000. = \$20,000 \\
0.27\overline{)\$5400.00}
\end{array}
$$

2. $64.27 \div 1.2$

```
        53.558 = $53.56
1.2)$64.2700
    60
    ──
    42
    36
    ──
    67
    60
    ──
    70
    60
    ──
   100
    96
   ───
     4
```

[Notice that in order to carry this answer to three decimal places (so it can be rounded off to cents), it was necessary to add two zeros to the right of the dividend. This does not change its value.]

Project 10 may be done now.

PROJECT 10   DECIMALS

A. Multiply the following.

1. $\begin{array}{r} 737,400 \\ \times 7.45 \end{array}$

2. $\begin{array}{r} 5.572 \\ \times 2.005 \end{array}$

3. $\begin{array}{r} 0.0018 \\ \times 0.24 \end{array}$

4. $\begin{array}{r} 82.92 \\ \times 1.782 \end{array}$

5. $\begin{array}{r} 0.629 \\ \times 0.35 \end{array}$

6. $\begin{array}{r} 301.4 \\ \times 0.402 \end{array}$

7. $80.92 \times 0.000062 =$

8. $3,754 \times 0.1132 =$

9. $30,007 \times 0.00601 =$

B. Divide each of the following and round off your answer to the nearest hundredth.

10. $0.312 \div 6 =$

11. $523.1 \div 32 =$

12. $29.543 \div 0.0013 =$

13. $82.714 \div 1,346 =$

14. $7.9103 \div 0.321 =$

15. $67.8 \div 3.04 =$

37

16. 7.369 ÷ 0.0036 =

17. 2.3652 ÷ 5.8 =

18. 17.02 ÷ 0.0067 =

C. Solve the following problems.

19. How many shares of TSU Corporation stock may be purchased with $26,400 if the stock is selling at $40.25 per share?

20. MINI Automobile, Inc., sold 193 automobiles in the first half of 1976 for a total price of $863,054. What was the average price per car?

21. The *Saratoga Sun* sells on the newsstand for 20¢ and the *Saratoga Sunday Advertiser* for 50¢. Together they offer home delivery every day for $6.25 per month. How much is saved by taking home delivery in a month of 30 days that includes four Sundays?

E. ALIQUOT PARTS

An *aliquot part* of any number is a portion of that number that is contained in the number an integral number of times. For example, 5, 10, 20, and 50 are aliquot parts of 100. There are twenty 5's, ten 10's, five 20's, and two 50's in 100. Aliquot parts often turn up as fractions. Thus 5 = 1/20 of 100, 10 = 1/10 of 100, etc. Similarly, 1/4, 1/2, 1/5, 1/10, and 1/20 are aliquot parts of 1. It saves time in multiplication and division if you know the decimal equivalents of common fractions (aliquot parts) or, conversely, the common fraction equivalents of decimal fractions.

Table of aliquot parts of 1 (and their multiples)

Common Fraction	Decimal Equivalent	Common Fraction	Decimal Equivalent
$\frac{1}{2}$	0.50	$\frac{3}{8}$	$0.37\frac{1}{2}$
$\frac{1}{3}$	$0.33\frac{1}{3}$	$\frac{5}{8}$	$0.62\frac{1}{2}$
$\frac{2}{3}$	$0.66\frac{2}{3}$	$\frac{7}{8}$	$0.87\frac{1}{2}$
$\frac{1}{4}$	0.25	$\frac{1}{9}$	$0.11\frac{1}{9}$
$\frac{3}{4}$	0.75	$\frac{1}{10}$	0.10
$\frac{1}{5}$	0.20	$\frac{1}{11}$	$0.09\frac{1}{11}$
$\frac{1}{6}$	$0.16\frac{2}{3}$	$\frac{1}{12}$	$0.08\frac{1}{3}$
$\frac{5}{6}$	$0.83\frac{1}{3}$	$\frac{1}{15}$	$0.06\frac{2}{3}$
$\frac{1}{7}$	$0.14\frac{2}{7}$	$\frac{1}{16}$	$0.06\frac{1}{4}$
$\frac{1}{8}$	$0.12\frac{1}{2}$	$\frac{1}{25}$	0.04

You should learn the aliquot parts in this table so their use becomes automatic.

Sometimes an aliquot part not included in the list may be needed to solve some problem. In such cases, the common fraction helps: you can find the decimal equivalent by dividing the denominator into the numerator.

$$\frac{11}{16} \overline{) \begin{array}{l} 0.68\frac{12}{16} = 0.68\frac{3}{4} \\ \overline{11.00} \\ 9\,6 \\ \overline{1\,40} \\ 1\,28 \\ \overline{12} \end{array}}$$

On the other hand, if you know the decimal fraction you can find the common fraction.

$$0.68\frac{3}{4} = \frac{68\frac{3}{4}}{100} = 68\frac{3}{4} \div 100 = \frac{275}{4} \div 100 = \frac{\overset{11}{\cancel{275}}}{4} \times \frac{1}{\underset{4}{\cancel{100}}} = \frac{11}{16}$$

PRACTICAL USES OF ALIQUOT PARTS

1. *Parts of $1.* Knowing the aliquot parts saves time in computing amounts on invoices and other business forms. For example:

Find the cost of 800 boxes at 25¢ each.

$$25¢ = \frac{1}{4} \text{ of } \$1.00$$

$$\frac{1}{\cancel{4}} \times \overset{200}{\cancel{800}} \times \$1 = \$200$$

Find the cost of 232 units at $37\frac{1}{2}$ ¢ each.

$$37\frac{1}{2}¢ = \frac{3}{8} \text{ of } \$1.00$$

$$\frac{3}{\cancel{8}} \times \$1 \times \overset{29}{\cancel{232}} = \$87$$

2. *Percentage of a whole.*

If 75% of a population of 20,000 voted, how many voted?

$$75\% = \frac{3}{4}$$

$$\frac{3}{\cancel{4}} \times \overset{5,000}{\cancel{20,000}} = 15,000 \text{ voted}$$

3. *Parts of 100.*

What is the cost of 25 bags at $5.36 per bag?

$$25 = \frac{1}{4} \text{ of } 100$$
$$\$5.36 \times 100 = \$536$$

$$\frac{1}{4} \text{ of } \$\overset{134}{\cancel{536}} = \$134$$

4. *Division.* It is difficult to divide a number by a mixed number. If the divisor is an aliquot part, the quotient may be found by multiplication.

If it costs $9,280. to produce 2,500 units, find the cost per unit.

$$2,500 \text{ is } \frac{1}{4} \text{ of } 10,000$$

$$\$9,280 \div 10,000 = \$.928$$

$$\$0.928 \times 4 = \$3.712$$

Project 11 may be done now.

PROJECT 11   ALIQUOT PARTS

A. Express the following as decimal fractions.

1. $\frac{7}{9} =$ 2. $\frac{1}{18} =$ 3. $\frac{7}{12} =$ 4. $\frac{3}{14} =$

B. Express the following as common fractions.

5. $0.03\frac{1}{8} =$ 6. $0.81\frac{1}{4} =$ 7. $0.13\frac{1}{3} =$ 8. $0.90\frac{10}{11} =$

C. Perform the indicated operations using aliquot parts.

9.   72 @ $\$0.16\frac{2}{3} =$ 10.   96 @ $\$0.12\frac{1}{2} =$

11.   77 @ $\$0.09\frac{1}{11} =$ 12.   48 @ 25¢ =

13.   56 @ $\$0.14\frac{2}{7} =$ 14.   940 @ 5¢ =

15.   81 @ $\$0.11\frac{1}{9} =$ 16.   132 @ $8\frac{1}{3}$¢ =

43

17. 75 @ 56¢ =

18. 396 ÷ 25 =

19. 5 @ $6.60 =

20. $5,230 \div 28\frac{4}{7} =$

21. 50 @ $3.80 =

22. $40 \div 6\frac{1}{4} =$

23. $3,292 \div 11\frac{1}{9} =$

24. 4,949 ÷ 875 =

25. A man has $112.50 and spends $75. What fraction of his money does he have left?

26. A factory normally employs 224 people. When the company lost a government contract, 32 employees were laid off. What fraction of the force continued to work?

$$32.92$$

$$\frac{3292}{1} \times \frac{90}{100}$$

$$\frac{4}{25} \times \frac{40}{1} = \frac{32}{5} \quad 6\frac{2}{5}$$

PAYMENT DUE

TV Repair MANAGER

2 CHECKING ACCOUNTS

KEY POINTS TO LEARN FROM THIS CHAPTER

1. **How to open a checking account**

2. **How to use a checking account**

3. **How to balance a checkbook**

MINICASE

Luis Santospago, a short-order cook in a local restaurant, recently had his television set repaired. Because the owner of the business was busy, he had one of his workers visit Mr. Santospago's apartment to fix the set. Luis paid for the repairs in cash and did not get a receipt because the worker had left the receipt book at the shop.

The owner of the repair shop sent a statement demanding payment. Luis explained that he had paid the worker. When the owner asked Luis for his receipt or proof of payment, Luis had none. As they discussed this further, the owner realized that the person who fixed Luis's set was the same one who had worked only three days and then had not shown up for work since. If Luis had written a check, he would have had proof of his payment when the canceled check was returned. Evidently the worker realized this and kept Luis's cash, not turning it into the owner of the repair shop.

A checking account provides an excellent proof of payment whenever a dispute arises. It also provides excellent protection from theft of cash.

A. SYSTEMS AND METHODS

In today's complex society, it would be futile to handle all business matters with paper money, and coins would be inconvenient if not impossible. Moving the money from place to place would cause great problems: risks of loss and theft would be very high. And so we rely on a vast banking system and its use of checks and checking accounts. At the end of 1973, the total money supply of the United States was $270 billion, but checking accounts in commercial banks accounted for nearly $209 billion of that total. Only $61 billion was in currency, coin, and other types of money.* Checking accounts, both personal and business, are basic to American life. Americans use checks to pay $9 out of every $10 they spend. There are 102 million checking accounts in the United States.‡

Two basic types of accounts are available, with many varieties of each.

(1) The *regular* account, which usually requires that a minimum amount of money, such as $100, be left in the account at all times. This type of account may or may not have a service charge (a small fee the bank sets for handling the paperwork). The service charge may be computed in various ways—a charge for a book of checks, a 10¢ charge for each check written, etc.

(2) The *special* account, which requires no minimum balance but does have a service charge. The service charge may be computed like those for the *regular* account. There may also be a monthly bookkeeping charge of 50¢, $1.00, etc., to maintain the account. This type of account is for the person who writes only a few checks each month and cannot leave excess cash in a checking account to cover the minimum balance.

Once you have chosen the type of account you want, you fill out a signature card (see Example1) on which you give certain

Statistical Abstract of the United States, 1974.
‡*The Story of Checks,* Federal Reserve Bank of New York, 6th ed., 1975.

Example 1 Signature card

Example 2 Deposit slip

personal information. It includes your signature so that the bank can verify the signature on a check. Some time after the account has been opened, you receive printed checks and deposit slips with your name, address, and account number printed on them. When you want to make a deposit, you write on the deposit slip the date and the amounts of cash and checks to be deposited (see Example 2). Checks are listed separately and identified by transit number (shown as a fraction, usually in the upper right-hand corner of the check). The transit number helps in routing a check back to its home bank.

Before depositing, cashing, or transferring a check you must endorse it. You simply write your name, as it appears on the check, on the back at the left end. If the form of the name on the front of the check differs from your usual signature, you must also sign your proper signature.

You should not endorse a check until you are ready to cash, deposit, or transfer it (see Example 3). If you sign it and don't add a restrictive phrase like ''For deposit only,'' the endorsed check is the same as cash. If you must endorse a check at home and carry or mail it, the endorsement should contain a restrictive phrase.

A check is a written order drawn on a deposit account instructing a bank to pay money to the person presenting the check. A check may be transferred from one person to another by endorsement. In such situations, the first person writes on the back of the check ''Pay to the order of Henry Smith'' and then signs his own name, ''William Doe.'' Notice the different parts of a check in Example 4.

You should always write your check clearly and completely. Don't leave any blanks. After you have filled out the stub in your checkbook and completed the arithmetic (to make sure your balance covers the check you plan to draw), write the items shown in Example 5 in ink on the face of the check. Don't cross out or change any part of your check. If you make a mistake, start a new check. Don't lend your check form to others (of course you can't if it has your name and account number printed on it).

Example 3   Check and endorsements

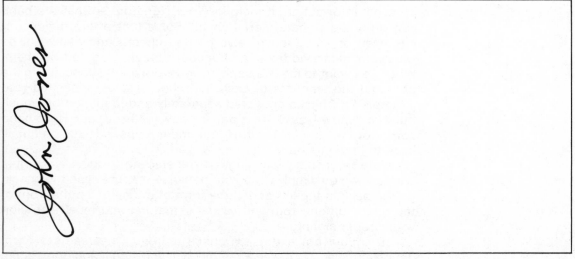

Face of check

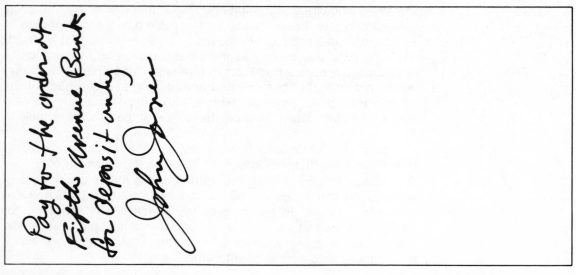

Blank endorsement

Restrictive endorsement

Example 4   Parts of a check

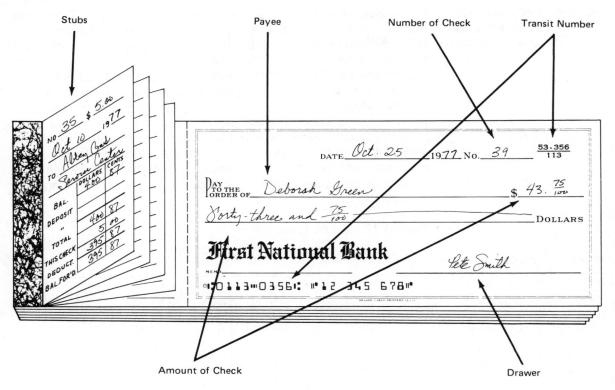

Example 5   How to write a check

1. **THE DATE** you write the check. Never write a future date.

2. **CHECK NUMBER** (sometimes printed on check). Numbering your checks is a great help in keeping your records and balancing your check book.

3. **THE PAYEE'S NAME** after "Pay to the order of."

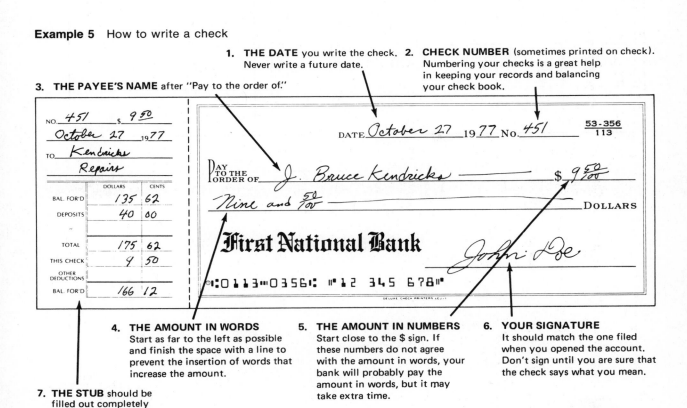

4. **THE AMOUNT IN WORDS** Start as far to the left as possible and finish the space with a line to prevent the insertion of words that increase the amount.

5. **THE AMOUNT IN NUMBERS** Start close to the $ sign. If these numbers do not agree with the amount in words, your bank will probably pay the amount in words, but it may take extra time.

6. **YOUR SIGNATURE** It should match the one filed when you opened the account. Don't sign until you are sure that the check says what you mean.

7. **THE STUB** should be filled out completely at the time the check is written.

B. THE CHECK AND THE CHECK STUB OR CHECK REGISTER

It is important to keep a record of every check written. This is the purpose of the *check stub*. The stub is a small piece of paper to the left of the check which is separated from the check by a perforated line. When the check is torn out, the stub is left bound in the checkbook as a permanent record of deposits made, checks written, and the balance in the account. Each check stub shows the balance after the preceding check. To this amount is added a deposit, if one is made. The amount of the check is then subtracted from the total to show the balance. Some types of checkbooks use stubs attached to the top or bottom of the check, while others do not have stubs but use a small record book called a *check register*. The check register (Example 6) is kept in a plastic folder along with the checkbook.

Project 12 may be done now.

Example 6   A check register

CHECK NO.	DATE	CHECK ISSUED TO	AMOUNT OF CHECK	✓	DATE OF DEP.	AMOUNT OF DEPOSIT	BALANCE	

PROJECT 12   CHECKS AND CHECK STUBS

You are Mr. Thomas White. Write the following two checks and complete the attached stubs in your checkbook. Check no. 84 is for $48.92 to Perez Manufacturing Company on June 2, 1977. Check no. 85 is for $37.48 to ABC Auto Sales on June 3, 1977.

NO. *84* $ *48.92*

June 2 19 *78*

TO *Perez Manufacturing Company*

	DOLLARS	CENTS
BAL. FOR'D	*123*	*62*
DEPOSITS		
"		
TOTAL	*123*	*62*
THIS CHECK	*48*	*92*
OTHER DEDUCTIONS		
BAL. FOR'D	*74*	*70*

DATE *June 2* 19*77* NO. *84*   53-356 / 113

PAY TO THE ORDER OF *Perez Manufacturing Company* $ *48.92*

Fourty-eight dollars and ninty two ——— DOLLARS

First National Bank
Peartree, Georgia

MEMO_____ *Thomas White*

⑆:0113⑈0356⑆ ⑈12 345 678⑈

NO. *85* $ *37.48*

June 3 19*77*

TO *ABC Auto Sales*

	DOLLARS	CENTS
BAL. FOR'D	*74*	*70*
DEPOSITS		
"		
TOTAL	*74*	*70*
THIS CHECK	*37*	*48*
OTHER DEDUCTIONS		
BAL. FOR'D	*37*	*22*

DATE *June 3* 19*77* NO. *85*   53-356 / 113

PAY TO THE ORDER OF *ABC Auto Sales* ——— $ *37.48*

Thirty seven dollars and fourty eight ——— DOLLARS

First National Bank
Peartree, Georgia

MEMO_____ *Thomas White*

⑆:0113⑈0356⑆ ⑈12 345 678⑈

Complete the stubs below for checks 86 through 94.

Check Stub No. 86 — NO. 86 — $ 10.00 — 19____ — TO____

	DOLLARS	CENTS
BAL. FOR'D	37	22
DEPOSITS		
"		
TOTAL	37	22
THIS CHECK OTHER DEDUCTIONS	10	00
BAL. FOR'D	27	22

Check Stub No. 89 — NO. 89 — $ 98.5 — 19____ — TO____ (crossed out)

	DOLLARS	CENTS
BAL. FOR'D	212	31
DEPOSITS		
"		
TOTAL	212	31
THIS CHECK OTHER DEDUCTIONS	98	15
BAL. FOR'D	114	26

Check Stub No. 92 — NO. 92 — $ 264.00 — 19____ — TO____

	DOLLARS	CENTS
BAL. FOR'D	541	73
DEPOSITS		
"		
TOTAL	544	73
THIS CHECK OTHER DEDUCTIONS	264	00
BAL. FOR'D	277	73

Check Stub No. 87 — NO. 87 — $ 24.91 — 19____ — TO____

	DOLLARS	CENTS
BAL. FOR'D	27	22
DEPOSITS	15	00
"		
TOTAL	42	22
THIS CHECK OTHER DEDUCTIONS	24	91
BAL. FOR'D	17	31

Check Stub No. 90 — NO. 90 — $ 31.27 — 19____ — TO____

	DOLLARS	CENTS
BAL. FOR'D	114	26
DEPOSITS		
"		
TOTAL	114	26
THIS CHECK OTHER DEDUCTIONS	31	27
BAL. FOR'D	83	89

Check Stub No. 93 — NO. 93 — $ 53.25 — 19____ — TO____

	DOLLARS	CENTS
BAL. FOR'D	277	73
DEPOSITS		
"		
TOTAL	277	73
THIS CHECK OTHER DEDUCTIONS	53	25
BAL. FOR'D	224	48

Check Stub No. 88 — NO. 88 — $ 125.00 — 19____ — TO____

	DOLLARS	CENTS
BAL. FOR'D	17	31
DEPOSITS	320	—
"		
TOTAL	337	31
THIS CHECK OTHER DEDUCTIONS	125	00
BAL. FOR'D	212	31

Check Stub No. 91 — NO. 91 — $ 42.16 — 19____ — TO____

	DOLLARS	CENTS
BAL. FOR'D	83	89
DEPOSITS	500	00
"		
TOTAL	583	89
THIS CHECK OTHER DEDUCTIONS	42	16
BAL. FOR'D	541	73

Check Stub No. 94 — NO. 94 — $ 110.00 — 19____ — TO____

	DOLLARS	CENTS
BAL. FOR'D	224	48
DEPOSITS		
"		
TOTAL	224	48
THIS CHECK OTHER DEDUCTIONS	110	00
BAL. FOR'D	114	48

C. RECONCILING THE BANK STATEMENT

Once a month (or sometimes less often), every checking account customer of a bank receives a statement from the bank. This statement lists all of the deposits made since the last statement, all the checks written that have been returned to the bank and subtracted from the balance in the account, and any other additions to or subtractions from the account (see Example 7). With the statement are all the checks that have been "canceled," that is, returned to your bank and subtracted from your account.

Example 7 A monthly bank statement

FIFTH AVENUE BANK
BUFFALO, NEW YORK

John H. / Eleanor Doe
365 W. Harwich Avenue
Buffalo, New York 14204   #132450

DATE	CHECKS	CHECKS	DEPOSITS	BALANCE
JUN 15 77			BALANCE FORWARD	* .00S
JUN 15 77			* 500.00	* 500.00*
JUN 16 77	* 2.00DM			* 498.00*
JUN 22 77	* 4.46			* 493.54*
JUN 23 77	* 25.00			* 468.54*
JUN 29 77	* 60.00			* 408.54*
JUL -2 77	* 94.50			* 314.04*
JUL -7 77			* 75.00	* 389.04*
JUL -9 77	* 4.65			* 384.39*
JUL 10 77	* 143.54	* 135.00		* 105.85*
JUL 11 77	* 61.08	* 22.00		* 22.77*
JUL 12 77	* 6.94	* 26.94		
	* 26.94EC			* 15.83*
JUL 21 77			* 40.00	* 55.83*
JUL 23 77	* 4.34			* 51.49*
JUL 28 77			* 40.00	* 91.49*
JUL 29 77	* 5.00			* 86.49*
JUL 30 77	* 4.20			* 82.29*
AUG -2 77	* 3.65			* 78.64*
AUG -3 77			* 40.00	* 118.64*
AUG -4 77	* 15.37	* 7.00		* 96.27*
AUG -9 77	* 22.16			* 74.11*

KEY

R.T. - Referred Transaction for Special Handling

E.C. - Error Corrected

LST. - List

O.D. - Overdraft

S.C. - Service Charges

D.M. - Checkbook Charge

The reconcilement of this statement with your records is essential. Any error or exception should be reported immediately.

The last amount in this column is your balance.

The first step in reconciling the *bank statement* with your checkbook (sometimes called *balancing the checkbook*) should be done before the statement arrives. The checkbook may be kept up to date by (1) saving all deposit slips; (2) numbering and dating all the checks written; (3) neatly entering every check on the stub *when it is written*, not later; and (4) double-checking all the arithmetic.

When the statement comes, the following procedure works best for reconciling the bank statement and checkbook:

1. Sort by number all checks returned with the statement.

2. Check off on checkbook stubs each returned check.

3. Add up the amounts of the checks not checked off on the stubs. These are the *outstanding checks*—checks that were written but have not come back to the bank to be withdrawn from the account. These checks must be subtracted from the balance on the bank statement.

4. Check deposit slips with the deposits listed on the statement. If you have deposit slips that do not appear on the statement, then those amounts must be added to the balance on the bank statement.

5. Finally, look over the statement for additions to the balance of items not entered as deposits on the check stubs. These should also be added to the *checkbook balance*. There may be items subtracted from the balance to cover bank charges for service fees, imprinting checks, collecting notes, bad checks returned, or other items. These should also be subtracted from the checkbook balance.

Next comes the reconcilation statement. Remember, reconciling involves adjusting *both* the bank statement and the checkbook balances to bring them up to date. They should be equal, without the equality being forced.

Mr. and Mrs. Doe, whose first monthly statement is shown in Example 7, notice that their bank statement balance is $74.11, while the balance on the checkbook is only $63.76. After comparing their returned, canceled checks with the stubs, they find that checks numbered 8 for $23.05, 18 for $8.92, and 19 for $15.38 are outstanding. Also they find that their deposit of $35.00 on August 9 does not appear on the statement. Their bank reconciliation appears in Example 8.

Projects 13, 14, and 15 may be done now.

Example 8 Bank reconciliation

```
                    John and Eleanor Doe
                    Bank Reconciliation
                     August 9, 1977


Bank statement balance  . . . . . . . $  74.11
Add: Late deposit of August 9            35.00
Deduct:                               $ 109.11
     Outstanding checks:
       # 8    $23.05
       # 18     8.92
       # 19    15.38                      47.35


Corrected bank statement balance. . . $  61.76


Balance in checkbook  . . . . . . . . $  63.76
Deduct:
       Charge for new checkbook . . . .    2.00

Corrected checkbook balance . . . . . $  61.76
```

PROJECT 13 CHECKING ACCOUNTS

A. Fill in the totals and the balances on Ms. Ginny Thompson's check stubs.

NO. *432* $ *27.19*
April 25, 19 77
TO *Sean's Hardware*
Miscellaneous Items

	DOLLARS	CENTS
BAL. FOR'D	297	49
DEPOSITS		
"		
TOTAL	297	49
THIS CHECK	27	19
OTHER DEDUCTIONS		
BAL. FOR'D	270	30

NO. *435* $ *42.97*
May 4, 19 77
TO *Arnold's Dept. Store*
April Purchases (charge acct)

	DOLLARS	CENTS
BAL. FOR'D	175	28
DEPOSITS		
"		
TOTAL	175	28
THIS CHECK	42	97
OTHER DEDUCTIONS		
BAL. FOR'D	132	31

NO. *438* $ *25.00*
May 12, 19 77
TO *Home Town Savings Bank*
SAVINGS DEPOSIT

	DOLLARS	CENTS
BAL. FOR'D	95	00
DEPOSITS		
"		
TOTAL	95	00
THIS CHECK	25	00
OTHER DEDUCTIONS		
BAL. FOR'D	70	00

NO. *433* $ *18.43*
April 28, 19 77
TO *Wilson's Dairy*
Milk for april

	DOLLARS	CENTS
BAL. FOR'D	270	30
DEPOSITS		
"	270	30
TOTAL	270	30
THIS CHECK	18	43
OTHER DEDUCTIONS		
BAL. FOR'D	251	87

NO. *436* $ *2.86*
May 5, 19 77
TO *Petro Company*
Gasoline

	DOLLARS	CENTS
BAL. FOR'D	132	31
DEPOSITS		
"		
TOTAL	132	31
THIS CHECK	2	86
OTHER DEDUCTIONS		
BAL. FOR'D	129	45

NO. *439* $ *19.08*
May 17, 19 77
TO *Happy Toy Co.*
Toys for children (b'day present)

	DOLLARS	CENTS
BAL. FOR'D	70	00
DEPOSITS	700	31
"		
TOTAL	770	31
THIS CHECK	19	08
OTHER DEDUCTIONS		
BAL. FOR'D	751	23

NO. *434* $ *76.59*
May 2, 19 77
TO *Hometown Credit Union*
payment (april)
on personal loan

	DOLLARS	CENTS
BAL. FOR'D	251	87
DEPOSITS		
"		
TOTAL	251	87
THIS CHECK	76	59
OTHER DEDUCTIONS		
BAL. FOR'D	175	28

NO. *437* $ *34.45*
May 9, 19 77
TO *Acme Tire Co.*
Tires (2)

	DOLLARS	CENTS
BAL. FOR'D	129	45
DEPOSITS		
"		
TOTAL	129	45
THIS CHECK	34	45
OTHER DEDUCTIONS		
BAL. FOR'D	95	00

NO. *440* $ *308.75*
May 18, 19 77
TO *The Sewing Center*
Sewing Machine

	DOLLARS	CENTS
BAL. FOR'D	751	23
DEPOSITS		
"		
TOTAL	751	23
THIS CHECK	308	75
OTHER DEDUCTIONS		
BAL. FOR'D	442	48

NO. _441_ $ _176.33_

May 21, 19_77_

TO _Commonwealth of Massachusetts_

Auto Excise Tax

	DOLLARS	CENTS
BAL. FOR'D	442	48
DEPOSITS		
"		
TOTAL	442	48
THIS CHECK	176	33
OTHER DEDUCTIONS		
BAL. FOR'D	266	15

NO. _442_ $ _33.99_

May 23, 19_77_

TO _Washington Drug Co._

Prescription (Penicillin)

	DOLLARS	CENTS
BAL. FOR'D	266	15
DEPOSITS		
"		
TOTAL	266	15
THIS CHECK	33	99
OTHER DEDUCTIONS		
BAL. FOR'D	232	16

NO. _443_ $ _41.86_

May 24, 19_77_

TO _Hometown Credit Union_

Car payment (May)

	DOLLARS	CENTS
BAL. FOR'D	232	16
DEPOSITS	300	00
"		
TOTAL	532	16
THIS CHECK	41	86
OTHER DEDUCTIONS		
BAL. FOR'D	490	30

SC – 1.00

489.30

FREEDOM BANK & TRUST COMPANY

Ms. Ginny Thompson
92 East Main Street
Lexington, New Hampshire

From: Apr. 24, 1977
To: May 24, 1977

DATE	CHECKS	CHECKS	CHECKS	DEPOSITS	BALANCE
				BALANCE FORWARD	297.49
5-01	27.19	18.43			251.87
5-03	76.59				175.28
5-10	42.97	2.86	34.45		95.00
5-15	25.00				70.00
5-16				700.31	770.31
5-19	308.75				461.56
5-24	33.99	19.08			408.49
5-24	1.00SC				407.49

Beginning balance this statement	Amount of checks paid	Amount of deposits	Service charge	Ending balance this statement
297.49	589.31	700.31	1.00	407.49

Account No.	Activity for service charge period			No. of debit entries	Please deduct this amount if any, from your checkbook balance before reconciling your account.
	No. of checks	No. of deposits	No. of items deposited		
0-840-7567	10	1	1	11	

DM-DEBIT MEMO	OD-OVERDRAWN BALANCE	DC-DEBIT CORRECTION
CM-CREDIT	RT-RETURNED CHECK	CC-CREDIT CORRECTION
LS -LIST OF CHECKS	DT-DORMANT CHARGE	SC-SERVICE CHARGE

B. In the space below, reconcile Ms. Thompson's checkbook and bank statement using the check stubs and bank statement above.

Ms. Thompson's Bank Recon.

Bank Statement Balance — $407.49

Add: late deposit — 300.00

707.49

Deduct: Outstanding Checks

#441 — 176.33
#443 — 41.86
218.19

218.19

Corrected Checkbook Balance — 489.30

PROJECT 14   RECONCILING BALANCES

Using the information given, reconcile the bank balances in the following problems. Solve each problem in the space below it.

1. Bank statement balance of Mary Thomas
    July 31, 1977: $811.57
    Checkbook balance: $32.55
    Bank service charge: $0.55
    Note collected by bank: $427.62
    Checks outstanding:

No. 11	$75.00	33	$ 7.65
13	20.00	34	31.80
20	20.00	35	58.50
26	49.50	36	73.00
32	16.50		

2. Bank statement balance of James Stone
    Jan. 31, 1977: $3,438.55
    Checkbook balance: $3,168.29
    Returned check charged to depositor's account by the bank: $151.46
    Collection charges: $3.50
    Checks outstanding:

No. 336	$ 35.80
387	179.39
395	5.25
396	120.00
397	84.78

3. Bank statement balance of
   M. A. Washington
   September 30, 1977: $915.11
   Checkbook balance: $328.08
   Collection made by the bank for the depositor: $450.00
   Receipts of Sept. 30, deposited on Oct. 1: $150.00
   Collection charge: $1.21
   Outstanding checks:
   No. 145 $ 39.89
        148   22.15
        156   15.50
        161   209.70
        165   1.00

4. Bank statement balance of
   Jane Lampty
   May 31, 1977: $1,830.50
   Checkbook balance: $979.60
   Service charges: $4.50
   Deposit entered May 31 but not deposited until June 1: $578
   Note collected by the bank: $100.00
   Checks outstanding:
   No. 812 $215.00
        823   372.75
        825   210.40
        828   535.25

PROJECT 15   RECONCILING BALANCES

In each of the following problems, reconcile the bank balance with the checkbook balance using the information given.

1.   The bank statement received by Madison Motel on November 30, 1977, showed a balance of $12,264.25, while the most recent check stub showed $12,223.10. After checking carefully, the book-keeper found the following: a $900.00 deposit in transit (didn't arrive at the bank in time to appear on the statement); five out-standing checks totaling $703.65 (no. 624, $24.70; no. 631, $210.05; no. 645, $310.20; no. 649, $80.00; no. 650, $78.70); a bank service charge of $2.25; and a $239.75 note collected by the bank but not recorded in the checkbook.

Madison Motel

Bank Statement Balance   12,264.25

add   *Deposit not recorded*   900.00

13164.25

deduct   *outstanding checks*   −703.65

12460.60

Check Book Balance   12,223.10

add   *Bank Note Collected*   239.75

12462.85

deduct   *Service charge*   −2.25

corrected Bank Balance   12460.60

65

2. The bank statement received by Greg's Greenhouse showed a balance of $23,593.85 on January 31, 1977. The checkbook balance on that date was $21,890.82. Six checks (no. 425, $183.10; no. 436, $400.00; no. 439, $198.95; no. 445, $73.60; no. 480, $736.50; no. 482, $200.83) were not returned by the bank and were presumed to be outstanding. Also, a customer's check for $89.95 that had been included in a deposit was returned by the bank because of insufficient funds; this item had not been deducted in the checkbook.

Greg's Greenhouse

Bank Balance —   23,593.85

Deduct
Outstanding Checks   7792.98
                         ‾‾‾‾‾‾‾‾‾‾
                         21800.87

                         21,890.82

Checkbook Balance
                         − 89.95
deduct   ‾‾‾‾‾‾‾‾‾
    Check Returned   21800.87

LARGER PAYCHECK

SMALLER PAYCHECK

3 PAYROLL

KEY POINTS TO LEARN FROM THIS CHAPTER

1. **How to figure what employees have earned**

2. **What deductions to make from employees' pay**

3. **What records are necessary for payroll work**

4. **How to compute an employer's payroll taxes**

MINICASE

Let's listen in as John and Tom discuss their recently received paychecks. John: "We both do the same type of work, were hired for the same wage, and worked the same number of hours this week, but your check is larger than mine! Why?" Tom: "Yes, we should get the same check. The only difference between the two of us is that I was hired in January and you were hired in August. Look! The payroll department didn't take any FICA tax out of my pay. I wonder if that was a mistake. Let's find out."

69

A. COMPUTATION OF GROSS EARNINGS

Payday is important—to the employee, to the payroll department, and to the employer. No matter what the job, an employee wants to be paid after working a full pay period. The payroll department wants to be sure the payroll is made up on time, with no errors. The employer wants to know that the payroll department will do the job carefully and accurately, with a minimum of wasted time.

In making up a payroll, four factors must be considered: gross earnings; deductions, giving net pay; payroll records; and employer's taxes.

Some companies have timeclocks in which employees insert their own timecards when they enter or leave work. The clock stamps the time of entrance or exit on the card. Other companies use cards that the employees fill out with the time worked, have approved by their supervisor, and turn in to the payroll department.

With both methods, the payroll department must add and verify the total number of hours worked during the pay period. Many companies count time worked in 15-minute periods only. An employee's time, if he or she arrives either a few minutes late or early, is counted only from the next 15-minute division on the clock. Some companies do not give an employee credit for arriving early.

John Blade, who is supposed to work an eight-hour day (8 A.M. to 5 P.M. with one hour for lunch) arrives and leaves at the following times during one week:

Monday—7:55 to 12:03 and 12:59 to 5:00 $\quad = 4 \ + 4 \ = \ 8$

Tuesday—8:05 to 12:00 and 1:00 to 3:50 $\quad = 3\frac{3}{4} + 2\frac{3}{4} = \ 6\frac{1}{2}$

Wednesday—8:00 to 11:55 and 1:10 to 5:00 $= 3\frac{3}{4} + 3\frac{3}{4} = \ 7\frac{1}{2}$

Thursday—8:00 to 12:05 and 1:00 to 6:30 $\quad = 4 \ \ + 5\frac{1}{2} = \ 9\frac{1}{2}$

Friday—8:00 to 12:30 and 1:30 to 7:30 $\quad = 4\frac{1}{2} + 6 \ \ = 10\frac{1}{2}$

Total hours worked during this period $\qquad\qquad = 42$

After they are totaled, the hours worked must be examined to see if the employee is entitled to overtime pay. Employers covered by the Federal Fair Labor Standards Act and certain state laws are required to pay a minimum of one and one-half times the regular rate for all hours worked over 40 hours per week. Other employers pay time and a half even though they are not required to do so; still others pay double and even triple the regular rate for any time worked over 40 hours (or the number of hours considered normal for that company). Sometimes an employee can earn overtime by working more than 8 hours in a day, even though she or he does not work more than 40 hours in a week.

Example   John Blade is paid at the rate of $7.00 per hour for the first 40 hours and $10.50 per hour for all hours over 40.

Total hours worked   = 42

Hours worked at regular time rate = 40 × $7   = $280

Hours worked at overtime rate   = 2 × $10.50 = ___21

Total (gross) earnings $301

The payroll for employees on a yearly salary is computed by taking the yearly salary and dividing it by the number of payroll periods, such as 12 months or 26 two-week periods.

Project 16 may be done now.

PROJECT 16   PAYROLL: GROSS EARNINGS

A.   Tim Grady is hired to work an 8-hour day (8 A.M. to 5 P.M. with one hour off for lunch). He is not paid for any work before 8 A.M., nor for any time period of less than 15 minutes if he is late or works a few minutes overtime. His arrivals and departures for the week of July 15 are listed below. Compute the total hours worked and his gross earnings, assuming he is paid $5.25 per hour and time and a half for overtime (over 38 hours per week).

Time Card and Payroll Sheet

Day	Arrive	Depart	Arrive	Depart	Total Hours	Reg.	Over-time
Monday	8:00	12:02	1:00	5:00	8	—	—
Tuesday	7:45	12:01	1:05	5:03	8	—	—
Wednesday	7:55	11:49	1:01	7:15	10 1/4	—	—
Thursday	8:05	12:15	12:55	7:30	10 1/2	—	—
Friday	8:00	12:05	12:50	5:00	8	—	—
Totals	—	—	—	—	44.75		

Date *July 15, 1977*   Regular 38 × $ 5.25 = $199.50
Name *Tim Grady* 6.75   Overtime × $ 7.87 = $ 53.19
                          Gross Pay   = $252.69

B.   Complete the following payroll sheet.

Name	M	T	W	T	F	Total Hours	Rate per hour	Gross Pay Earned
ATHERTON, DONALD	8	8	8	8	8	40	4.75	190.00
DORIO, JOHN	8	8	3	5	8	32	3.25	104.00
HENRIQUE, LORI	7	8	8	6	8	37	5.80	214.60
HOGAN, LINDA	8	6	9	8	5	36	4.15	149.40
KOLLIOS, ROBERT	7	8	5	8	6	34	4.85	164.90
LEVY, CLAIR	9	8	5	7	9	38	2.95	112.10
O'ROURKE, OSCAR	4	—	8	9	10	31	4.60	142.6
O'TOOLE, WAYNE	6	8	6	8	7	35	4.75	166.25
PENDER, PAULA	8	7	5	9	9	38	3.35	127.30
PRINCE, TODD	5	8	8	4	9	34	4.50	153.00
STEINER, JOAN	10	3	—	8	10	31	4.15	128.65
ZEKE, BERTHA	9	6	—	9	9	33	2.90	95.70
Totals	95	78	71	98	98	419	—	1748.51

73

C. Sometimes workers are paid by the number of pieces of work they turn out rather than by the number of hours worked. In this case the total number of pieces completed is multiplied by the rate (called *piece rate*) to find the gross earnings. The number of pieces completed by each worker and the amount paid per piece are given in the payroll sheet below. Complete the payroll sheet. (Check total pieces completed by getting daily totals and adding them together.)

Payroll Sheet for the Week Ended November 22, 1977

Name	Pieces Completed*							Rate	Gross Earnings	Employee Tax Exempt
	M	T	W	Th	F	Sat	Total			
ANTONIO, WILLIAM	55	31	42	37	55	19	249	$0.45	222.05	2
DAWSON, JANE	33	23	40	24	48	10	178	.79	140.62	2
GRAYSON, BARBARA	33	19	25	37	35	16	165	.68	112.20	1
KOHL, HARRY	45	44	29	50	66	30	264	.44	116.16	3
LARSON, THOR	59	26	38	49	41	18	231	.50	115.50	3
MENDES, GAIL	28	57	36	40	39	13	213	.55	117.15	2
PINTO, TONY	49	60	44	30	36	19	298	.41	122.18	4
Totals	302	260	254	267	320	125	1598	—	945.86	—

*Check total pieces completed by getting daily totals and adding them together.

D. Complete the partial payroll record given below. The workers are paid for any time worked over 40 hours a week at the rate of one and a half times the regular hourly rate.

Name	M	T	W	Th	F	Total Hours	Reg. (40) Hours	Reg. Rate	Over-time Hours	Over-time Rate	Reg. Pay	Over-time Pay	Gross Earnings
ADAMS, ROBERT	9	9	4	10	8	40	40	3.65	—	5.48	146.00	—	146.00
BENEDICT, DAN	7	9	8	10	8	42	40	3.90	2	5.85	156.00	11.70	167.70
CURTIS, LINDA	6	7	8	10	8	39	39	4.30	—	6.45	167.70	—	167.70
DODD, PARKER	5	9	8	7	10	39	39	3.90	—	5.85	152.10	—	152.10
EVANS, JEAN	7	8	9	11	4½	39½	39½	2.80	—	4.20	110.60	—	110.60
FRANKLIN, SIMON	7	8	10½	8	10	43½	40	4.10	3½	6.15	164.00	21.53	185.53
HILLMAN, SWAN	7	8	4½	8	7	34½	34½	3.85	—	5.78	132.83	—	132.83
INCORVATI, TOM	9	8	9½	9	10½	46	40	3.90	6	5.85	156.00	35.10	191.10
MEEKS, DEAN	8	8	8	8	8	40	40	2.80	—	4.20	112.00	—	112.00
TERRILL, CAROL	8	6½	10	10	9	43½	40	3.95	3½	5.93	158.00	19.76	177.76
WALKER, LINDA	8	10½	4½	9	9	41	40	4.75	1	7.13	190.00	7.13	197.13
WHALEN, PAUL	9	10	9	8	9	45	40	4.80	5	7.20	192.00	36.00	228.00
Totals	90	101	93	108	101	493½	472	—	21	—	1867.23	61.22	1998.45

B. PAYROLL DEDUCTIONS

Employers are required by law to withhold (deduct) from their workers' wages certain amounts that they forward to city, state, or federal government offices at specified times. Also, the employee may request in writing that the employer deduct certain amounts for union dues, health and life insurance premiums, retirement plans, contributions to charity, savings bonds, etc. The required deductions are:

1. *FICA tax.* The Federal Insurance Contributions Act requires that an employer deduct from each employee's wages every year a percentage of earnings up to a specified maximum. At the time of the printing of this book, the rate is 5.85% on the first $15,300 earned in a calendar year.* All earnings above $15,300 in the calendar year are not taxable. The rates and maximum amount subject to tax are constantly being changed by Congress and therefore are not important for you to memorize. It is more important to understand the basic system of payroll computation into which any rate may be inserted. This tax pays for federal programs for old age and disability benefits, insurance benefits to survivors, and health insurance to the aged (Medicare).

2. *Federal income tax.* Employees must file with their employers a withholding exemption certificate in which they report the number of exemptions they claim (see Example 1). Taking this information, along with each employee's marital status and gross earnings, the payroll department computes the deduction for federal income tax. This amount may be computed either by the "percentage" method or by the "wage bracket" method from tables. Again, these rates and tables vary from year to year.

*This is the rate for 1976. The law states that the rate for 1978 will be 6.05% but at the present time there is considerable demand for an additional increase in rates.

Example 1   An exemption certificate

Form **W-4**
(Rev. Dec. 1971)

Department of the Treasury—Internal Revenue Service
Employee's Withholding Exemption Certificate

Type or print full name   *JOHN A. BLADE*

Social security number   *071-23-1972*

Home address (Number and street or rural route)   *2721 EASTERN AVE.*

City or town, State and ZIP code   *DAYTON, Ohio   44284*

Marital status—check one (if married but legally separated, or spouse is a nonresident alien, check "Single"): ☐ Single ☒ Married

If you expect to owe more tax than will be withheld, you may either claim fewer or zero exemptions or ask for additional withholding on line 8.

1 Personal exemption for yourself. Write "1" if claimed . . . .

2 If married, personal exemption for your wife (or husband) if not separately claimed by her (or him). Write "1" if claimed *2*

3 Special withholding allowance.¹ (See instruction 2.) Write "1" if claimed . . . .

4 Exemptions for age and blindness (applicable only to you and your wife but not to dependents):

   (a) If you or your wife will be 65 years of age or older at the end of the year, and you claim this exemption, write "1"; if both will be 65 or older, and you claim both of these exemptions, write "2" . . . .

   (b) If you or your wife are blind and you claim this exemption, write "1"; if both are blind, and you claim both exemptions, write "2" . . .   *2*

5 Exemptions for dependents. (Do not claim an exemption for a dependent unless you are qualified under instruction 5.) . . . .

6 Additional withholding allowances for itemized deductions. See table on reverse . . . .

7 Add the exemptions and allowances (if any) which you have claimed above and enter total *4*

8 Additional withholding per pay period under agreement with employer . . . . $

Under the penalties of perjury, I certify that the number of withholding exemptions and allowances claimed on this certificate does not exceed the number to which I am entitled.

(Date) *January 4,* 19 *77* (Signed) *John A. Blade*

C. NET PAY

John Blade's gross earnings for the week of November 15 were $332.50 (cumulative earnings for the year thus far were $15,100.05). The FICA tax is 5.85% on the first $15,300, the federal income tax is $48.29. He has arranged for the following voluntary deductions: United Fund, $5; health insurance, $13.50; and U.S. Savings Bonds, $10.

Gross earnings for the week $332.50
Deductions:
  FICA tax
  5.85% of ($15,300 − $15,100.05) ...... $11.70   (There is no tax
  Federal income tax ....   48.29   on the earnings
  United Fund ....   5.00   over $15,300.)
  Health insurance 13.50
  U.S. savings bonds 10.00
                                        $88.49
Total deductions .... −88.49
Net pay $244.01

Project 17, Part A (p. 81) may be done now.

D. PAYROLL RECORDS

There are two basic forms of payroll records. The *employee's earnings record* shows the complete payroll story of *each* employee on a separate page or card (see Example 2). Information from the time cards is copied onto this record, then the net pay of each employee is computed.

The second form is known by various names, such as *payroll register*, *payroll records*, *payroll sheet*, etc. (see Example 3). Its purpose is to show on one sheet all the information about *all* the employees being paid *in one payroll period*. There are many variations of this form, depending on the kind of company involved. The information on each employee's earnings record is copied onto the payroll register, where the total company payroll for the time period is computed.

In completing an employee's earnings record or a payroll register, the computations are checked by adding the totals across to check with the totals of the summary columns at the right side of each form.

Two other payroll forms are helpful for a company that pays in cash—the *change tally sheet* and the *change slip* (see Examples 4 and 5). The number of particular coins and bills that will be needed for the pay envelope of each employee must be figures. The employer must take each employee's pay and break it down into the largest denomination of bills and coins possible. Once this is done, the columns on the change tally sheet must be totaled and the totals must be transferred to the change slip.

If an employer pays by check, the check should have a detachable payroll information slip on which the employer lists gross pay, all deductions itemized, and net pay. If the employer pays by cash, this same information is listed on the outside of the envelope or on a separate slip of paper inside.

Example 2 Employee's earnings record

Name JOHN A. BLADE						Soc. Sec. # 071-23-1972				M or F: MALE		# 73		
Address 2721 EASTERN AVE						Phone # 849-2267				Exempt: 4		Birth: 7/27/45			
DAYTON, OHIO 44284						Pay rate $ 7/HOUR ($280)				Mar. or Sin. MARRIED		Date of employ: 1/4/77			

Line No.	Period ended	Total hours	Earnings			Cumulative total	Deductions					Total	Net amount	Check no.
			reg.	o.t.	total		FICA tax	Fed. inc. tax	U.S. bonds	Other	Other			
43	OCT. 25	45	$280.	52.50	332.50	$14,492.80	19.45	48.29	10-	—	UNION 20-	97.74	234.76	426
44	NOV. 1	43½	280.	36.75	316.75	14,809.55	18.53	45.10	10-	—	—	73.63	243.12	523
45	NOV. 8	41	280.	10.50	290.50	$15,100.05	16.99	41.50	10-	U.F. 5.00	—	73.49	217.01	561
46	NOV. 15	45	280.	52.50	332.50	$15,432.55	11.70	48.29	10-	U.F. 5.00	HEALTH INS. 13.50	88.49	244.01	606
47	NOV. 22	40	280.	—	280.-	15,712.55	—	40.20	10-	—	UNION 20-	70.20	209.80	652
52	DEC. 27	40	280.	—	280.	$16,986.75	—	40.20	10-	—	—	50.20	229.80	942
Yearly totals		—	16,201.45	785.30	16,986.75	—	895.05	2,080	520-	U.F. 10.00	UN. 240 H.I. 162	3,895.05	13,091.70	—

E. EMPLOYER'S PAYROLL TAXES

The following taxes are levied on employers simply because they have employees. They are *not deductions* from the employee's gross pay, but are related to the employee's gross earnings.

1. *FICA tax.* An employer must contribute an amount equal to the amount deducted from an employee's earnings. This now would be 5.85% of the first $15,300 earned by each employee. Therefore, John Blade's employer would deduct $11.70 from Blade's gross pay, and he would also contribute an additional $11.70 from company funds.

2. *Federal unemployment compensation tax.* The employee makes no contribution towards unemployment compensation: the employer does, through taxation. The funds collected by the federal government are not paid directly as benefits to the unemployed but are allocated among the states for their use in administering state unemployment compensation programs. The current rate (which may be changed at any time) is 0.5% on the first $4,200 of earnings in one calendar year.

3. *State unemployment compensation tax.* Although a few states require employee contributions, the amounts paid as benefits to unemployed persons in most states generally come from taxes levied on employers. The rates vary from state to state and from employer to employer, depending on the employer's employment record. The fewer people an employer lays off, the lower is the rate. The most common tax base is the first $4,200 of earnings of each employee for the calendar year, with rates varying from 0 to over 5% (more commonly from 0.10% to 2.7%).

Example 3 Payroll register

Payroll for week ending November 15, 1977

| Name | Total hours | Earnings | | | Tax.earnings | | Deductions* | | | | | | | Net amount paid | Check no. |
		Regular	Overtime	Total	Unempl.	FICA	FICA	Fed. inc. tax	U.S. sav. bonds	Other	Other	Other	Total		
ALLEN, JEAN	40	165.00	—	165.00	70.00	165.00	9.65	19.10	—	—	U.D. —	H.I. 8.63	42.38	122.62	604
BEAN, SAM	45	170.00	38.00	208.00	208.00	208.00	12.17	25.30	—	U.F. 10.00	U.D. 5.00	H.I. 8.63	61.10	146.90	605
BLADE, JOHN	45	280.00	52.0	332.50	—	199.95	11.70	48.29	10.00	U.F. 5.00	—	H.I. 13.50	88.49	244.01	606
HOWARD, ED	—	300.00	—	300.00	—	—	—	71.30	20.00	U.F. 30.00	—	H.I. 14.63	135.93	164.07	607
TENNACE, ANN	40	110.00	—	110.00	—	110.00	6.44	13.15	—	—	—	H.I. —	19.59	90.41	647
WHITE, SEAN	—	290.00	—	290.00	—	100.00	5.85	45.20	15.00	U.F. 20.00	—	H.I. 14.63	100.68	189.32	648
Totals	—	6,110.41	872.54	6,983.01	3,810.10	4,231.15	247.51	910.30	235.00	182.00	55.00	410.30	2,300.14	3,822.87	—

*Other deductions:
U.F. = United Fund; U.D. = Union dues; H.I. = health insurance.

Example 4 Change tally sheet

Name	Net pay	$50	$20	$10	$5	$1	25¢	10¢	5¢	1¢
ALLEN, JEAN	$ 122.62	2	1	—	—	2	2	1	—	2
BEAN, SAM	146.90	2	2	—	1	1	3	1	1	—
BLADE, JOHN	244.01	4	2	—	—	4	—	—	—	1
HOWARD, ED	164.07	3	—	1	—	4	—	—	1	2
TENNACE, ANN	90.41	1	2	—	—	—	1	1	1	1
WHITE, SEAN	189.32	3	1	1	1	4	1	—	1	2
Totals	$ 957.33	15	8	2	2	15	7	3	4	8

Example 5 Change slip

Denom-ination	No.	Amount
$50	15	$ 750 —
$20	8	160 —
$10	2	20 —
$ 5	2	10 —
$ 1	15	15 —
25¢	7	1.75
10¢	3	0.30
5¢	4	0.20
1¢	8	0.08
Total		$ 957.33

Computation of these three taxes is based on the totals of the taxable earnings columns on the payroll register (see Example 3). Multiplication of the appropriate total by the corresponding percentage yields the proper amount of tax. In preparing a payroll register, an employer computes the taxable earnings columns by comparing the cumulative earnings column of each employee's earnings record with the limit of $15,300 for FICA or $4,200 for unemployment compensation.

Example Taxable earnings for FICA

$$\$4{,}231.15 \times 0.0585 = \$247.52$$

Taxable earnings for federal unemployment compensation

$$\$1{,}810.10 \times 0.005 = \quad \$9.05$$

Taxable earnings for state unemployment compensation

$$\$1{,}810.10 \times 0.027 = \quad \$48.87$$

Total employer's payroll taxes

$$\$247.52 + 9.05 + 48.87 = \$305.44$$

Project 17, Part B, and Projects 18 and 19 may be done now.

Table 3.1 How much you've paid in Social Security taxes, based on maximum rate since 1937

Year	Earnings Ceiling	Rate	Annual Amount	Employee Contribution Cumulative for Years After 1950	Employee Contribution Cumulative for Years After 1936
1937	$ 3,000	1 %	$ 30.00		$ 30.00
1938	3,000	1	30.00		60.00
1939	3,000	1	30.00		90.00
1940	3,000	1	30.00		120.00
1941	3,000	1	30.00		150.00
1942	3,000	1	30.00		180.00
1943	3,000	1	30.00		210.00
1944	3,000	1	30.00		240.00
1945	3,000	1	30.00		270.00
1946	3,000	1	30.00		300.00
1947	3,000	1	30.00		330.00
1948	3,000	1	30.00		360.00
1949	3,000	1	30.00		390.00
1950	3,000	1.50	45.00		435.00
1951	3,600	1.50	54.00	$ 54.00	489.00
1952	3,600	1.50	54.00	108.00	543.00
1953	3,600	1.50	54.00	162.00	597.00
1954	3,600	2	72.00	234.00	669.00
1955	4,200	2	84.00	318.00	753.00
1956	4,200	2	84.00	402.00	837.00
1957	4,200	2.25	94.50	496.50	931.50
1958	4,200	2.25	94.50	591.00	1,026.00
1959	4,800	2.50	120.00	711.00	1,146.00
1960	4,800	3	144.00	855.00	1,290.00
1961	4,800	3	144.00	999.00	1,434.00
1962	4,800	3.125	150.00	1,149.00	1,584.00
1963	4,800	3.625	174.00	1,323.00	1,758.00
1964	4,800	3.625	174.00	1,497.00	1,932.00
1965	4,800	3.625	174.00	1,671.00	2,106.00
1966	6,600	4.20	277.20	1,948.20	2,383.20
1967	6,600	4.40	290.40	2,238.60	2,673.60
1968	7,800	4.40	343.20	2,581.80	3,016.80
1969	7,800	4.80	374.40	2,956.20	3,391.20
1970	7,800	4.80	374.40	3,330.60	3,765.60
1971	7,800	5.20	405.60	3,736.20	4,171.20
1972	9,000	5.20	468.00	4,204.20	4,639.20
1973	10,800	5.85	631.80	4,836.00	5,271.00
1974	13,200	5.85	772.20	5,608.20	6,043.20
1975	14,100	5.85	824.85	6,433.05	6,868.05
1976	15,300	5.85	895.05	7,328.10	7,763.10

Reprinted courtesy of *Boston Herald-American*.

PROJECT 17   PAYROLL TAXES

A.   In the following situations, assume an FICA tax rate of 5.85% on the first $15,300 and compute (a) the FICA tax to be withheld and (b) the net pay.

1.   Gross earnings, $295.42; cumulative earnings, $15,182.98; and federal income tax, $41.32.

2.   Gross earnings, $305.00; cumulative earnings, $14,935.84; and federal income tax, $49.74.

3.   Gross earnings, $371.98; cumulative earnings, $15,507.48; and federal income tax, $60.15.

4.   Gross earnings, $225.80; cumulative earnings, $9,500.71; and federal income tax, $30.98.

5.   Gross earnings, $269.73; cumulative earnings, $15,210.15; and federal income tax, $39.98.

81

B. In each of the situations below, compute the following *employer's* payroll taxes: (a) FICA tax (5.85% on the first $15,300), (b) federal unemployment compensation tax (0.5% on the first $4,200), and (c) state unemployment compensation tax (2.7% on the first $4,200).

1. Cumulative earnings, $15,169.54; gross earnings, $373.19

2. Cumulative earnings, $6,391.71; gross earnings, $192.25.

3. Cumulative earnings, $3,781.25; gross earnings, $115.54

4. Cumulative earnings, $16,100.99; gross earnings, $401.83

5. Cumulative earnings, $4,091.71; gross earnings, $165.35

PROJECT 18   PAYROLL RECORDS

A.   Complete the employee's earnings records of Tim Bray and Luke Snow shown below. Overtime is paid at the rate of one and a half times the regular rate for any time worked over 40 hours in one work week for both men. The FICA rate is 5.85% on the first $15,300. Bray's cumulative earnings on October 15 were $14,653.19; Snow's cumulative earnings on June 1 were $4,044.92.

Name _BRAY, TIM S._   Soc. Sec. No._089-34-6281_   _MARRIED_   _#611_

Address _Rt. 9, FARGO, N.D._   Pay rate _$8.00/HR. ($320)_ _3 EXEMPTIONS_   _1/22/72_

| Week | Per. Ended | Total Hours | Earnings | | | | Deductions | | | | Net Amt. Paid | Check No. | Misc. |
			Reg.	O.T.	Total	Total	FICA	Fed. Inc. Tax	Other	Total			
43	Oct. 22	45	320	60	380	15033.19	22.23	30.11	H.I. 35.21	87.55	292.45	542	
44	29	40	320	—	320	15353.19	15.61	27.19	B 20—	62.80	257.00	601	
45	Nov. 5	36	288	—	288	15641.19	—	23.51	—	23.51	264.49	672	
46	12	44	320	48	368	16.009.19	—	28.94	—	28.94	339.06	744	
47	19	42	320	24	344	16,353.19	—	28—	U 31.50	59.50	284.44	813	
48	26	40	320	—	320	16673.19	—	27.19	H.I. 35.21	62.40	257.34	887	

Other deductions: B = U.S. Sav. bonds; H.I. = health ins.; U = union dues; C = Community Fund

Name _SNOW, LUKE A._   Soc. Sec. No._023-78-9213_   _MARRIED_   _#850_

Address _GRAND FORKS, N.D._   Pay rate _$4.50/HR ($180)_ _4 EXEMPTIONS_   _9/15/75_

| Week | Per. Ended | Total Hours | Earnings | | | | Deductions | | | | | Net Amt. Paid | Check No. |
			Reg.	O.T.	Total	Cumul. Total	FICA	Fed. Inc. Tax	Other	Other	Total		
23	June 8	40	180	—	180	4224.92	10.53	17.13	B 10—		37.66	142.34	419
24	15	37	166.50	—	166.50	4391.42	9.14	15.75	H.I. 25.21		50.10	116.40	492
25	22	42½	180	16.88	196.88	4588.30	11.52	18.35	C 10—		39.87	157.01	563
26	29	46	180	40.50	220.50	4808.80	12.90	20.54	U 20—		53.44	167.06	639
27	July 6	40	180	—	180	4988.80	10.53	17.13	B 10—		37.66	142.34	705
28	13	44	180	27.00	207.00	5195.80	12.11	19.11	H.I. 25.21	C 10—	66.42	140.58	781

Other deductions: B = U.S. Sav. bonds; C = Community Fund; H.I. = health ins.; U = union dues

83

B. Compute the employer's payroll taxes to be paid on Bray's wages for the weeks of October 22 and November 19 and on Snow's wages for the weeks of June 8 and 15. The unemployment compensation tax rates are: federal, 0.5%, and state, 2.7% on the first $4,200 earned in one year.

		FICA	State	Federal
Bray	Oct. 22	22.23		
	Nov. 19			
Snow	June 8	10.53	4.19	.78
	June 15	9.14		

PROJECT 19 PAYROLL

A. Complete the payroll register of the Boston Furniture Co. for the period ended November 20, 1977. Overtime is paid for time worked over 40 hours in one week. Cumulative earnings prior to the current week were, in order starting with Alden: $3,258.84, $2,962.12, $16,975.49, $4,059.37, $4,170.85, $6,354.72, $18,492.57, $15,178.29, $9,184.62. The payroll tax rates are FICA, 5.85% on the first $15,300; federal unemployment compensation, 0.5% on the first $4,200; and state unemployment compensation, 2.7% on the first $4,200.

Payroll Register for the period ended November 20, 1977														
Name	Total Hrs.	Hrly. Rate	Earnings			Taxable Earnings		Deductions					Net Amt. Paid	Check No.
			Reg.	O.T.	Total	Unemploy. Compen.	FICA	FICA	Fed. Inc. Tax	Other	Other	Total		
ALDEN, S.	42	4.30	172.00	12.90	184.90	92	184.90	10.72	23.20	U.F. 10.00		43.92	140.98	779
BONNEAU, K.	37	4.75	175.75	—	175.75	.88	175.75	9.97	21.95	B. 5.00	H.I. 17.00	53.92	121.83	780
BRENNAN, B.	43	8.25	330.00	37.14	367.14		—	—	47.82	B 7.50		55.32	311.82	781
GLOVER, T.	32	7.00	224.00	—	224		224	13.10	27.57			40.67	183.33	782
MOREY, A.	40	5.80	232	—	232		232	13.67	28.71	B 7.50	U.F. 20.00	69.88	162.12	783
QUILL, P.	40	7.50	300	—	300		300	17.55	36.79	H.I. 27.00		81.34	218.66	784
RUSK, D.	44	9.00	360	54	414		—	—	50.85	B. 20.00	H.I. 25.00	95.85	318.15	785
STEP, C.	41	6.90	276.00	10.35	286.35		121.71	7.12	32.61	B. 6.00		45.73	240.62	786
TOWLE, H.	44	4.70	188	28.20	216.20		216.20	12.65	25.11	B. 5.00	H.I. 25.00	67.76	148.44	787
Totals	—	—	2251.75	152.04	2400.34				294.61	88.00	87.00	469.61		—

Other deductions: B = U.S. sav. bonds; U.F. = United Fund; H.I. = health insurance.

Compute the employer's payroll taxes for this period.
FICA
Federal unemployment
State unemployment

85

B. Complete the change tally sheet and the change slip shown below for the November 20, 1977, payroll of the Boston Furniture Company as computed in Part A assuming payment by cash, instead of by check. The largest denomination of bills and coins possible up to $20 will be used.

Name	Net Pay	$20	$10	$5	$1	25¢	10¢	5¢	1¢
ALDEN, SANDRA	140.98	7	—	—	—	3	2	—	3
BONNEAU, KEN	121.83	6	—	—	1	3	—	1	3
BRENNAN, B.	314.82	15	1	—	1	3	—	1	2
GLOVER, TOM	183.33	9	—	—	3	1	—	1	3
MOREY, ANN	162.12	8	—	—	2	—	1	—	2
QUILL, PETER	218.66	10	1	1	3	2	1	1	1
RUSK, DAWN	318.15	15	1	1	3	—	1	1	—
STEP, CAROL	240.62	12	—	—	—	2	1	—	2
TOWLE, HARRY	148.44	7	—	1	3	1	1	1	4
Totals $	1845.95	89	3	3	16	15	7	6	20

Denomination	Number	Amount
$20	89	$1786.00
$10	3	30.00
$5	3	15.00
$1	16	16.00
25¢	15	3.75
10¢	7	.70
5¢	6	.30
1¢	20	.20
Total		$ 1845.95

25   1841 3.75
30
20

1780
30
15
10

4 BASIC MATH: PART TWO

KEY POINTS TO LEARN FROM THIS CHAPTER

1. How to find unknown quantities in a business-like manner—by using algebra

2. Basics of handling and applications of percentages

3. How to compare two numbers by use of a ratio

4. How to *think metric*

MINICASE

Tim Moran read the following item in his newspaper one Saturday:

U.S. HAS 20% OF COAL   Washington: U.S. coal reserves remaining in the ground were estimated at 3.968 billion tons on Jan. 1, 1975, by the U.S. Geological Survey. This was about one-fifth of the world's total reserves.

He was concerned about the rising price of energy (coal, oil, natural gas, and gasoline). He was also concerned about the effect on the environment of using some of the "dirty" forms of energy; therefore, he chose energy as the topic of his term paper in his international politics class at Seashore Community College.

Tim needs to know what the world's total reserves of coal are. He could experiment with different numbers to see if one would fit the situation. Unless he were lucky, he would have to try many numbers and waste a lot of time. Or, Tim could use basic algebra to find his answer quickly and accurately. First, he should state his problem in a simple sentence and then write it in mathematical symbols the same way he stated it in English:

20% of the world's reserves are 3.968 billion tons

$$20\% \times (\text{``times''})\ r\ (\text{unknown}) = 3.968$$
$$20\% \times r = 3.968$$
$$0.2 \times r = 3.968$$
$$\frac{0.2 \times r}{0.2} = \frac{3.968}{0.2}$$
$$r = \frac{39.68}{2} = 19.84 \text{ billion tons}$$

Tim now knows that the world's estimated reserves of coal are 19.84 billion tons. He can check his answer by multiplying 20% by 19.84 and getting 3.968.

89

A. BASIC ALGEBRAIC OPERATIONS

A knowledge of basic algebra is very useful—it will save you a great deal of time. Only the more common and useful principles of algebra will be discussed in this chapter.

The operating signs ($+$, $-$, $\times$, and $\div$) mean the same thing in algebra as in arithmetic. But algebra also uses some other signs. For example, the centered dot $\cdot$, parentheses ( ), and sometimes no sign at all indicate multiplication. Thus, s multiplied by t may be written $s \times t$, $s \cdot t$, $s(t)$, or simply st. Likewise, 3 multiplied by b may be written $3 \times b$, $3 \cdot b$, $3(b)$, or simply $3b$.

Using letters instead of numbers should not bother you. Letters stand for either known or unknown numbers and may be handled in the same way as numbers. When looking for an unknown number, use the first letter of the word that describes the number, such as r for reserves.

An equation shows equality between two numbers. It is a statement that uses mathematical symbols and letters in place of words.

In order to find the value of the unknown (the letter) in an equation, the letter must be left standing alone on one side of the equation. It doesn't matter whether the unknown is on the left or the right. Although certain operations (add, subtract, multiply, and divide) can be performed on the equation, the equality must never be destroyed. Both sides of the equation must be equal after each operation.

An equation is like a seesaw. The pivot point is the equal sign. If two children, each weighing 50 pounds, are on opposite ends of a seesaw, the board will stay flat or balanced (equal), assuming that

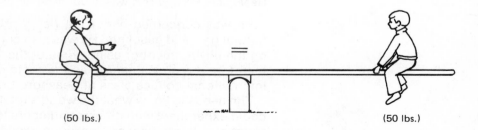

(50 lbs.) (50 lbs.)

the children remain the same distance from the center. If you add three boys, each weighing 50 pounds, to the left side, you must add three boys of the same weight to the right side in order to keep the board balanced. This shows the process of addition on an equa-

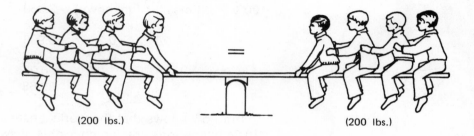

(200 lbs.) (200 lbs.)

tion; whatever you add to one side of an equation, you must add to the other side. Likewise, the action shows multiplication, because if you add three boys (50 pounds + 50 pounds + 50 pounds) to the one (50 pounds) already on the seesaw (on each side), you are really multiplying the original 50 pounds by 4. Then you must also multiply the right side by 4. Whenever you multiply one side of an equation by a number, you must multiply the other side by it too. If there are eight boys on the seesaw (four on each side), and you remove two from the right side, you must also remove two boys from the left side. This removal shows the processes of subtraction

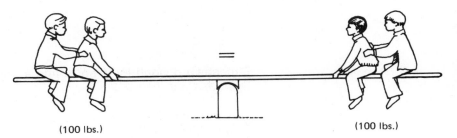

(100 lbs.)   (100 lbs.)

and division. To keep the equation in balance, you must subtract the same number from each side or divide both sides by the same number ($4 \div 2 = 2$).

To solve an equation, you must remember:

1. To copy the equation onto paper, and on each succeeding line show the equation as it appears after *one* operation has been performed. Don't try to combine two steps into one line before you have a good working knowledge of algebra.

2. To isolate the unknown on one side of the equation.

3. That isolation of the unknown requires the transfer of all other terms (each part of the equation preceded by a plus or minus sign) to the other side of the equation. To transfer you do the opposite of each term to every term on both sides of the equation. If one side of the equation is $x + 8$, then subtract 8 from each side. This both transfers the term $+8$ and isolates x.

4. To combine similar terms.

5. That you can add or subtract numbers and letters only if they are on the same side of the equation.

EXAMPLES OF EQUATIONS
(SIMPLE TYPES)

1. $g + 6 = 55$

To find g, do the opposite of "+6": *subtract 6* from each side.

$$g + \cancel{6} - \cancel{6} = 55 - 6$$

$$g = 49$$

2.* $a - 48 = 99$

To find a do the opposite of "-48": *add 48* to each side.

$$a - \cancel{48} + \cancel{48} = 99 + 48$$

$$a = 147$$

*For those students more familiar with algebra, this same effect can be accomplished by means of *transposition*—shifting a term from one side of an equation to the other and changing its sign.

3. $6x = 18$

$6x$ means 6 multiplied by x, so to find x divide both sides by 6.

$$\frac{6x}{6} = \frac{18}{6}$$

$$x = 3$$

4. $\frac{a}{9} = 2$

$\frac{a}{9}$ means a divided by 9, so to find a, multiply both sides by 9.

$$\frac{a}{9}(9) = 2(9)$$

$$a = 18$$

5. $\frac{f}{16} + 5 = 7$

Usually it is better to handle the addition and subtraction terms first and then the multiplication and division terms. To find f, subtract 5 from each side.

$$\frac{f}{16} + 5 - 5 = 7 - 5$$

$$\frac{f}{16} = 2$$

Then multiply by 16.

$$16\frac{(f)}{16} = 16(2)$$

$$f = 32$$

This equation may also be solved by eliminating the fraction as the first step (remember to multiply *each term* by 16):

$$16\left(\frac{f}{16}\right) + 5(16) = 7(16)$$

$$f + 80 = 112$$

$$f + 80 - 80 = 112 - 80$$

$$f = 32$$

6. $\frac{4y}{5} = 16$

This equation can also be written as $\frac{4}{5}(y) = 16$, showing that y is multiplied by $\frac{4}{5}$. To find y, divide $\frac{4}{5}$ (the opposite operation), which is the same as multiplying by $\frac{5}{4}$.

$$\frac{5}{4}\left(\frac{4y}{5}\right) = \overset{4}{\cancel{16}}\left(\frac{5}{\cancel{4}}\right)$$

$$y = 20$$

7. $9(m - 3) = 27$

To find m, first multiply 9 (the coefficient) by *each term* within the parentheses.

$$9m - 27 = 27$$

Then add 27 to each side.

$$9m - \cancel{27} \underline{+ \cancel{27}} = 27 \underline{+ 27}$$

$$9m = 54$$

Now divide ech side by 9.

$$\frac{\cancel{9}m}{\cancel{9}} = \frac{54}{9}$$

$$m = 6$$

8. Remember:
a. Numbers and letters can be added or subtracted only if they are on the same side of the equation.
b. Combine similar terms.

$$2p + 8 = 11 - p$$

To find p, first add p to each side.

$$2p \underline{+ p} + 8 = 11 - \cancel{p} \underline{+ \cancel{p}}$$

$$3p + 8 = 11$$

Next, subtract 8 from each side.   Then divide each side by 3.

$$3p + \cancel{8} \underline{- \cancel{8}} = 11 \underline{- 8}$$ $$\frac{3p}{\cancel{3}} = \frac{3}{3}$$

$$3p = 3$$ $$p = 1$$

Projects 20 and 21 may be done now.

PROBLEM SOLVING   Take a simple, clear statement of the problem in English and re-write it in mathematical symbols (see, for example, the problem of Tim Moran, p.89).   [Some hints: (a) The verb in the sentence is usually the equals sign, and (b) the word "of" means multiply.] Then proceed according to the rules of algebra given above.

Example   If a number is added to 2 times the number, the sum is 66. Find the number:

Let n = the number n $+$ $2n$ $= 66$

Combine terms.

$3n = 66$

Divide each side by 3.

$$\frac{3n}{3} = \frac{66}{3}$$

$$n = 22$$

Project 22 may be done now.

PROJECT 20   ALGEBRA

Solve the following equations.

1. $4x = 16$

2. $x + 8 = 52$

3. $x - 5 = 0$

4. $6x + 8 = 38$

5. $2x + 15 = 5x$

6. $\dfrac{D}{3} = 8$

7. $\dfrac{Y}{3} + 6 = 11$

8. $3M + 5M - M = 56$

9. $7c = 2c + 15$

10. $3(2x - 6) = 9$

11. $7x - 10 = 480$

12. $4T - 6 = 2T$

95

13. $10x + 5 = 45$

14. $28 + 5b = 8b + 4$

15. $49x - 4 = 37x + 20$

16. $2 = \dfrac{2A}{5} - 4$

17. $6(K - 1) = 3K + 12$

18. $6x + 6 = 4x + 16$

19. If 3 is subtracted from 4 times a number, the remainder is 45. Find the number.

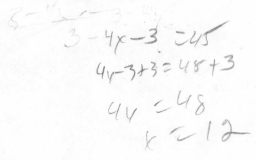

PROJECT 21   ALGEBRA

Solve the following equations.

1. $s - 48 = 22$

2. $89 = x - 57$

3. $2r = 3 + r$

4. $7y - 9 = 2y$

5. $2m + 5 = 7m$

6. $12 - s = 5s$

7. $9x + 46 = x + 86$

8. $12r - 3 = 4 - 2r$

9. $16 + 4k = 10k - 20$

10. $5m + 2 = m + 7$

11. $\frac{n}{9} - 2 = 11$

12. $8t + 16 = 3t + 17$

13. $12 + x = 5x - 8$

14. $3z + 17 = 5z - 75$

15. $3(2h + 1) = 4h + 19$

16. $4(x + 1) + 9 = 2(3x - 4)$

17. If five times a certain number is increased by 2, the result is 67. What is the number?

18. If 35 is decreased by four times a certain number, the result is equal to the certain number. Find the number.

PROJECT 22   ALGEBRA PROBLEMS

1.   Ann's sales on Opening Day were $150 less than Terry's sales. If Ann sold $2,985 worth of merchandise, how much did Terry sell?

[handwritten work]
$A - 150 = 2.985.00$
$A - 150 + 150 = 2985 + 150$
$A = 3,135.00$

2.   The city of Rockville agreed to pay 3/4 of the cost of a road building project. The remaining cost will be paid by the state. If the city's share of the project is $300,000, what is the total cost of the project?

[handwritten work]
$300,000 = 3/4 x$
$\frac{4}{3} \times 300,000 = \frac{3}{4} x \times \frac{4}{3}$
$400,000 = x$

3.   Howe and Wiggins together sold 90 automobiles. If Howe sold twice as many autos as Wiggins, how many cars did each sell?

[handwritten work]
$x + 2x = 90$
$3x = 90$
$x = 30$

Wiggins
$90 - 2x = x$
$90 - 2x + 2x = x + 2x$
$90 = 3x$
$30 = x$

$30 \times 2 = x$
$60 = x$ Howe

4. How can 120 be divided into two parts in such a way that one part will be five times the other?

$$5x + x = 120$$
$$6x = 120$$
$$x = 20$$

5. A man's estate of $33,120 was to be divided among his wife, four sons, and four daughters. The wife was to receive three times as much as each son, and each son twice as much as each daughter. How much was each to receive?

$$6x + 4(2x) + 4(x) = 33,120$$
$$6x + 8x + 4x = 33,120$$
$$18x = 33,120$$
$$x = 1840$$
$$2x = 3680$$
$$6x \quad 11,040$$

6. Lynn and Deb together have $2,582. If Lynn has $452 more than Deb, how much does Lynn have?

$$x + x + 452 = 2582$$
$$2x + 452 = 2582 - 452$$
$$2x = 2130$$
$$x = 1015$$

Lyn
1517
Deb.
1065

7. A man is five times as old as his son. The difference between their ages is 24 years. What is the man's age?

$$5x - x = 24$$
$$5x - x = 24$$
$$4x = 24$$
$$x = 6$$

$$5(6) - 6 = 24$$
$$30 - 6 = 24$$

8.   A student made B grades on $\frac{3}{7}$ of his semester's assignments and C grades on $\frac{1}{3}$ of the assignments. The remaining 5 assignments were not handed in. What was the total number of assignments in the semester?

9.   The sum of three numbers is 95. The second number is 4 times the first and the third is 11 more than the first. What are the three numbers?

B. WORKING WITH PERCENTAGES

Percentage is another aspect of fractions, specifically numbers expressed as fractions of 100. By expressing two or more numbers in the same terms—as *parts of 100*—we can compare them directly. Thus, 100 is the denominator of the fraction, and the number is said to be so many *hundredths* or so many *percent* of the total. *Percent* is the Latin expression for *hundredths*.

CHANGING A DECIMAL TO A PERCENT

Because percent means hundredths, we can change the expression 0.02 (read as 2 hundredths) to 2% (read as 2 percent). To change a decimal to a percent: *Move the decimal point two places to the right* (two places stand for hundredths), *and place a percent sign to the right of the number.*

CHANGING A FRACTION TO A PERCENT

1. Convert the fraction to its decimal equivalent by dividing the numerator by the denominator.

2. Then change the decimal to a percent as explained above.

Examples

1. $\dfrac{1}{4} = 4\overline{)1.00} = 0.25$ (quotient 0.25)

$0.25 = 0.25\% = 25\%$

[*Hint:* The use of aliquot parts (Chapter 1, Section E) will save time and work in many of these examples.]

2. $\dfrac{1}{6} = 6\overline{)1.00} = 0.16\frac{2}{3}$ (quotient $0.16\frac{2}{3}$)

$0.16\frac{2}{3} = 0.16\frac{2}{3}\% = 16\frac{2}{3}\%$

3. $3\dfrac{1}{8} = \dfrac{25}{8} = 8\overline{)25.000} = 3.125$ (quotient 3.125)

$3.125 = 3.125\% = 312.5\%$

CHANGING A PERCENT TO A DECIMAL

To convert a percent to a decimal, *move the decimal point two places to the left and remove the percent sign.* Remember that whole number percents between 1% and 99% are written in the first *two* decimal places.

Examples

1. 4% = 4 hundredths (% sign means hundredths) = 0.04
2. 85% = 85.% = 0.85
3. 46.7% = 46.7% = 0.467 (46% = 0.46)
4. 243.2% = 243.2% = 2.432 (43% = 0.43)
5. 0.8% = 00.8% = 0.008 (0% = 0.00)

A fractional percent is less than 1%. Note, therefore, that two zeros precede the decimal equivalent of the fraction (1% = 0.01; 0% = 0.00). To change a fractional percent to a decimal:

1. Convert the fractional percent to a decimal percent by dividing the numerator of the fraction by the denominator.

2. Change the decimal percent to an ordinary decimal.

Example $\dfrac{5}{8}\%$

$$\dfrac{5}{8} = 8\overline{)5.000}^{0.625} = 0.625$$

$$\dfrac{5}{8}\% = 0.625\% = 00.625\% = 0.00625$$

CHANGING A PERCENT TO A FRACTION

1. Change the percent to its decimal equivalent.

2. Read the value of the decimal as "—hundredths," and write this value as a fraction.

3. Reduce the fraction to lowest terms.

4. The only exception to this procedure is with a percent containing a fraction. Because percent means hundredths (1/100), take the percent containing a fraction and multiply by 1/100. Reduce the resulting fraction to lowest terms (see Examples 4 and 5 below).

Examples

1. $94\% = 0.94 = 94$ hundredths $= \dfrac{94}{100} = \dfrac{47}{50}$

2. $150\% = 1.50 =$ one and 50 hundredths $= 1\dfrac{50}{100} = 1\dfrac{1}{2}$

3. $25.5\% = 0.255 = 255$ thousandths $= \dfrac{255}{1000} = \dfrac{51}{200}$

4. $16\dfrac{2}{3}\% = 16\dfrac{2}{3} \times \dfrac{1}{100} = \dfrac{\overset{1}{50}}{3} \times \dfrac{1}{\underset{2}{100}} = \dfrac{1}{6}$

5. $\dfrac{1}{2}\% = \dfrac{1}{2} \times \dfrac{1}{100} = \dfrac{1}{200}$

Project 23 may be done now.

PROJECT 23   PERCENTS

A.   Express each of the following as a percent.

1. $0.34 =$ 34%

2. $0.063 =$ 6.3%

3. $0.209 =$ 20.9%

4. $0.0073 =$ .73%

5. $2.81 =$ 281%

6. $\dfrac{1}{25} =$ .04%

7. $1\dfrac{5}{8} =$ 162.5%

8. $10.13 =$ 1013%

9. $\dfrac{1}{16} =$ 6.25%

10. $4\dfrac{4}{5} =$ 480%

11. $0.0003 =$ .03%

12. $7\dfrac{4}{25} =$ 716%

105

B. Express each of the following as a decimal.

1. 23% =   .23

2. 67.3% =   .673

3. 0.08% =   .0008

4. 212.08% =   2.1208

5. $\frac{1}{8}$% =   1.25

6. $32\frac{1}{6}$ =   .3216⅔

C. Express each of the following as a common fraction in lowest terms.

1. 42% =   .42 $\frac{42}{100} = \frac{21}{50}$

2. 184% =   1.84 $\frac{184}{100} = 1\frac{21}{25}$

3. 3.9% =   .039 $\frac{39}{1000}$

4. $16\frac{2}{3}$% = $16\frac{2}{3} \times \frac{1}{100} = \frac{50}{3} \times \frac{1}{100}$ $\frac{1}{6}$

5. 0.045% =   .00045 $\frac{45}{100000} = \frac{9}{20,000}$

6. 0.0084% =   .00.0084 $\frac{84}{1,000,000} = \frac{21}{250,000}$

C. APPLICATIONS OF PERCENTS

Percents are always expressed in some variation of the form

$$R \times B = P \qquad \text{where} \qquad R \text{ is the rate}$$
$$B \text{ is the base}$$
$$P \text{ is the percentage.}$$

The *base* is the number or quantity taken as a whole, the total, or 100%. It may be total students in a school, gross or net sales for the year, the population of a city in a particular year, etc.

The *rate* is the number of hundredths of the total (the base) under consideration. Without a base, the rate is meaningless. If one says that 50 students represent 10%, the question immediately arises, 10% of what?

The *percentage* is the product of the rate times the base. It is easy to compute any one of the three parts of the formula if you know the other two parts. Simply substitute the two known figures in the equation and solve by basic algebra.

Examples

1. What is 35% of $756?

$$P = R \times B$$

$$P = 0.35 \times 756 \; (\textit{of} \text{ means multiply})$$

$$P = \$264.60$$

2. What percent of $428 is $64.20?

$$R \times B = P$$

$$R \times \$428 = 64.20$$

$$\frac{R \times 428}{428} = \frac{64.20}{428} \qquad \text{Divide by 428.}$$

$$R = \frac{64.2}{428} = 0.15 = 15\%$$

[*Note:* When computing the rate, remember that the final answer must be expressed in percent form.]

3. 12.5% of what is 625?

$$R \times B = P$$

$$0.125 \times B = 625$$

$$\frac{0.125B}{0.125} = \frac{625}{0.125} \qquad \text{Divide by 0.125.}$$

$$B = \frac{625.000}{0.125} = 5,000$$

There are many uses of this basic percentage formula. One is finding the rate of increase or decrease (sometimes called percent of change). When computing rate of change, always use the *origi-*

nal, or beginning, quantity as the *base*. The formula $R \times B = P$ may be restated as

Rate $\times$ base = amount of increase or decrease.

4. The price of a pound of ground beef was $1.00 last year and $1.50 this year. What was the rate of increase?

$$R \times B = \text{amount of increase}$$

$$\text{amount of increase} = 1.50 - 1.00 = 0.50$$

$$R \times 1.00 = 0.50$$

$$\frac{R \times 1.00}{1.00} = \frac{0.50}{1.00} \qquad \text{Divide by 1.00.}$$

$$R = \frac{1}{2} = 50\%$$

5. The population of Herman, a rural town, as 1,500 in 1960 and 1,100 in 1970. What was the rate of decrease?

$$R \times B = \text{amount of decrease}$$

$$\text{amount of decrease} = 1,500 - 1,100 = 400$$

$$R \times 1,500 = 400$$

$$\frac{R \times 1,500}{1,500} = \frac{400}{1,500} \qquad \text{Divide by 1,500.}$$

$$R = \frac{4}{15} = 26\frac{2}{3}\%$$

6. What number increased by $5\frac{1}{2}\%$ of itself is 42.20?

$$N \qquad + \qquad 0.055 \qquad \times \quad N \quad = \quad 42.20$$

$$N + 0.055N = 42.20$$

$$\frac{1.055N}{1.055} = \frac{42.20}{1.055} \qquad \text{Divide by 1.055.}$$

$$N = \frac{42.2}{1.055} = 40$$

7. A portable radio bought for $24.50 is sold for $32. What percent of the cost is the profit?

$$R \times 24.50 = (32.00 - 24.50)$$

$$R \times 24.50 = 7.50$$

$$\frac{R \times 24.50}{24.50} = \frac{7.50}{24.50} \qquad \text{Divide by 24.50.}$$

$$R = 30.6\%$$

Project 24 may be done now.

PROJECT 24   PERCENTS: APPLI

1. What is 35% of $425?

2. Joan bought a camera for $45. She made a down payment of 20% of the price. (a) How much was the down payment? What percent of the price was the unpaid balance?

3. What percent of $78 is $12?

4. $62.50 is what percent of $750?

5. If $12\frac{1}{2}$% of a number is 64, what is the number?

6. 24% of what number is 60?

109

7. $17 is what percent more than $10?

8. $192 is what percent less than $320?

9. There were 750 freshmen last year and 900 this year in a small midwestern college. Find the percent increase.

10. What number increased by 10% of itself is 2,640?

11. Sally Silver received a dividend of $375, which is 5% of her investment. What is the size of the investment?

12. Last year's taxes on a house were $1,160. This year's taxes were $1,420. What percent were this year's taxes of last year's taxes?

D. RATIOS   A *ratio* is a method of comparing two or more numbers. It may be written $\frac{2}{3}$, or 2 to 3, or 2:3. In comparing more than two items, we may express the comparison as 2 to 3 to 7, or 2:3:7.

Often ratios are used instead of percent in expressing comparisons in business. A common form of ratio is a "comparison to one." Take the ratio expressed as a fraction and divide the numerator by the denominator. [Hint: The number following the word "to" in the statement of the problem is usually the denominator of the fraction.]

Examples

1. In 1971, Jerry Morgan earned $10,000 as a sales representative, while Ed Francis earned $25,000 as sales manager for the same firm. (a) Express in all four forms the ratio of Morgan's earnings *to* Francis's. (b) Express in all four forms the ratio of Francis's earnings to Morgan's.

a. Morgan *to* Francis $= \dfrac{10,000}{25,000} = \dfrac{2}{5}$

$$5)\overline{2.0} \quad 0.4$$

$\dfrac{2}{5}$, 2 to 5, 2:5, 0.4 to 1

b. Francis *to* Morgan $= \dfrac{25,000}{10,000} = \dfrac{5}{2}$

$$2)\overline{5.0} \quad 2.5$$

$\dfrac{5}{2}$, 5 to 2, 5:2, 2.5 to 1

2. A man divides his estate of $648,000 among his three sons in the ratio 2:3:7. He is really saying one son will get 2 parts, a second 3 parts, and the last 7 parts, making a total of 12 parts, or ratios of 2/12, 3/12, and 7/12.

$\dfrac{2}{12} \times \$648,000 = \$108,000$ first son $= \$108,000$

$\dfrac{3}{12} \times \$648,000 = \$162,000$ second son $= 162,000$

$\dfrac{7}{12} \times \$648,000 = \$378,000$ third son $= \underline{378,000}$

Total estate $\underline{\underline{\$648,000}}$

Project 25 may be done now.

PROJECT 25 RATIOS

A. Reduce the following ratios to their lowest terms and express the answer in the four ratio forms.

1. 35 to 5 =

2. 7 to 63 =

3. 93 in 744 =

4. 39 out of 52 =

5. 94 to 28 =

6. 7.5 to 3.5 =

7. $12\frac{2}{3}$ to $8\frac{1}{4}$ =

8. 45 minutes to 12 hours =

113

B.   Solve the following problems.

9.   In a freight-carload of 120,000 lb of paneling, 36,000 lb were Grade A. What is the ratio of Grade A to the total carload? (Express in the four ratio forms.)

10.   6,000,000 out of 10,800,000 cars produced in a year were compacts. What is the ratio of compacts to total cars produced? (Express in four ratio forms.)

11.   A retail store sold a rug for $80. The cost including expenses of the rug sold is $65. Find the ratios of (a) the cost to the selling price, (b) the profit to the selling price, and (c) the profit to the cost. (Note: profit = selling price − cost.)

12.   In 1977, Liz earned $4,200 from dividends on the stocks she owned and $24,000 in salary. Determine to two decimal places the ratio of her dividend income to her salary. Also determine to two decimal places the ratio of her dividend income to her total income (assume this consists only of dividends and salary).

13.   Divide 720 into four numbers in the ratios 2:3:7:6.

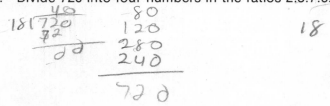

14.   Three partners, Collins, Henry, and Nessen, agree to share profits in the ratio 6:4:7, respectively. This year the partnership has a profit of $68,000. How much does each partner receive?

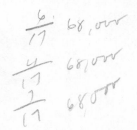

E. METRIC SYSTEM

The Metric Conversion Act, which became law on December 23, 1975, gives the people of the United States until 1986 to become familiar with the metric system. The United States is the only industrialized country in the world that does not use the metric system. This is costing businesses millions of dollars each year because each product must be made in two models—one with "English" measurements for sale in this country and another with metric measurements for sale in other countries. Various leaders of our country have been trying to get the United States to go metric since George Washington's time. In fact, the United States adopted a metric system for money in 1792—100 cents in a dollar. Even though the 1975 law does not have the "teeth" in it that proponents would like, many manufacturers have begun to switch their products to metric measurements.

Our "English" system is based on various arbitrary measures, such as the length of an English King's foot and the distance from his nose to the tip of the middle finger of his outstretched arm. By contrast, the metric system is built on blocks of *10, 100, 1000,* etc. To multiply or divide you simply shift the decimal point. While metrics are simple, the difficulty will be in changing our habits and thought processes to the new system. The government has suggested that rather than converting we should *think metric*. Elementary school students are being taught the new system. Older children and adults will have to train themselves to *use* the metric system, rather than thinking in the "English" system and then converting to metrics. Manufacturers of consumer products now show weights and measures in both systems, but already a few companies have marketed new-size boxes and jars measured only in whole-number metric measurement, such as a large-size soft drink bottle of one liter (formerly this would be a one-quart or 0.95 liter bottle). The following charts are presented, not for conversion purposes, but more for comparison purposes. The important thing is to learn the meaning of the new terms (and their *approximate* sizes), not the conversion factors.

A. Common prefixes (to be used with meters, liters, grams):

Milli: One-thousandth (0.001), such as millimeter, which is one-thousandth of a meter or about the diameter of paper clip wire.

Centi: one-hundredth (0.01), such as a centimeter, which is a one-hundredth of a meter or about the width of a paper clip (about 0.4 inch).

Kilo: one-thousand times (1,000) such as a kilometer, which is 1,000 meters or about 0.6 miles.

B. Conversion Factors* (*approximate* conversions to metric measures):

	When You Know	Multiply by	To Find	Symbol
LENGTH	inches	2.5	centimeters	cm
	feet	30	centimeters	cm
	yards	0.9	meters	m
	miles	1.6	kilometers	km
AREA	square inches	6.5	square centimeters	cm²
	square feet	0.09	square meters	m²
	square yards	0.8	square meters	m²
	square miles	2.6	square kilometers	km²
	acres	0.4	hectares	ha
MASS (weight)	ounces	28	grams	g
	pounds	0.45	kilograms	kg
	short tons (2000 lb)	0.9	tonnes	t
VOLUME	teaspoons	5	milliliters	ml
	tablespoons	15	milliliters	ml
	fluid ounces	30	milliliters	ml
	cups	0.24	liters	l
	pints	0.47	liters	l
	quarts	0.95	liters	l
	gallons	3.8	liters	l
	cubic feet	0.03	cubic meters	m³
	cubic yards	0.76	cubic meters	m³
TEMPERATURE (exact)	Fahrenheit temperature	5/9 (after subtracting 32)	Celsius temperature	°C

*NBS Letter Circular 1051, July, 1973, U.S. Department of Commerce, National Bureau of Standards, Washington, D.C. 20234

C. Temperature scale:

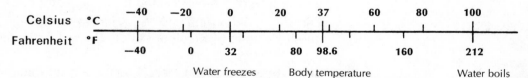

Source: NBS Letter Circular 1051, July, 1973, U.S. Department of Commerce, National Bureau of Standards, Washington, DC 20234.

D. Common approximate measures:

1. Water freezes 32°F—0°C
2. Body temperature 98.6°F—37°C
3. Water boils 212°F—100°C
4. One liter of milk equals 1.06 quarts
5. One teaspoon equals 5 milliliters

6. One kilogram (1,000 grams) equals 2.2 pounds

7. One meter equals 1.1 yards

8. One kilometer equals 0.6 miles

9. Speed: 50 miles per hour equals 80 kilometers per hour

E. Typewriting—common equivalents:

1. a. One inch margin equals 2.5 centimeters
($1\frac{1}{2}$ inches equals 3.75 centimeters, 2 inches equals 5 centimeters)

b. Ten pica spaces or 12 elite spaces equal 2.5 centimeters. (Or stating it differently, 4.7 elite spaces or 3.9 pica spaces to the centimeter.)

c. Six vertical lines equal 2.5 centimeters.

or

2. When we adopt the metric system, most likely we will also adopt the universal paper sizes that are specified by the International System of Weights and Measures. Standard paper sizes used in business are known as the "A" Series, which are slightly different from the U.S. system's $8\frac{1}{2}$ inch $\times$ 11 inch, etc. Because inches will disappear and the spacing on a typewriter is not comparable with the metric system, margins can be expressed in vertical and horizontal spaces, rather than in inches or centimeters.

International Paper Sizes

Series	Metric	In Inches (Approx.)
A4	210 $\times$ 297 mm	$8\frac{1}{4} \times 11\frac{3}{4}$
A5	148 $\times$ 210 mm	$5\frac{7}{8} \times 8\frac{1}{4}$
A6	105 $\times$ 148 mm	$4\frac{1}{8} \times 5\frac{7}{8}$

Project 26 may be done now.

PROJECT 26   REVIEW: ALGEBRA, PERCENTS, AND METRICS

A. ALGEBRA

1. One number is twice the size of another number. Their sum is 87. Find the numbers.

2. Jones and Johnson, partners in a business, earned $356. By agreement, Jones received three times as much as Johnson. How much did each partner receive?

3. Mary's mother is twice as old as Mary. If the sum of their ages is 126 years, how old is Mary?

4. Shannon traveled 859 miles in two days. On the second day, he traveled 63 miles farther than on the first day. How many miles did he travel the first day?

5. The sum of two numbers is 326. One of the numbers is 48 larger than the other number. Find the numbers.

119

B. PERCENT

1. Jim Baker earned $880 in commissions for the month of October. His commission rate was $12\frac{1}{2}$%. What were his October sales?

2. Mrs. Forman's jewels are appraised at $2,000, and are insured for $1,700. What percent of their appraised value are they insured for?

3. The stock of the XYZ Corporation was $50 per share. The stock dropped 40% in the first month, and dropped another 40% in the next month. What is the stock selling for now?

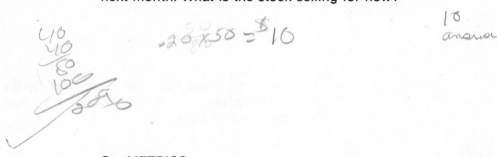

C. METRICS

1. Give the *approximate* equivalent of the following:

(a) One meter (m) equals ___1.1___ yards.

(b) One quart equals ___1.95___ liters (l).

(c) Ten pica spaces on a typewriter equal ___2.5___ centimeters (cm).

(d) One's body temperature of 98.6°F equals ___37___ °C.

(e) An automobile traveling at 50 miles per hour (mph) can be said to be traveling at ___80___ kilometers per hour (km/h).

Test
11-29-78 No Payroll

Pg 120

1) Percents
2) fractions
3) decimals

Pg 103

SAVINGS & LOAN

INTEREST RATE

LOANS

5 INTEREST: BASIC COMPUTATION

KEY POINTS TO LEARN FROM THIS CHAPTER

1. How to find loan maturity dates
2. How to count days between loan dates and maturity dates
3. How to figure ordinary and exact simple interest on a loan
4. Ways to estimate interest

MINICASE

Terry and Joan were responsible for organizing a class discussion on one aspect of inflation in their economics class at Harbor City Community College. They spent an afternoon in the library trying to decide on the specific topic.

Terry: "Joan, look at this index of articles in periodicals for last year! There are almost two dozen articles listed for the topic of interest for last year alone. Most of them are on rising or high interest rates."

Joan: "Yes, interest rates are very important to all parts of our economy. Let's use interest rates as our topic for the class discussion. The cost of borrowing money has become more and more important as the rates have gone up. Apparently there is not much hope for the rates to fall very far in the next few years."

A. BORROWING MONEY

Government, businesses, and individuals alike must be careful to keep the money they borrow and the items they buy on credit to a minimum. Doing so holds down the charges for the money used, which is called interest. The amount paid for interest in a year can mean success or failure for a business.

In a fast-moving economy, business people often need large sums of money quickly to take advantage of low prices on carload purchases or to pay debts early and receive cash discounts. Because it is unprofitable to let cash sit idle, a business may not have these funds in its own accounts and instead borrows from a local bank. The money borrowed is called the *principal*. The charge for the use of this money is called *interest*, and it is similar to the rent a person pays for the use of a building, an apartment, or a car.

Likewise, one business may buy goods from another (the supplier) and promise to pay in the future. The supplier may charge interest on the amount owed.

If the promise to pay is made orally or by signing a sales slip, the account is considered to be an *open account*. A department store charge account or a gasoline credit card are open accounts.

If the amount is large, or if the loan is for a long period, the seller normally will ask the buyer to sign a formal legal paper that shows all the information about the loan. Often this paper is in the particular legal form known as a *negotiable instrument*. The two most common forms of negotiable instruments are *promisory notes* and *trade acceptances*.

B. THE MATURITY DATE

The *maturity date* is the day on which the business must repay the loan or pay the seller for the goods. That date is found by subtracting the day the loan was made from the total number of days in that month, and then taking this difference from the total time of the loan. Then the total number of days in each succeeding month must be subtracted from the answer until the last answer is smaller than the total number of days in the next month. There is no need to worry about counting or not counting the first or last days of the loan. The above arithmetic method will give the correct answer each time.

Example

A 90-day loan is made on June 21. When is it due?

$$
\begin{array}{ll}
& 90\text{-day loan} \\
& \underline{-\ \ 9}\ \text{days left in June} \\[6pt]
30\ \text{days in June} & 81\ \text{days left after the end of June} \\
\underline{-21}\ \text{June 21} & \underline{-31}\ \text{days in July} \\
\ \ 9\ \text{days left in June} & 50\ \text{days left after the end of July} \\
& \underline{-31}\ \text{days in August} \\
& \ \ 19
\end{array}
$$

Maturity date = September 19

Remember: If a loan is expressed in *days*, compute it in *days*; if it is expressed in *months*, compute it in *months*.

To find the maturity date expressed in months, the number of months the loan is to run must be counted. The date on which it falls is the same day of the month as that on which the loan was made. The only exception occurs when the loan becomes due in a month that has fewer days than the month in which it was made. Then it is due on the last day of the month.

Example

A two-month note dated October 31 is due *December 31.*

A one-month note dated October 31 is due *November 30.*

A four-month note dated October 31 is due *February 28* (or February 29 in leap year).

Sometimes it is necessary to compute the number of days of the loan when given only the loan date and the maturity date. To do this, simply find the number of days between the loan date and the end of that month. Then add this figure to the number of days in each month until the maturity date.

Example

A loan is dated August 5 and due on October 4. How many days does it run?

31 days in August
-5 August 5
26 days left in August
30 days in September
  4 days in October
60 -day loan

C. SIMPLE INTEREST FORMULA: ORDINARY

Any amount of simple interest at any rate for any length of time can be computed by using the formula

Interest = Principal $\times$ Rate $\times$ Time

$I = PRT,$

where *principal* is the amount borrowed or owed
   rate is a percent of the principal (unless otherwise stated, this is always based on *one year*)
   time, as a multiple or portion of *one year*.

While decimals can be used, common fractions make this formula much clearer and give a more orderly solution. Always set up the formula first with all the amounts, and then solve, canceling wherever possible.

Example

1. What is the interest for one year on a loan of $500 at a rate of 8%?

$$I = 500 \times \frac{8}{100} \times 1 = \overset{5}{\cancel{500}} \times \frac{8}{\underset{1}{\cancel{100}}} \times 1$$

$$I = \$40$$

Example   **2.** What is the interest for three years on a loan of $500 at a rate of 8%?

$$I = 500 \times \frac{8}{100} \times 3$$

$$I = \overset{5}{\cancel{500}} \times \frac{8}{\underset{1}{\cancel{100}}} \times 3$$

$$I = \$120$$

If the time is less than one year, it is expressed as a fraction of a year. For example, 5 months = 5/12, 1 month = 1/12, 30 days = 30/360. Usually the number of days is placed over 360 because the 360-day year is most often used by banks and businesses. This 360-day year is known as the *bank year*, the *commercial year*, or the *business year*. As in computing the maturity date, do not change months to days or days to months. This method is called the *ordinary interest method* or the *banker's interest method*. It is both convenient and legally acceptable even though it is not exact.

Example   **3.** What is the interest for 60 days on a loan of $500 at a rate of 8%?

$$I = 500 \times \frac{8}{100} \times \frac{60}{360}$$

$$I = \overset{5}{\cancel{500}} \times \frac{\overset{4}{\cancel{8}}}{\underset{1}{\cancel{100}}} \times \frac{\overset{1}{\cancel{60}}}{\underset{\underset{3}{\cancel{6}}}{\cancel{360}}} = \frac{5 \times 4 \times 1}{1 \times 3}$$

$$I = \$6.67$$

If the interest rate is expressed as a fractional percent, this percentage should be converted to a common fraction; for example, $8\frac{1}{2}\% = 0.085$.

This is read as 85 thousandths. Therefore $\frac{85}{1000}$ is used in the formula.

Example   **4.** What is the interest for 75 days on a loan of $500 at a rate of $8\frac{1}{2}\%$?

$$I = \overset{1}{\cancel{500}} \times \frac{85}{\underset{2}{\cancel{1000}}} \times \frac{\overset{5}{\cancel{75}}}{\underset{24}{\cancel{360}}} = \frac{425}{48} = \$8.85$$

D. SIMPLE INTEREST FORMULA: EXACT

Exact interest is computed by using the interest formula in the same way as in computing ordinary or bank interest, except that the denominator of the time fraction is 365, instead of 360. The United States government makes interest computations on the basis of a 365-day year. Exact interest is somewhat less than ordinary interest.

Example   What is the exact interest on $500 at 8% for 60 days?

$$I = 500 \times \frac{8}{100} \times \frac{60}{365}$$

$$I = \overset{1}{\underset{1}{\cancel{500}}} \times \frac{8}{\underset{1}{\cancel{100}}} \times \frac{60}{\underset{73}{\cancel{365}}} = \frac{1 \times 8 \times 60}{1 \times 73}$$

$I = \$6.58$ (See Example 3 above, where the ordinary interest was computed to be $6.67.)

Project 27 may be done now.

PROJECT 27   DATES, TIME, AND INTEREST

1.   What is the maturity date of a three-month note dated August 31?
November 30

2.   (a) What is the maturity date of a 30-day loan dated January 31?
(b) of a one-month note dated January 31?   _Feb. 28 (29 leap year)_
March 2

31 days in Jan
_28_
_3_

_30_
_0_
_30_
_28_
2 March

3.   A three-month note dated April 30 is due on
July 30

4.   Compute the due date of a 90-day note dated July 21.

_31_
_21_
_10_

_90_
_10_
_80_
31 aug.
_49_
30 Sep
_19_

Oct 19.

5.   Find the maturity date of a 120-day loan dated March 14.

_31_
_14_
_17_

_126_
_17_
_103_
30 apr
_73_
31 may
_42_
30 June
_12_

July 12

6.   When will a 40-day note dated November 17 be due?

_30_
_17_
_13_

_40_
_13_
_27_

Dec. 27

7.   Find the number of days of a note dated October 1 and due on November 30.

_31_
_1_
30 Oct.
_30_
60-day loan

8.   How many days of interest are due on a note dated May 28 and due on September 25?

120 days

_31_
_28_
3 - May
30 - Jun
31 July
31 aug
25 Sep
_120_

9.   How many days of interest are there on a loan dated January 20 and due on April 20 of the same year?

90 days

_31_
20 Jan
_11_
_28 fe_
31 Mar
_20 ap._
_90_

129

Find the interest on each of the following loans by using the interest formula.

10. $700 at 8% for 8 months

11. $900 at 9% for 120 days

12. $584 at 8% for 76 days

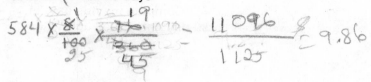

13. $1,000 at 6¼% for 40 days

14. $840 at 8½% for 4 months

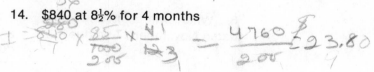

15. $1600 at 7¾% for 270 days

16. $584 at 9% for 175 days (exact interest)

17. $730 at 10% for 218 days (exact interest)

E. SIMPLE INTEREST (ORDINARY): OTHER METHODS

When it is necessary to compute interest at 6% for various numbers of days, the answer can be found quickly by using the *60-day, 6% method.* This type of calculation usually produces about the same answer as that computed by the formula method. Use of this method requires moving the decimal point in the principal two places to the left to find the interest for 60 days at 6%. The reason for this is that

$$\text{Principal} \times \frac{\overset{1}{\cancel{6}}}{100} \times \frac{\overset{1}{\cancel{60}}}{\underset{\underset{1}{\cancel{6}}}{\cancel{360}}} = \frac{\text{principal}}{100}$$

is the same as moving the decimal point two places to the left in the principal.

Example

1. What is the interest for 60 days on a loan of $600 at a rate of 6%?

$$\$6\underset{\curvearrowleft}{00}.00 = \$6 \qquad Proof: I = \overset{6}{\cancel{600}} \times \frac{\overset{1}{\cancel{6}}}{\underset{1}{\cancel{100}}} \times \frac{\overset{1}{\cancel{60}}}{\underset{\underset{1}{\cancel{6}}}{\cancel{360}}} = \$6$$

2. What is the interest for 15 days on a loan of $600 at a rate of 6%?

$$\$6\underset{\curvearrowleft}{00}.00 = \$6 = \text{interest for 60 days}$$

15 is $\frac{1}{4}$ of 60 days

Therefore, interest for 15 days is $\frac{1}{4}$ of $6.00 or $1.50

$$Proof: I = \overset{\overset{1}{\cancel{6}}}{\underset{1}{\cancel{600}}} \times \frac{\overset{1}{\cancel{6}}}{\underset{1}{\cancel{100}}} \times \frac{\overset{3}{\cancel{15}}}{\underset{\underset{\underset{2}{\cancel{10}}}{\cancel{60}}}{\cancel{360}}} = \frac{\overset{3}{\cancel{6}}}{\underset{2}{\cancel{4}}} = \$1.50$$

3. What is the interest for 20 days on a loan of $600 at a rate of 9%?

$$\$6\underset{\curvearrowleft}{00}.00 = \text{interest for } \textit{60 days} \text{ at } 6\%$$

20 days is $\frac{1}{3}$ of 60 days

Therefore, interest for *20 days* at *6%* is $\frac{1}{3}$ of $6, or $2.

$$6\% + 3\% = 9\% \qquad 3\% \text{ is } \frac{1}{2} \text{ of } 6\%$$

Therefore, interest for 20 days at 3% is $\frac{1}{2}$ of $2, or $1.

Therefore, interest for 20 days at 9% is $2 + $1, or $3.

$$Proof: I = 600 \times \frac{9}{100} \times \frac{20}{360} = \$3$$

While this 60-day 6% method may be used for various other numbers of days at various rates (as in Example 3), it often takes longer than the formula method. Also, there may be a few cents difference in the answers. The short-cut method is useful for those who feel confident about it and actually find it shorter. Otherwise, when in doubt, it is safest to use the formula. The short-cut method is an excellent way to approximate or to estimate an answer.

The above examples may also be worked with the *6*-day, 6% method, in which the decimal point in the principal moves *three* places to the left. Sometimes it is useful to combine the 60-day and the 6-day methods.

Example What is the interest for 66 days on a loan of $350 at a rate of 6%?

Interest for 60 days = $3̶5̶0̶. = $3.50
Interest for 6 days   = $3̶5̶0̶. = 0.35
Interest for 66 days = $3.85

$$Proof: I = 350 \times \frac{6}{100} \times \frac{66}{360} = \frac{11 \times 7}{20} = \frac{77}{20} = 3.85$$

There are other methods, such as the 30-day, 12% method and the 90-day, 4% method, which also provide ways to compute interest quickly. In both, the decimal point in the principal moves *two* places to the left, for the same reason as with the 60-day, 6% method.

30-day, 12%

$$\frac{30}{360} \times \frac{12}{100} = \frac{principal}{100}$$

90-day, 4%

$$\frac{90}{360} \times \frac{4}{100} = \frac{principal}{100}$$

Example **1.** What is the interest for 10 days at 10% on $2,400?

$24̶0̶0̶. = $24 for 30 days at 12%

$$10\% = \frac{5}{6} \text{ of } 12\% \left(\frac{10}{12} = \frac{5}{6}\right)$$

$$\frac{\overset{4}{\cancel{5}}}{\underset{1}{\cancel{6}}} \times 24 = \$20 \text{ for 30 days at } 10\%$$

10 days is $\frac{1}{3}$ of 30 days $\left(\frac{10}{30}\right)$

$$\frac{1}{3} \times \$20 = \$6.67 = \text{interest for 10 days at } 10\%$$

$$Proof: I = \overset{20}{\cancel{2400}} \times \frac{\overset{1}{\cancel{10}}}{\underset{\underset{1}{\cancel{10}}}{\cancel{100}}} \times \frac{\overset{1}{\cancel{10}}}{\underset{3}{\cancel{360}}} = \frac{20}{3} = \$6.67$$

2. What is the interest for 90 days at 8% on $600?

$6.00, = $6.00 for 90 days at 4%
8% is two times 4%
$6.00 × 2 = $12.00 = interest for 90 days at 8%

$$Proof: I = \overset{1}{\cancel{600}} \times \frac{\overset{4}{\cancel{8}}}{\underset{1}{\cancel{100}}} \times \frac{\overset{3}{\cancel{90}}}{\underset{\underset{\underset{1}{\cancel{2}}}{\cancel{60}}}{\cancel{360}}} = \$12.00$$

F. MATURITY VALUE

The *maturity value* of a single-payment loan or note is the amount the borrower must pay on the maturity date. It is found by adding the principal (amount of the loan) and the interest (computed by any method).

Projects 28 and 29 may be done now.

PROJECT 28   INTEREST

A. Compute the ordinary interest on the following loans by the 60-day, 6% method; the 6-day, 6% method; the 30-day, 12% method; or the 90-day, 4% method.

1. $610 for 240 days at 6%

2. $900 for 33 days at 8%

3. $750 for 52 days at 10%

4. $450 for 17 days at 6%

5. $755.15 for 22 days at 9%

135

6. $850 for 105 days at $7\frac{1}{2}$%

B. Compute the maturity date, the amount of ordinary interest, and the maturity value of each of the following loans.

1. $300 at 8% for 90 days, dated August 27

2. $740 at 10% for 75 days, dated May 9

3. $2,640 at $7\frac{1}{2}$% for 120 days, dated March 15

C.   Compute the ordinary interest and the maturity value for each of the following loans.

1. $275.50 at 8% from June 22 to October 20

2. $3,275.40 at 9% from July 2 to September 30

3. $720.40 at 10% from August 23 to December 21

PROJECT 29   INTEREST: REVIEW

A. Find the ordinary interest by the formula method and then by the 60-day, 6% method.

1. $4,500.00 at 6% for 126 days

2. $950.75 at 10% for 75 days

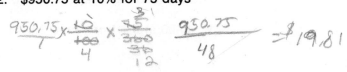

3. $650.35 at $7\frac{1}{2}$% for 102 days

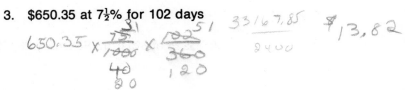

4. $540 at 9% for 84 days

5. $1,250.20 at 8% for 132 days

139

6. $200.00 at $7\frac{1}{2}$% for 150 days

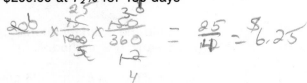

B.   Find the ordinary interest (360-day year) and then the exact interest (365-day year) on the following loans.

1. $450 at 9% from June 20, 1977 to November 17, 1977

2. $225 at 8% from February 28, 1977, to October 26, 1977

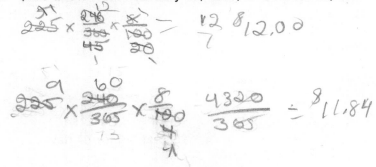

C.   Hilda Johnson borrowed $3,500 on October 21, 1977, promising to pay interest at the rate of 7%. She agreed to pay off the loan on February 18, 1978. (a) Find the interest charge if the time used in computing the interest was based on the 360-day banker's year. (b) Find the interest charge if the time used in computing the interest was based on the 365-day government year.

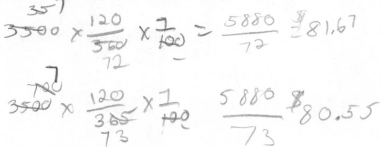

6 INTEREST: NOTES AND INTEREST

KEY POINTS TO LEARN FROM THIS CHAPTER

1. **Kinds of negotiable instruments**

2. **Bank discount vs. interest**

3. **Simple vs. compound interest**

4. **How to compute present value**

MINICASE

George and Martha Adams have been married two years. Recently Martha gave birth to a beautiful baby girl. Martha required a great deal of medical help and hospitalization. George is trying to finish his degree program at Lakefront Junior College. He is also working 40–45 hours per week to take care of his new family. In order to save money, he rather foolishly (he now admits) decided not to take out health insurance. He now has very large hospital and medical bills.

George asked his father for help in paying these bills. His father approved and asked George to sign an I.O.U. for the money, even though they were father and son. The loan would run for three years at an interest rate of 6% per year. At the end of the three years, George could repay the entire amount of the loan, pay back part of it, or extend the full amount for a longer time. If he chose the second or third possibility, he would have to sign a new I.O.U. for the money still on loan.

Many businesses and families start with loans of one kind or another. And others find it is better to borrow at times than to keep money available. Therefore, knowledge of loans and interest is very useful.

143

Example 1 Negotiable promissory note

$1000.00 St. Paul, Minn. _____ April 16, _____ 19 77

_____ Sixty days _____ After date I promise to pay to

the order of _____ Samuel J. Boone _____

At the **Guaranty Bank of St. Paul, Minnesota**

_____ One Thousand & 00/100 _____ Dollars

and interest at __8__%

No. 95   Due __June 15, 1977__   Elva H. Nader

A. NEGOTIABLE INSTRUMENTS

When the amount of a credit sale or loan is large, or the terms are long, the seller normally asks the buyer to sign a formal legal paper. This paper, containing all the information about the loan, is called a *negotiable promissory note.* Of the many types of credit instruments in business, the negotiable promissory note is used most often when interest is charged. The Uniform Commercial Code defines this note as an unconditional promise in writing made by one person to another. Signed by the maker (or promissor), the note states the maker's promise to pay on demand or at a particular future time a certain sum of money to order or to the bearer (see Example 1).

There are many different forms of promissory notes, but each note should contain all the necessary information about the promise made. The amount written on the note is called the *face value* (principal) of the note. The face value plus the interest is the *maturity value.* A promissory note may be either interest bearing or non-interest bearing. The note in Example 1 is interest bearing, that is, the borrower (Nader, the *maker of the note*) promises to repay on June 15, 1977, the $1,000 borrowed plus interest at 8% to the lender (Boone, the *payee*).

B. BANK DISCOUNT: NON-INTEREST-BEARING NOTE

On a non-interest-bearing note, the maturity value equals the face value. There are two types of non-interest-bearing notes. In the less common note, the lender does not charge the borrower any interest. More usually, the lender *does* charge interest but subtracts it from the face value before giving the money to the borrower. We say that the borrower receives the *proceeds* of the note. The interest that is subtracted from the principal at the time of the loan is called *discount,* or *bank discount.* The note is said to be non-interest-bearing because the lender gets back only the face value on the maturity date. Let us look at a note for $600 at 6% for 120 days as an interest-bearing and a non-interest-bearing note and compare the two.

	Interest-bearing Note	*Non-interest-bearing Note*
Borrower needs	$600.00	$600.00
Borrower signs a note for	600.00 + interest	600.00
Interest	12.00	12.00 (called *discount*)
Borrower receives (proceeds)	600.00	588.00 ($600.00 − $12.00)
Borrower pays (maturity value)	612.00	600.00

Notice that the computation of discount ($D = PRT$) is exactly the same as the computation of interest ($I = PRT$). Discount can be defined as interest collected in advance (on the date of the loan), whereas interest is collected on the maturity date. This means that the non-interest-bearing note (with discount) is slightly more expensive for borrowers because they have the use of the proceeds (in this case $588), rather than the face value ($600), even though the discount is computed on $600. Also, if the borrower really needs $600 to use, he or she must borrow more than $600 and pay discount on this higher amount.

C. BANK DISCOUNT: INTEREST-BEARING NOTE

In the foregoing case, either customers gave *their* note (their written promise) to a store in payment for goods purchased or borrowers gave a bank *their* note in return for the bank's lending them money. Much the same situation occurs with an interest-bearing note involving discount except that the circumstances are different.

Suppose a store has received a number of promissory notes from its customers. The store needs cash to pay bills and buy more merchandise, so it "sells" some of these notes to a bank. This process also is called "discounting" because, as with the non-interest-bearing note, the bank receives notes and pays out cash. The bank pays out the *maturity value* less the *discount*. It is happy to do this because it keeps the discount and will receive the face value from the maker of the note on the maturity date. The store is glad to get its money early so it can buy more merchandise to sell and therefore earn more profit. True, the store doesn't receive the full maturity value of the note, but normally the profit it can make on the additional merchandise sales far exceeds the loss of part of the maturity value (the discount).

Here again the bank lends money on a note—but it is the borrower's *customer's note* rather than the *borrower's note*—and deducts the interest in advance (discount). Again, the discount is computed by using $D = P \times R \times T$, but the *maturity value* represents the principal because the full value of the note is turned over to the bank. When computing the proceeds, the discount is subtracted from the *maturity value*.

Example   A $500, 60-day, 8% note dated March 23 is discounted at the bank on April 7 at 9%. Find the proceeds of the note.

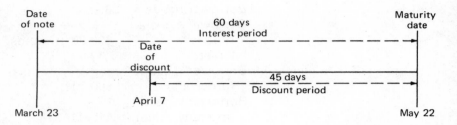

$$I = P \times R \times T$$

$$I = \overset{5}{\cancel{500}} \times \frac{\overset{4}{\cancel{8}}}{\underset{1}{\cancel{100}}} \times \frac{\overset{1}{\cancel{60}}}{\underset{\underset{3}{\cancel{6}}}{\cancel{360}}} = \frac{20}{3} = \$6.67 \text{ interest for 60 days}$$

Maturity value = face value + interest
$MV = 500 + 6.67 = 506.67 -$ value on May 22

Discount $= MV \times R \times T$

$$D = 5{,}06.67 \times \frac{9}{\underset{1}{\cancel{100}}} \times \frac{\overset{1}{\cancel{45}}}{\underset{8}{\cancel{360}}} = \frac{45.6003}{8} = \$5.70$$

Bank charge (discount) to the store for giving the store the value of the note 45 days before the maturity date.

Proceeds $= MV -$ Discount

$$P = \$506.67 - \$5.70$$

$$P = \$500.97$$

Project 30 may be done now.

PROJECT 30   DISCOUNT

Compute the amount of the bank discount and the net proceeds for each of the non-interest-bearing notes below.

	Date of Note	Face of Note	Time of Note	Discount Rate	
1.	May 15	$ 450.00	90 days	8%	Aug 13
2.	August 7	$1,050.00	120 days	$7\frac{1}{2}$%	Dec 5
3.	March 2	$ 912.00	2 months	9%	May 2
4.	November 9	$ 539.50	30 days	7%	Dec 9
5.	February 26	$ 720.00	50 days	8%	May 6
6.	July 15	$1,248.24	90 days	9%	Oct 13

Find the amount of interest, the maturity value, the amount of discount, and the proceeds of each of the interest-bearing notes below. (When a note expressed in *months* is discounted, use the *exact* number of days between the day of the discount and the maturity date.)

	Face of Note	Time of Note	Interest Rate	Date of Note	Discount Date	Discount Rate
7.	$6,200.00	3 months	$7\frac{1}{2}$%	Aug. 3	Aug. 14	8%
8.	$7,350.00	60 days	9%	June 15	July 3	10%
9.	$5,475.00	60 days	8%	Jan. 31	Feb. 2	7%
10.	$3,580.00	90 days	$7\frac{1}{2}$%	Feb. 15	Mar. 17	8%
11.	$786.00	90 days	9%	June 5	July 17	$7\frac{1}{2}$%
12.	$580.50	6 months	8%	Aug. 5	Nov. 28	9%

D. COMPOUND INTEREST AND PRESENT VALUE

When money is loaned or borrowed for longer than one interest period, the interest for that period may be added to the principal, unless it is paid. Then the next month's interest is computed on the original principal plus the interest of the first period. Likewise, when money is left on deposit in a savings bank account, the bank will add the interest to the balance in the account, then compute the interest for the next period on the new, higher balance. This process of adding the interest for each period to the principal before interest is calculated for the next period is called *compound interest*. The process may be repeated as many times as there are interest periods. The final result will be the amount due or the *compound total.* This total less the original principal is the compound interest paid or due.

$100.00	original note
×0.07	annual interest rate
$ 7.00	interest for first year
+100.00	principal (note) for first year
$107.00	new principal (for second year)
× 0.07	annual interest rate
$ 7.49	interest for second year
+107.00	second year principal
$114.49	principal for third year
× 0.07	annual interest rate
$ 8.01	interest for third year
+114.49	third year principal
$122.50	amount due at end of third year (compound total)
−100.00	original note
$ 22.50	total amount of compound interest paid

If only *simple interest*—interest on the principal only—was paid, the amount of interest would be calculated as follows:

$$I = P \times R \times T$$

$$I = \overset{1}{\cancel{100}} \times \frac{7}{\underset{1}{\cancel{100}}} \times 3 = \$21$$

The compound interest is $1.50 more than the simple interest. This amount would be even larger if the note were larger or the interest were compounded more often (daily, monthly, etc.).

Short cut: Normally, it is not necessary to know the amount of interest for each interest period, only the amount due at the end of the last interest period. We may compute the amount due by multiplying the original note by the interest-rate-plus 100% and each succeeding new principal by the same rate. For example:

$100.00	
×1.07	
$107.00	due at end of first year
×1.07	
$114.49	due at end of second year
×1.07	
$122.50	due at end of third year

COMPOUND INTEREST
TABLES

If interest on an amount must be compounded for many periods, computation becomes a time-consuming chore. Tables are available that greatly reduce the time and effort needed to compute the compound amount (see Table 6.1).

To determine the compound amount of $1,000 at 6% for five years, compounded annually:

Example

1. Find the 5 in the periods column, then go across to the 6% column and find the number 1.3382. 1.3382 represents what $1 today at compound interest will be worth five years from now. That is to say, each dollar today will have earned a little less than 34¢ at the end of five years.

2. Multiply that figure by $1,000, since the table is computed for $1 amounts of principal; the compound amount becomes $1,338.20.

MORE FREQUENT
COMPOUNDING

Many banks, credit unions, and savings and loan associations compound interest monthly or even daily in the intense competition for the saver's dollar. The computer has made this practical.

To compound more frequently than once a year:

1. Multiply the number of years by the number of times compounding occurs per year to determine the number of interest periods.

2. Divide the annual rate by the number of times compounding occurs per year to determine the rate for each interest period.

3. Then follow the same steps used in annual compounding.

This procedure may be followed whether interest is computed by arithmetic or the use of tables.

Therefore in calculating the compound amount of $1,000 at 8% for three years compounded quarterly, find the compound interest on $1,000 at 2% (8% ÷ 4) for 12 (3 yrs. × 4) interest periods.

PRESENT VALUE

The value at the present time of a sum of money that will yield a desired amount of money at a particular date in the future is known as the *present value* of that sum of money. From a personal viewpoint, present value may be used to determine the amount that you must save in order to have a certain sum of money in a definite number of years to send children to college, start a business, or buy a home. In the business world, this method is often used to determine how much must be saved periodically or regularly to provide a definite income or pension in a given number of years or to accumulate the face value of a bond issue to be paid off at maturity.

To compute *present value,* determine the rate of compound interest, the number of years or interest periods for which the amount is to be held, and the amount desired at the end of the specified time. (Present value is really the computation of compound interest in reverse—taking what is computed as the answer in compound interest and finding the beginning number.)

Table 6.1 Growth of $1 at compound interest (to 4 decimal places)

Interest Periods	1%	$1\frac{1}{2}$%	2%	$2\frac{1}{2}$%	3%	$3\frac{1}{2}$%	4%	$4\frac{1}{2}$%	5%	$5\frac{1}{2}$%	6%	7%	8%	Interest Periods
1	1.0100	1.0150	1.0200	1.0250	1.0300	1.0350	1.0400	1.0450	1.0500	1.0550	1.0600	1.0700	1.0800	1
2	1.0201	1.0302	1.0404	1.0506	1.0609	1.0712	1.0816	1.0920	1.1025	1.1130	1.1236	1.1449	1.1664	2
3	1.0303	1.0457	1.0612	1.0769	1.0927	1.1087	1.1249	1.1412	1.1576	1.1742	1.1910	1.2250	1.2597	3
4	1.0406	1.0614	1.0824	1.1038	1.1255	1.1475	1.1699	1.1925	1.2155	1.2388	1.2625	1.3108	1.3605	4
5	1.0510	1.0773	1.1041	1.1314	1.1593	1.1877	1.2167	1.2462	1.2763	1.3070	1.3382	1.4026	1.4693	5
6	1.0615	1.0934	1.1262	1.1597	1.1941	1.2293	1.2653	1.3023	1.3401	1.3788	1.4185	1.5007	1.5869	6
7	1.0721	1.1098	1.1487	1.1887	1.2299	1.2723	1.3159	1.3609	1.4071	1.4547	1.5036	1.6058	1.7138	7
8	1.0829	1.1265	1.1717	1.2184	1.2668	1.3168	1.3686	1.4221	1.4775	1.5347	1.5938	1.7182	1.8509	8
9	1.0937	1.1434	1.1951	1.2489	1.3048	1.3629	1.4233	1.4861	1.5513	1.6191	1.6895	1.8385	1.9990	9
10	1.1046	1.1605	1.2190	1.2801	1.3439	1.4106	1.4802	1.5530	1.6289	1.7081	1.7908	1.9672	2.1589	10
11	1.1157	1.1779	1.2434	1.3121	1.3842	1.4600	1.5395	1.6229	1.7103	1.8021	1.8983	2.1049	2.3316	11
12	1.1268	1.1956	1.2682	1.3449	1.4258	1.5111	1.6010	1.6959	1.7959	1.9012	2.0122	2.2522	2.5182	12
13	1.1381	1.2136	1.2936	1.3785	1.4685	1.5640	1.6651	1.7722	1.8856	2.0058	2.1329	2.4098	2.7196	13
14	1.1495	1.2318	1.3195	1.4130	1.5126	1.6187	1.7317	1.8519	1.9799	2.1161	2.2609	2.5785	2.9372	14
15	1.1610	1.2502	1.3459	1.4483	1.5580	1.6753	1.8009	1.9353	2.0789	2.2325	2.3966	2.7590	3.1722	15

Table 6.2 Present value of one at compound interest (to 4 decimal places)

Interest Periods	1%	$1\frac{1}{2}$%	2%	$2\frac{1}{2}$%	3%	$3\frac{1}{2}$%	4%	$4\frac{1}{2}$%	5%	$5\frac{1}{2}$%	6%	7%	8%	Interest Periods
1	.9901	.9852	.9804	.9756	.9709	.9662	.9615	.9569	.9524	.9479	.9434	.9346	.9259	1
2	.9803	.9707	.9612	.9518	.9426	.9335	.9246	.9157	.9070	.8985	.8900	.8734	.8573	2
3	.9706	.9563	.9423	.9286	.9151	.9019	.8890	.8763	.8638	.8516	.8396	.8163	.7938	3
4	.9610	.9422	.9238	.9060	.8885	.8714	.8548	.8386	.8227	.8072	.7921	.7629	.7350	4
5	.9515	.9283	.9057	.8839	.8626	.8420	.8219	.8025	.7835	.7651	.7473	.7130	.6806	5
6	.9420	.9145	.8880	.8623	.8375	.8135	.7903	.7679	.7462	.7252	.7050	.6663	.6302	6
7	.9327	.9010	.8706	.8413	.8131	.7860	.7599	.7348	.7107	.6874	.6651	.6227	.5835	7
8	.9235	.8877	.8535	.8207	.7894	.7594	.7307	.7032	.6768	.6516	.6274	.5820	.5403	8
9	.9143	.8746	.8368	.8007	.7664	.7337	.7026	.6729	.6446	.6176	.5919	.5439	.5002	9
10	.9053	.8617	.8203	.7812	.7441	.7089	.6756	.6439	.6139	.5854	.5584	.5083	.4632	10
11	.8963	.8489	.8043	.7621	.7224	.6849	.6496	.6162	.5847	.5549	.5268	.4751	.4289	11
12	.8874	.8364	.7885	.7436	.7014	.6618	.6246	.5897	.5568	.5260	.4970	.4440	.3971	12
13	.8787	.8240	.7730	.7254	.6810	.6394	.6006	.5643	.5303	.4986	.4688	.4150	.3677	13
14	.8700	.8118	.7579	.7077	.6611	.6178	.5775	.5400	.5051	.4726	.4423	.3878	.3405	14
15	.8613	.7999	.7430	.6905	.6419	.5969	.5553	.5167	.4810	.4479	.4173	.3624	.3152	15
16	.8528	.7880	.7284	.6736	.6232	.5767	.5339	.4945	.4581	.4246	.3936	.3387	.2919	16
17	.8444	.7764	.7142	.6572	.6050	.5572	.5134	.4732	.4363	.4024	.3714	.3166	.2703	17
18	.8360	.7649	.7002	.6412	.5874	.5384	.4936	.4528	.4155	.3815	.3503	.2959	.2502	18
19	.8277	.7536	.6864	.6255	.5703	.5202	.4746	.4333	.3957	.3616	.3305	.2765	.2317	19
20	.8195	.7425	.6730	.6103	.5537	.5026	.4564	.4146	.3769	.3427	.3118	.2584	.2145	20

Example   How much money must be invested for five years at 6% interest, compounded annually, to provide $1,000 at the end of that period?

Look at the present value table (Table 6.2), under the 6% column across from Period 5. That figure, 0.7473 (about 75 cents) represents the amount you would have to invest now at 6% compound interest in order to have $1.00 in five years. Multiplying the 0.7473 by the desired amount, $1,000 gives $747.30. This means that to accumulate $1,000 in five years, $747.30 must be invested this year at 6% compound interest. To prove this, turn back to the compound interest table (Table 6.1) and look in the 6% column across from Period 5. Multiply the 1.3382 from the table by $747.30, which gives $1,000.03686. The difference of three or four cents is caused by the rounding off in the tables.

Remember, for more frequent compounding, divide the interest rate and also multiply the number of periods by the number of times compounding occurs per year. To compute the above problem at 6%, compounded semiannually (instead of 6% annual interest), look for the present value figure in Table 6.2 under the 3% column on the line for 10 interest periods.

Projects 31 through 34 may be done now.

PROJECT 31   COMPOUND INTEREST; PRESENT VALUE

Find the total amount due for the following notes at compound interest. Check your answer by using Table 6.1.

	Principal	Term (Years)	Rate of Compound Interest	How Compounded
1.	$1,000	3	6%	semiannually
2.	1,200	4	7%	semiannually
3.	2,400	2	8%	quarterly
4.	3,000	6	7%	annually
5.	800	1	10%	quarterly
6.	2,500	3	7%	semiannually

Find the amount of money to the nearest dollar that must be invested under the following conditions to accumulate the required amount. (Use Table 6.2.)

Required Amount	Number of Years Invested	Rate of Compound Interest	How Compounded
7. $ 600	5	7%	annually
8. 3,500	3	6%	quarterly
9. 5,000	3	9%	semiannually
10. 1,800	6	8%	annually
11. 2,700	2	8%	quarterly

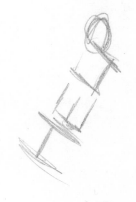

PROJECT 32   PROBLEMS ON NOTES

1. Find the bank discount and proceeds on a note for $2,500.00 dated August 8 and due in three months with 8% interest, discounted October 1 at 9%.

2. What are the proceeds of a note for $450, dated April 18 and due in 90 days with interest at $7\frac{1}{2}\%$, discounted June 17 at 7%?

3. Find the date of maturity, the term of discount, the bank discount, and the proceeds of a 60-day non-interest-bearing note for $1,250.00 dated October 15 and discounted October 27 at $9\frac{1}{2}\%$.

157

4. Find the date of maturity, term of discount, bank discount, and proceeds of a $850 non-interest-bearing note, dated September 30, due in five months, and discounted January 14 at $8\frac{3}{4}$%.

5. Ann Keller deposited $3,600 in a mutual savings bank. If the money earned a 6% annual dividend, compounded quarterly, how much compound interest did she receive at the end of two years if she permitted the earnings to accumulate? Check your answer by using Table 6.1.

6. Tom Howe's investment club pays interest at the rate of 8% compounded quarterly. If he opened his account with a $600 deposit, how much will he have in his account in two years (assume no withdrawals are made during this period)? Check your answer by using Table 6.1.

PROJECT 33 MORE PROBLEMS

1. How much must Arthur Jones invest today at 8% interest, compounded quarterly, to accumulate $5,000 at the end of five years to help provide for his son's education? (Use Table 6.2.)

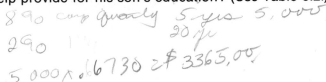

2. Find the proceeds of the following interest bearing note if it is discounted November 27 at 9%.

$2,250.00   August 27,   19 77

Four Months   after date I   promise to pay to

the order of George K. Hatch

Two Thousand Two Hundred Fifty 00/100   Dollars

Payable at Farmer's National Bank of Topeka, Kansas

Value received with interest at 8%

No. 645   Due December 27, 1977   Kenneth Corey

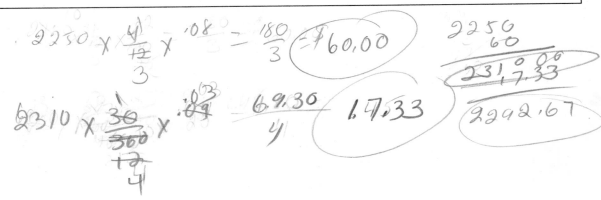

3. Four years from now, Tina Travers will need about $6,100 for a summer tour of Europe. How much must she invest today at 7% compounded semiannually to have enough for her vacation? (Use Table 6.2.)

4. On March 3, Joan Kelley discounted a 100-day, 7% interest-bearing note in the amount of $1,550, which she received from Marcia Holmes on January 10. If the bank charged 8% discount, how much did Joan receive for the note?

5. Henderson Corporation's sales increased an average of 6% per year over a six-year period. If the sales the first year were $422,000, what were the sales for the seventh year?

6. The contract of the sales manager of a local store provided for a beginning yearly salary of $14,500, with annual increases of 5%. What was his salary for the fifth year?

PROJECT 34   NOTES: REVIEW

Al's Auto Shop received the following notes during the three-month period March 1 to May 31:

	Date	Face Amount	Term	Interest Rate	Date Discounted
1.	March 15	$2,500	90 days	8%	March 20
2.	March 24	4,200	30 days	—	April 5
3.	April 8	3,000	2 months	$8\frac{1}{2}$%	May 4
4.	April 17	940	120 days	9%	May 27
5.	May 1	3,600	60 days	7%	May 31

These notes were discounted at the California Commerce Bank on the dates indicated at a discount rate of 9%. Find for each note: (a) the due date, (b) the amount of interest, (c) the maturity value, (d) the discount period, (e) the discount, and (f) the proceeds.

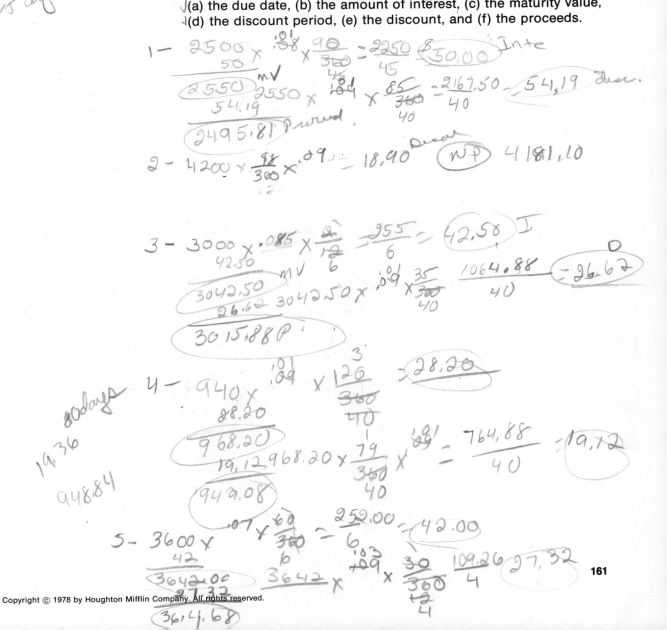

6. Jerry Smith deposited $10,000 in the Fisherman's Savings Bank, which pays 6% compounded quarterly. At the same time he deposited another $10,000 in Harrison National Bank, which pays 6% compounded semiannually. Compare the interest received from the two banks at the end of 3 years. Which bank pays more interest? What is the difference?

7. Find the amount you must invest now to have $1,700 at the end of five years assuming interest of (a) 8% compounded quarterly, or (b) 9% compounded semiannually.

8. On May 15, Ann Rigo borrowed $930 for 66 days. She paid $13.64 interest. What was the rate of interest?

9. Arthur Green received a check on July 19 from a customer in payment of a loan made on April 20 at 7% interest. The amount of the interest was $16.45. What was the amount of the loan?

LEMONADE 5¢

SHORT-TERM LOANS 15½% INTEREST

7 INTEREST: CONSUMER APPLICATIONS

KEY POINTS TO LEARN FROM THIS CHAPTER

1. **How to figure the interest on savings accounts**

2. **How to compute the actual interest paid on an installment loan**

3. **How to figure the rebate of interest on a loan paid off early**

4. **How different kinds of charge accounts work**

5. **How home mortgages are computed**

MINICASE

Marty and Joan Baker were students at Ocean Park Community College. After graduation, they were married and went to work— Marty as a sales representative for a local manufacturer and Joan as an assistant buyer for a specialty store. They planned to live on Marty's salary and put Joan's salary in the bank to save for a down payment on their own home. A few months later, their car began to require many repairs, so they decided to trade it in for a newer, more reliable vehicle. The following Friday night they went to the bank so Joan could deposit her check, and they inquired about paying off the small loan on the old car and taking out a new loan.

When the teller returned Joan's passbook, the interest since last time had been added—$8.33. She had expected it to be $25.00 because she had computed her interest at the bank's advertised rate of 5%, and there was a $500 balance in her account.

Next, they talked with a loan officer about paying off the $433.33 balance on their old car loan and getting a new loan for $2,000. Two years ago Marty had borrowed $1,000 at 10% for three years. The bank had added $300 for interest to the balance, giving a total amount owed of $1,300. Now that the loan was two-thirds paid, they figured they would need $333.33 to pay off the loan because the bank would not charge the final year's interest ($100) if the loan was paid a year early. The loan officer said they were mistaken; they would need $398.19.

Neither Marty nor Joan really understood how banks figure interest on savings and loans.

165

A. SAVINGS ACCOUNTS

Example 1 shows Joan Baker's savings account ledger card after her interest and new deposit were added. She had expected to receive $25 interest but got only $8.33. The teller explained that although the first $200 was in the bank for the entire six-month period, the $200 deposited on March 28 was in the bank only three months (April, May, and June), and the $100 deposited on May 1, only two months (May and June). Naturally, she received no interest on the newest deposit made that day. The interest is computed as follows:

$$I = P \times R \times T$$

Dec. 31 $I = 200 \times \dfrac{5}{100} \times \dfrac{6}{12} = \$5.00$

Mar. 28 $I = 200 \times \dfrac{5}{100} \times \dfrac{3}{12} = \ 2.50$

May 1 $I = 100 \times \dfrac{5}{100} \times \dfrac{2}{12} = \ 0.83$

Interest for the six-month period $\overline{\$8.33}$

This bank pays interest to depositors every six months on money deposited by the tenth of each month. Many banks today pay interest every three months or every month or even every day. Whatever the time period, four basic facts should be remembered:

1. The advertised rate of interest is an annual (yearly) rate; therefore, interest is computed by multiplying the deposit by the rate and by the number of months the deposit is in the bank.

Example 1   Savings account ledger card

#336274

Name: Joan or Martin Baker
Address: 11 B Gull Place
Truro, Massachusetts

	Date	Withdrawals	Deposits	Balance	Memo
1	Dec. 31, '76	Bal. brought forward		600—	
2	Dec. 31, '76	400—		200—	6 mos.
3	Mar. 28, '77		200—	400—	3 mos.
4	May 1, '77		100—	500—	2 mos.
5	June 30, '77	6 mos. int.	8.33	508.33	
6	June 30, '77		100—	608.33	
7					
8					
9					

2. Interest is paid for the length of time the money has been on deposit, not for the interest period. (Credit is often given for a whole month if money is deposited within the first 10 days of the month.)

3. No interest is paid on money withdrawn *before* the end of the interest period even though that money may have been on deposit for a long time during the period. With a daily interest account, an interest period ends every day, and all deposits earn interest. (Interest on these accounts is usually *paid* monthly, however.)

4. Interest is added automatically (unless it is withdrawn) to the balance and is computed on the new balance at the end of the next interest period (see Chapter 6, Section D, compound interest).

There are numerous kinds and varieties of savings accounts—each with its own advantages and disadvantages as to flexibility, interest rates, options, and methods of computing interest on both deposits and withdrawals. The method shown here is not necessarily used at every bank, but rather is presented as a way to help you understand the basic computation of interest on savings accounts. While daily interest eliminates most of the penalties in the system shown here, and also the depositor receives a slightly larger amount of interest by compounding daily, the daily interest account is usually offered at a lower rate of interest. This type of account should be chosen when money (especially larger amounts) is deposited and withdrawn within a short period of time. Before opening an account, one must carefully consider all the advantages and disadvantages.

See Example 2 for a comparison of interest rates compounded at varying lengths of time. If a depositor plans to leave money in the bank for a period of time, a higher paying regular (or 90-day notice)

Example 2 True annual rate of interest (yield)

Nominal Annual Rate	The True Annual Rate if Compounded . . .				
	Semiannually	Quarterly	Monthly	Weekly	Daily
5.25	5.3189	5.3542	5.3781	5.3874	5.3898
5.50	5.5756	5.6144	5.6407	5.6509	5.6536
5.75	5.8326	5.8751	5.9039	5.9151	5.9180
6.00	6.0900	6.1363	6.1677	6.1799	6.1831
6.25	6.3476	6.3980	6.4321	6.4454	6.4488
6.50	6.6056	6.6601	6.6971	6.7115	6.7152
6.75	6.8639	6.9227	6.9627	6.9783	6.9823
7.00	7.1225	7.1859	7.2290	7.2457	7.2500
7.25	7.3814	7.4495	7.4958	7.5138	7.5185
7.50	7.6406	7.7135	7.7632	7.7825	7.7875
7.75	7.9001	7.9781	8.0312	8.0519	8.0573
8.00	8.1600	8.2432	8.2999	8.3220	8.3277
8.25	8.4201	8.5087	8.5692	8.5927	8.5988

Reprinted with permission from *Changing Times* magazine, © 1973 Kiplinger Washington Editors, Inc., December 1973.

account would be more profitable. Using Example 2, annual interest on $1,000 left on deposit for a year, at $5\frac{1}{2}\%$ compounded at various times, would be:

Compounded Semiannually

$1,000 \times 5.5756 = \$55.76$

Compounded Quarterly

$1,000 \times 5.6144 = \$56.14$

Compounded Monthly

$1,000 \times 5.6407 = \$56.41$

Compounded Daily

$1,000 \times 5.6536 = \$56.54$

But $5\frac{3}{4}\%$, Compounded Semiannually

$1,000 \times 5.8326 = \$58.33$

Project 35 may be done now.

PROJECT 35   SAVINGS ACCOUNTS

1.   Compute the amount of interest (5%—according to the four basic facts listed on pp. 166–167) or the balance for each box marked with an asterisk(*) on p. 170. Label each answer "interest" or "balance" for a particular date. (Show your work in the space below.)

2.   Compute the amount of interest (5%—according to the four basic facts listed on pp. 166–167) or the balance for each box marked with an asterisk(*) on p. 170. Label each answer "interest" or "balance" for a particular date. (Show your work in the space below.)

IN ACCT. WITH _____ Sarah Shaw   #982111

	DATE	WITHDRAWALS	DEPOSITS	MEMO	BALANCE	TELLER	MEMO
A							
1	Aug 1/73		100.00		100.00	A	
2	Aug 27/73		45.00		145.00	C	
3	Oct 12/73		10.00		155.00	B	
4	Oct 30/73	25.00			130.00	G	
5	Nov 11/73		15.00		145.00	B	
6	Dec 10/73		35.00		180.00	A	
7	Dec 29/73		40.00		220.00	C	
8	Dec 31/73	6 mos. int.	*3.17		*223.17	A	
9	Jun 30/74	6 mos. int.	*5.58		*228.75	G	
10	Oct 7/74	40.00			*188.75	E	
11	Dec 31/74	6 mos. int.	*4.72		*193.47	B	
12	Jun 7/75		671.43		*864.90	A	
13	Jun 30/75	6 mos. int.	*7.63		*872.53	G	
14	Dec 31/75	6 mos. int.	*21.81		*894.34	C	
15	May 31/76	355.00			*539.34	F	
16	Jun 30/76	6 mos. int.	*17.16		*556.50	C	
17	Dec 31/76	6 mos. int.	*13.91		*570.41	E	
18	Feb 9/77		50.00		*626.41	A	
19	May 14/77	22.50			*597.91	B	
20	Jun 9/77		30.00		*627.91	E	
21	Jun 30/77	6 mos. int.	*15.52		*643.43	A	
22	Dec 31/77	6 mos. int.	*16.09		*659.52	C	
23							

IN ACCOUNT WITH
CONSUMERS SAVINGS BANK
TOLLAND, IDAHO

IN ACCT. WITH __George M. Gilkson   #3 924 673__

	DATE	WITHDRAWALS	DEPOSITS	MEMO	BALANCE	TELLER	MEMO
A							
1	Feb 14/74		2,000.00		2,000.00	A	
2	Jun 30/74	6 mos. int.	* 50.00		*2050.00	E	
3	Aug 6/74		575.00		*2625.00	G	
4	Sept 15/74	100.00			*2525.00	B	
5	Oct 10/74		75.00		*2700.00	A	
6	Nov 12/74		72.14		*2772.14	C	
7	Dec 4/74	25.00			*2747.14	F	
8	Dec 31/74	6 mos. int.	*		*	A	
9	Jun 30/75	6 mos. int.	*		*	A	
10	July 6/75		263.50		*	B	
11	Dec 31/75	6 mos. int.	*		*	G	
12	Feb 11/76		235.25		*	C	
13	May 29/76	300.00			*	D	
14	Jun 30/76	6 mos. int.	*		*	F	
15	Sept 24/76	375.00			*	G	
16	Dec 1/76		300.00		*	A	
17	Dec 31/76	6 mos. int.	*		*	C	
18	Jun 30/77	6 mos. int.	*		*	D	
19							
20							
21							
22							
23							

**IN ACCOUNT WITH
DOLLAR SAVINGS BANK
LINCOLN, NEW HAMPSHIRE**

B. INTEREST ON INSTALLMENT PURCHASES AND LOANS

In Chapters 5 and 6, you learned how to compute interest on single payment loans in which the entire amount of the loan was to be paid on the maturity date. Many people who cannot pay cash for their purchases would rather make small monthly payments than face one large payment some time in the future. Indeed, businesses believe that customers are more likely to settle their debts if they pay a small part every month. From this belief and the desire to buy now regardless of ability to pay, has come an important part of American business—the *installment loan*. Whether a customer borrows money from a bank and repays it in monthly payments or buys merchandise in a store and pays for it weekly or monthly, that customer is doing the same thing—using someone else's money for his or her own purpose.

When merchandise is bought on the installment plan, the customer makes a deposit, called a *down payment*, then pays the remainder of the price weekly or monthly in equal parts. The total price on an installment purchase is the price for cash plus a *service* or *carrying charge*—really an interest charge. The amount of the carrying charge can be computed by subtracting the cash price from the installment price.

Example

Jack Taylor bought a $459 television set for $534 with a down payment of $70. He promised to repay the balance in 12 equal monthly installments. What were the carrying charge and monthly installment on this purchase?

$534	installment price	$534.00	installment price
−459	cash price	−70.00	down payment
$ 75		12)$464.00	amount to be financed
		$ 38.67	monthly installment

Jack actually borrows $389 ($459 − 70) when he buys on the installment plan. The procedures are similar to borrowing $389 from the store owner and paying interest on this debt. He pays $75 for the use of the $389 for one year, even though he won't have its full use for the entire year. Because he is slowly repaying his loan, he has the use of less and less of the $389 each month. This is a very expensive way to buy merchandise. Many Americans do not realize the high interest rates they pay when interest is computed on the *original* balance. The truth-in-lending acts have compelled stores, banks, credit unions, and finance companies to tell the customer in writing the *actual* interest rate they are paying.

In the Jack Taylor example, the store computed the amount of the monthly payment by adding the interest, or carrying charge, to the cash price. Then they subtracted the down payment and divided the result by the number of payments to be made. This is the *level-payment* plan, in which the customer makes equal payments throughout the life of the loan.

$459	cash price	$534.00	installment price
+75	carrying charge (interest)	−70.00	down payment
$534	installment price	12)$464.00	
		$ 38.67	amount to be financed per month

Some loans and installment plans compute interest by other methods. Interest on the unpaid balance will be discussed later in this chapter (see Section F, Home Mortgages).

C. ACTUAL RATE OF INTEREST ON INSTALLMENT LOANS

Because Jack Taylor *actually borrowed* $389 and is regularly paying off a portion of this loan,

during the first	month he has the use of	$389.00
" " second	" " " " " "	362.00*
" " third	" " " " " "	334.00*
" " fourth	" " " " " "	305.00*
" " fifth	" " " " " "	275.00*
" " sixth	" " " " " "	244.00*
" " seventh	" " " " " "	212.00*
" " eighth	" " " " " "	179.00*
" " ninth	" " " " " "	145.00*
" " tenth	" " " " " "	110.00*
" " eleventh	" " " " " "	74.00*
" " twelfth	" " " " " "	37.00*

The *actual* rate of interest that Jack Taylor is paying can be computed by using the formula:

$$R = \frac{2mi}{P(n + 1)}$$

where R = the actual rate of interest per year

m = the number of payment periods in one year

i = the dollar cost of interest or carrying charge

P = cash price minus the down payment (the amount borrowed)

n = the total number of installment payments one makes

$$R = \frac{2mi}{P(n + 1)} = \frac{2(12)(75)}{(389)(12 + 1)} = 35.6\%$$

The $75 Jack paid may seem rather small, but it is really a 35.6% interest rate. If this had been a one-payment loan, like those in Chapters 5 and 6 (not paid by installment payments each month), then the $75 carrying charge would be equivalent to a 19% interest rate. The problem arises because the interest is computed on the $389, but Jack does not have the use of the $389 for the full year. Jack might have saved money by finding a bank or credit union that would give him a loan at a much lower rate.

Example

In the story at the beginning of this chapter, Marty Baker borrowed $1,000 for three years at an advertised rate of 10%. The interest was $300. What was the actual rate he paid?

$$R = \frac{2mi}{P(n + 1)} = \frac{2(12)(300)}{1,000(36 + 1)} = 19.5\%$$

*The payment minus interest charge per month, based on the Rule of 78's.

Again, because the interest charge was computed on the original balance, and Marty repaid his loan in installments, the actual interest rate was 19.5% rather than the 10% advertised.

D. RULE OF 78'S

When the bank officer told him he needed $398.19 to pay off his auto loan, Marty was surprised. He thought he owed only the $333.33 of the principal. The officer explained that the bank uses the "Rule of 78's" to compute rebates on loans that are paid off early. The bank applied most of his early installment payments to the interest instead of reducing the principal. Most consumer loans use this method. Another name for this method, which can be applied to a loan of any duration, is the *sum-of-the-digits* method.

A bank assumes that on a 12-month loan 12 units of principal are outstanding the first month, 11 units the next month, and so on, down to the last month, when one unit of principal remains. Since the sum of the numbers (digits) from 12 to 1 is 78, the total interest or charge for the loan is divided into 78 parts. (There are 300 parts to a 24-month loan, 666 parts to a 36-month loan, etc.) For the first month of the loan, 12/78 of the total interest is considered to be earned by the bank. At this point, 66/78 would be the rebate. The next month the bank earns 11 *more* parts, for a total of 23/78, leaving a rebate of 55/78 of the total interest after 2 months. When a loan is repaid in full, the rebate is simply the unearned charge. Banks often use tables that give the rebate figure at a glance.

12-Month Loan	24-Month Loan	36-Month Loan
12	24	36
11	23	35
10	22	34
9	21	33
8	20	32
7	19	31
6	18	30
5	17	.
4	.	.
3	.	.
2	2	2
+1	+1	+1
78	300	666

To save time or to compute a loan of a longer term, use the formula:

$$\text{Sum of digits} = N\,\frac{(N+1)}{2}$$

Example

1. How would this work for a 36-month loan?

$$S = \overset{18}{\cancel{36}}\,\frac{\overset{37}{\cancel{(36+1)}}}{\underset{1}{\cancel{2}}} = 666$$

2. To compute Marty's rebate:

$1,300.00 balance including interest on a three-year loan
$\underline{-866.67}$ payments for two years
$433.33 balance at end of second year

Total Interest Charge = $300

$$\text{Rebate} = \frac{78}{666} \times \$300 = \$35.14$$

36
·
·
·
12
11
10
9 } sum of digits of remaining year = 78
·
·
·
2
$\underline{1}$
666 for a 3-year loan

$433.33 balance owed
$\underline{-35.14}$ rebate
$398.19 payoff figure

Projects 36 and 37 may be done now.

Example 3 Portion of a personal loan note (note circled items)

$..............

————— ....19..

FOR VALUE RECEIVED, I/We (jointly and severally, if more than one) promise to pay to—————Savings Bank on order, at its principal office in—————,

.... dollars repayable in........monthly installments of $..............each, and a final installment of $..............plus any accumulated late charges due, the first installment being payable on......................and the remaining installments on the same date in each successive month, together with interest at the rate of 6% per annum on each installment after maturity until fully paid, having deposited with, transferred to, or executed and delivered to said Bank as security for the payment of this and any and all other liabilities, direct or indirect, absolute or contingent, due or to become due, now existing or hereafter existing, of mine/ours or either of us to said Bank, its successors or assigns, the following property, viz:

....

Any deposits or other sums at any time credited by or due from the holder to any maker, co-maker, endorser, or guarantor hereof and any securities or other property of any maker, co-maker, endorser or guarantor hereof in the possession of the holder may at all times be held and treated as collateral security for the payment of this note and any and all other liabilities, direct or indirect, absolute or contingent, due or to become due, now existing or hereafter arising, of said respective maker, co-maker, endorser, or guarantor to the holder. The holder may apply or set off such deposits or other sums against said liabilities on or after maturity of the liabilities.

Any Unpaid Balance May Be Paid, At Any Time, Without Penalty and Any Unearned Finance Charge Will Be Refunded Based on the Rule of 78's.

This note shall, at the option of the holder, become immediately due and payable without notice or demand upon the occurrence of any of the following events: (a) failure to pay any monthly installment on the due date thereof; (b) if at any time the

PROCEEDS ....$.......
OFFICIAL FEES ....
OTHER PERMITTED CHARGES (ITEMIZE) ....
AMOUNT FINANCED ....$.......
FINANCE CHARGE ....
TOTAL OF PAYMENTS ....$.......
ANNUAL PERCENTAGE RATE ....%

PROJECT 36 INSTALLMENT INTEREST: RULE OF 78'S

1. Jean Adams bought a $448 color television set for $500 on the installment plan. She made a $60 down payment and promised to pay the balance in 12 equal payments. Compute the carrying charge and the monthly payment.

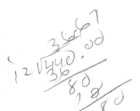

2. Brian James bought his first car for $1,200 on the installment plan. The cash price was $950. He put $400 down and promised to repay the balance in 30 equal payments. How much was the interest charge, and how much did he have to pay each month?

3. Using the formula $R = \dfrac{2mi}{P(n+1)}$, compute the actual rate of interest in Problem 1 above.

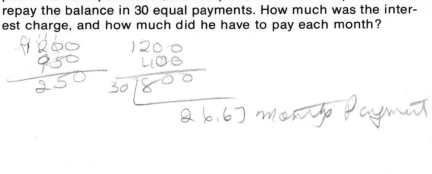

179

4. Using the formula $R = \dfrac{2mi}{P(n+1)}$, compute the actual rate of interest in Problem 2 above.

$$\frac{2(12)(250)}{550(30+1)} \quad \frac{6000}{17050} = 35.29\%$$

5. If Jean Adams in Problem 1 paid off the balance on her account shortly after she made her sixth monthly payment, would she get one-half of the carrying charge returned to her? Find (a) the total of the six payments made, (b) the balance owed after the sixth payment, (c) the rebate of carrying charge to be made, and (d) the amount needed to pay off the debt.

440

$$36.67 \quad -\$220.02$$
$$219.98$$

$$\frac{39}{78} \times 52 = \frac{2028}{78} \quad 26.00$$

$$219.98$$
$$-26.00$$
$$193.98$$
Pay off
figer

6. (a) Compute the sum of the digits for a 30-month loan.
(b) Compute the sum of the digits for an 18-month loan.

$$30 \frac{30+1}{2} = 450$$

$$18 \frac{18+1}{2} = 171$$

$$\left(N \frac{N+1}{2} \right)$$

PROJECT 37 INSTALLMENT INTEREST; RULE OF 78'S

1. If Brian James in Problem 2 of Project 36 paid off his car loan after one year of payments, how much would he have to pay? Find (a) the total of the 12 payments made, (b) balance owed after the twelfth payment, (c) rebate of carrying charge to be made (see Problem 6 of Project 36), (d) the amount needed to pay off the debt.

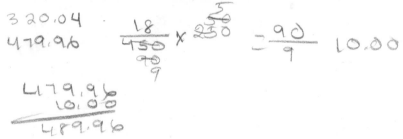

2. Dottie Gendron bought a stereo system for $800 plus interest charges of 10% on the balance owed for two years. She paid 10% down and promised to pay the balance in 24 equal installments. Now she has paid 18 installments, and she is considering paying off the loan. Find (a) the interest charge, (b) the monthly payment, (c) the actual rate of interest (d) the total of the 18 payments made, (e) the balance owed after the eighteenth payment, (f) the rebate of the interest charge, and (g) the payoff figure.

181

3.   The Gifford family bought a station wagon for $6,500 plus 10% on the balance owed for three years. They turned in their two-year-old car (worth $2,600) and promised to pay the balance in three years. After making 12 payments, they decide to pay off the loan and trade in the car. Find (a) the total installment cost, (b) the balance owed and monthly payment, (c) the actual rate of interest, (d) the total of the 12 payments made, (e) the balance owed after the twelfth payment, (f) the rebate of the interest charge (compare this with two-thirds of the interest charge), and (g) the payoff figure.

E. CHARGE ACCOUNTS

REGULAR CHARGE ACCOUNTS

Generally speaking, *regular charge accounts* are 30-day accounts. Any purchases made during a month appear on the next month's statement, and the balance shown is due within 25 to 30 days from the date of the statement. Extended terms are not available, and interest is not charged for use of the store's money.

REVOLVING CHARGE ACCOUNTS

Most so-called *revolving charge accounts* are 30-day accounts with optional payment plans. The name "revolving" comes from the fact that each account has a limit ($200, $300, or $500, for example) on the total that may be owed at one time. As soon as any amount of the balance is paid, the customer may charge additional merchandise until the outstanding balance reaches the limit again. Although this kind of account is handled in much the same way as the regular account (use of charge plate, signature on sales slip, etc.), the optional payment plans make the difference. On most such accounts you have the following choices:

1. You may pay your bill in full within each monthly billing period and avoid a finance charge. This way, the account operates exactly the same as a *regular* charge account.

2. You may pay the minimum amount requested on the statement. To maintain a good credit record and be able to continue to use the account you must pay *at least* this minimum. The minimum payment is often computed by taking 10% of the unpaid balance, but many stores vary this method. The store may require full payment if the balance is under $10 or $15, or provide a table of boundaries within which a certain payment is due (a balance of $100 to $150 would require a minimum payment of $15, etc.)

3. You may pay an amount larger than required, thereby decreasing future finance charges.

Choices 2 and 3 incur a finance charge. This charge may be computed on the unpaid balance at the end of the previous month *or* on the unpaid balance less any payments made in the current month. The interest rate varies from store to store and from state to state. Many states allow $1\frac{1}{2}$% per month (18% per year), while others permit a maximum of only 1% or $1\frac{1}{4}$% per month. Often the rate is $1\frac{1}{2}$% per month on balances up to $500 and 1% on any amount over $500 (rates of 18% and 12% per year). Many stores put an arbitrary 50¢ or 75¢ charge on any balance below a certain amount, say $25 or $35. As a rule, interest is not charged on purchases of the current month. Thus, the revolving charge account customer has the same 30-day period to pay for purchases, without finance charge, as the regular charge account customer.

Example

Debbie Lynn's revolving charge account balance on her June statement from Apex Department Store was $152.33. During June she bought three articles valued at $5.75, $19.89, and $11.39. On June 21, she made a payment of $25.00. Apex requires a minimum payment of 10% and adds a finance charge of $1\frac{1}{2}$% on the previous balance less payments made this month.

(a) Did she satisfy the minimum payment? (b) What was the finance charge on the July statement? (c) Find the new balance on the July statement.

(a) 10% of $152.33 = $15.23
Yes, her $25 more than met the minimum payment.

(b) $152.33   previous balance
    $\underline{-25.00}$ this month's payment
    $\$127.33 \times 1\frac{1}{2}\% = \$1.91$ finance charge

(c) $152.33   previous balance
    5.75 ⎫
    19.89 ⎬ purchases
    11.39 ⎭
    $\underline{\quad 1.91}$ finance charge
    $191.27
    $\underline{-25.00}$ payment
    $166.27   new balance on July statement

BANK CHARGE CARDS

A bank charge card is really a revolving charge account issued by a bank for use at a variety of stores, restaurants, and service businesses. For the customer, it is the same as having revolving accounts at an untold number of businesses. Generally speaking, the maximum balance and the computation of both the minimum payment and the finance charge are the same as for the revolving charge account. Because it is so easy to use, a bank charge card must be handled very carefully to avoid getting deeply in debt before one realizes it. Eighteen percent per year is a very high interest rate to pay for items that might be more wisely bought for cash or, if necessary, bought with a regular bank loan at a lower interest rate.

In addition to the charge account advantages of bank charge cards, small amounts ($25, $50, $100, $200, etc.) can be borrowed simply by presenting the card at the bank. Some banks supply card holders with blank checks that may be written for any amount as long as the total of checks and the present balance does not exceed the maximum allowed for the account. Writing one of these checks is the same as negotiating a loan by presenting the card at the bank. Many banks do not give 30 days of freedom from finance charges on the loans and checks but compute interest beginning the very first month.

Project 38 may be done now.

PROJECT 38   CHARGE ACCOUNTS

1. Based on the revolving charge account statement shown below, compute the following: (a) total purchases and charges, (b) total payments and refunds, (c) finance charge—$1\frac{1}{2}\%$ of the previous balance less any payments made during the month, (d) new balance, (e) minimum payment due—for balances up to $10, the minimum is the full amount; for balances up to $100, it is $10. (f) If a $25 payment is made in November and no more purchases are made, what finance charge will appear on the December statement?

Big Bargain Stores, Inc.				Date: 11–5–77	
Date	Reference Number	Dept. #	Transaction Description	Purchases and Charges	Payments and Refunds
Oct. 6	543169	10	Gloves	$11.95	
Oct. 10	913245	2	Film, Bulbs	6.29	
Oct. 15			Payment, Thank You		45.00
Oct. 22	621543	7	Girl's Coat	41.10	
Oct. 22	562194	8	Boy's Pants	15.95	
Oct. 24	913245	2	Return – Bulbs		1.29
Previous Balance	Total Purchases and Charges	Total Payments, Etc.	Finance Charge	New Balance	Minimum Payment
52.79	*75.29*	*46.29*	*.42*	*82.21*	*$10.00*

Handwritten work:

5.28

52.79
25.00
———
27.79

$27.79 \times 1\frac{1}{2} = \$.42$

128.50
-46.29
———
82.21

$_5\ 7.21 \times 1\frac{1}{2} = .86$

$(.71)$

2. Based on the bank charge card statement shown below, compute the following: (a) total purchases and charges, (b) total payments and refunds, (c) finance charge—$1\frac{1}{2}\%$ of the previous balance less any payments made during the month plus any cash advances, (d) new balance, (e) minimum payment due—10% of new balance. (f) If a $50 payment is made in April and no more purchases are made, what finance charge will appear on the May statement?

Date: April 8, 1977

County Bank & Trust Co. Charge Card

Date	Transaction	Purchases and Charges	Payments and Returns
Mar. 10	Smith Hardware	12.76	
14	Harold's Drug Stores	14.39	
17	Don's Mens Store	35.89	
22	Payment – Thank You		140.00
30	Cash Advance	100.00	

Previous Balance	Total Purchases and Charges	Total Payments	Finance Charge	New Balance	Minimum Payment
$320.25	163.04	140.00	4.20	347.49	34.75

320.25
163.04

$220.25 \times 1\frac{1}{2} = \$4.20$

487.49
140
347.49

f) 262.74 — $3.94

F. HOME MORTGAGES

Once you have selected the home you want to buy, you must arrange the financing. You have to make certain decisions about where to go for the financing, how large a down payment you can make, and the type of loan to ask for—conventional, FHA, or GI.

A *conventional loan* is made directly to the homeowner by a bank or other lending institution. *FHA* and *GI loans* also are made by lending institutions, but the United States government guarantees their repayment, at least in part. The GI loan is guaranteed for certain war veterans, and the FHA loan is guaranteed when the homeowner meets certain standards for housing and pays an insurance premium in addition to other mortgage-loan costs. All three types of home loans are *direct-reduction mortgages*. In contrast, the older straight mortgage requires repayment of the principal in one lump sum at the end of the loan. The direct-reduction mortgage is so named because the borrower makes a fixed monthly payment that both includes interest (and perhaps taxes and insurance) *and reduces the principal of the mortgage debt*.

In the first few months, installments cover mostly interest and only small amounts are for repayment of principal. As the principal is gradually reduced, a larger and larger portion of the monthly payment applies to repayment of principal. Interest at the agreed-upon rate is figured on the *unpaid balance* of the loan.

Examples

1. Table 7.1 shows the first 10 payments on a five-year direct-reduction loan of $3,300 at 6%. Regular monthly payment of $63.80 repays the principal and pays interest on the unpaid balance. Notice that even by the end of 10 months the interest has dropped from $16.50 to $14.33, while payment on the principal has increased from $47.30 to $49.47. The last payment at the end of five years is $0.32 for interest and $63.39 for principal (only $63.71 is needed on the final payment to pay off the loan).

2. Notice that the interest is always computed on the outstanding, or unpaid balance. See the interest for the third and the seventh month in Table 7.1.

Table 7.1

	Time		Payment on		Balance
Yrs.	Mos.	Periods	Interest	Principal	of Loan
0	1	1	16.50	47.30	3,252.70
0	2	2	16.26	47.54	3,205.16
0	3	3	16.03	47.77	3,157.39
0	4	4	15.79	48.01	3,109.38
0	5	5	15.55	48.25	3,061.13
0	6	6	15.31	48.49	3,012.64
0	7	7	15.06	48.74	2,963.90
0	8	8	14.82	48.98	2,914.92
0	9	9	14.57	49.23	2,865.69
0	10	10	14.33	49.47	2,816.22

Interest for third month: Outstanding balance = $3,205.16; time = 1 month.

$$I = P \times R \times T$$

$$I = \underset{3{,}205.16}{\overset{1{,}602.58}{\cancel{3{,}205.16}}} \times \frac{\cancel{6}}{100} \times \frac{1}{\underset{1}{\overset{2}{\cancel{12}}}}$$

$$= 16.0258 = \$16.03$$

Interest for seventh month: Outstanding balance = $3,012.64; time = 1 month.

$$I = P \times R \times T$$

$$I = \underset{3{,}012.64}{\overset{1{,}506.32}{\cancel{3{,}012.64}}} \times \frac{\cancel{6}}{100} \times \frac{1}{\underset{1}{\overset{2}{\cancel{12}}}}$$

$$= 15.0632 = \$15.06$$

The total fixed payment each month is applied first to pay the interest and then to reduce the unpaid balance or principal.

Third month		Seventh month	
$63.80	payment	$63.80	payment
−16.03	interest	−15.06	interest
$47.77	principal	$48.74	principal

Other costs that may increase the monthly payment are:

1. One-twelfth of the annual real estate tax bill.

2. One-twelfth of the annual insurance payment on an FHA loan or of the property insurance if required.

3. Penalty or late charges (usually computed as a percent of the monthly payment) if payments are made after the due date.

The mathematics of direct-reduction loans of 15, 20, or 25 years, payable in monthly installments, are too complicated for the average borrower to compute; even banks use tables. The amount of a loan is influenced, of course, by the price of the house purchased and the amount of the down payment. The monthly payments are also determined by the length (time) of the loan and the interest rate. The longer the loan period, the smaller the monthly payments needed to pay it off, but the size of the payments do not decrease in proportion to the increase in the number of payments, because the amount of interest is much larger on a longer-term loan. The FHA estimates that a 30-year mortgage costs about 60% more in interest than a 20-year mortgage; but on a 20-year loan, monthly payments are only about 20% higher than on the 30-year loan. See Table 7.2 to compute approximate monthly payments.

Table 7.2 Annual payment necessary to amortize a loan of $1000

Terms in Years	Interest Rate								
	7	$7\frac{1}{4}$	$7\frac{1}{2}$	$7\frac{3}{4}$	8	$8\frac{1}{4}$	$8\frac{1}{2}$	$8\frac{3}{4}$	9
2	553.10	555.01	556.93	558.85	560.77	562.70	564.62	566.55	568.47
3	381.06	382.80	384.54	386.29	388.04	389.79	391.54	393.30	395.06
4	295.23	296.90	298.57	300.25	301.93	303.61	305.29	306.98	308.67
5	243.90	245.53	247.17	248.81	250.46	252.11	253.77	255.43	257.10
6	209.80	211.42	213.05	214.68	216.32	217.96	219.61	221.27	222.92
7	185.56	187.18	188.81	190.44	192.08	193.72	195.37	197.03	198.70
8	167.47	169.10	170.73	172.37	174.02	175.67	177.34	179.00	180.68
9	153.49	155.13	156.77	158.42	160.08	161.75	163.43	165.11	166.80
10	142.38	144.03	145.69	147.36	149.03	150.72	152.41	154.11	155.83
11	133.36	135.03	136.70	138.39	140.08	141.78	143.50	145.22	146.95
12	125.91	127.59	129.28	130.99	132.70	134.42	136.16	137.90	139.66
13	119.66	121.36	123.07	124.79	126.53	128.27	130.03	131.79	133.57
14	114.35	116.07	117.80	119.55	121.30	123.07	124.85	126.64	128.44
15	109.80	111.54	113.29	115.06	116.83	118.62	120.43	122.24	124.06
16	105.86	107.62	109.40	111.18	112.98	114.79	116.62	118.46	120.30
17	102.43	104.21	106.01	107.81	109.63	111.47	113.32	115.18	117.05
18	99.42	101.22	103.03	104.86	106.71	108.56	110.44	112.32	114.22
19	96.76	98.58	100.42	102.27	104.13	106.01	107.91	109.81	111.74
20	94.40	96.24	98.10	99.97	101.86	103.76	105.68	107.61	109.55
21	92.29	94.16	96.03	97.93	99.84	101.76	103.70	105.65	107.62
22	90.41	92.29	94.19	96.11	98.04	99.98	101.94	103.92	105.91
23	88.72	90.62	92.54	94.48	96.43	98.39	100.38	102.37	104.39
24	87.19	89.12	91.06	93.01	94.98	96.97	98.97	100.99	103.03
25	85.82	87.26	89.72	91.69	93.68	95.69	97.72	99.76	101.81
26	84.57	86.53	88.50	90.50	92.51	94.54	96.59	98.65	100.72
27	83.43	85.41	87.41	89.42	91.45	93.50	95.57	97.64	99.74
28	82.40	84.39	86.41	88.44	90.49	92.56	94.64	96.74	98.86
29	81.45	83.47	85.50	87.55	89.62	91.71	93.81	95.93	98.06
30	80.59	82.62	84.68	86.75	88.83	90.94	93.06	95.19	97.34

Reproduced from Financial Mortgage Guide Publication No. 149, pages 110–111, copyright 1970, Financial Publishing Company, Boston.

1. To find the annual payment, locate the term (in years) of a mortgage, then trace across that line to the column headed by the interest rate of the loan.

2. Take the annual payment, multiply by the number of times $1,000 goes into the loan, and then divide by 12.

Example   Find the approximate monthly payment of a $15,000 loan at 9% amortized over (payments spread over) 25 years.

$1,000 at 9% for 25 years = $101.81

$$\frac{\$101.81}{\underset{4}{\cancel{12}\ \text{months}}} \times \overset{5}{\cancel{15}} = \frac{509.05}{4}$$

$$= 127.2625 = \$127.26 \quad \text{approximate monthly payment}$$

Project 39 may be done now.

PROJECT 39 HOME MORTGAGES

A. Using Table 7.2, find the approximate monthly payment needed to amortize the loan and pay taxes and other costs.

	Size of Loan	Interest Rate	Term (Years)	Taxes	FHA Insurance (per Year)	Fire Insurance (per Year)
1	$30,000	8%	20	$1,100	—	—
2	21,000	$8\frac{1}{4}$%	25	750	$87.29	$172
3	22,500	$8\frac{1}{2}$%	30	1,425	110.70	205
4	15,000	9%	25	1,000	—	—
5	25,000	$7\frac{1}{2}$%	15	1,600	—	—

(handwritten work)

1 — 101.86

$\dfrac{101.86}{\frac{12}{2}} \times 30^{5} = \dfrac{509.30}{2}$ \$254.65

$\dfrac{101.86}{12} \times 31 = \dfrac{3157.66}{12} = \$263.14$

2. $\dfrac{95.69}{12} \times 21 = \dfrac{2009.49}{12}$ 167.46

$\dfrac{95.69}{\frac{12}{6}} \times \dfrac{11}{12} = \dfrac{1052.59}{6} =$ 175.43

3. $\dfrac{93.06}{12} \times 24^{2} = -$ 186.12

$\dfrac{93.06}{\frac{12}{6}} \times \dfrac{11}{12} = \dfrac{1023.66}{6} = 170.61$

4. $\dfrac{101.81}{\frac{12}{4}} \times 15^{5} = \dfrac{509.05}{4} = 127.26$

$\dfrac{101.81}{\frac{12}{3}} \times \dfrac{4}{12} = \dfrac{407.24}{3} = 135.75$

5. $\dfrac{113.29}{\frac{12}{6}} \times 26^{13} = \dfrac{1472.77}{6} = 245.46$

$\dfrac{113.29}{12} \times 25 = \dfrac{2832.25}{12} = 236.02$

191

B. Compute the amount of interest payment and the amount of principal payment to be applied against the loan for the first two months of each of the loans in Problem A above.

BETTY BALANCE
CERTIFIED PUBLIC ACCOUNTANT

RECEIPTS BALANCE INCOME

8 THE BALANCE SHEET AND THE INCOME STATEMENT

KEY POINTS TO LEARN FROM THIS CHAPTER

1. **How to prepare a balance sheet**
2. **Different types of income statements**
3. **How to use the information on the statements**

MINICASE

The students majoring in retailing at South Shore Community College have been given permission to open a campus store for textbooks, supplies, and other student needs. John Montgomery, president of the Retailing Club, appointed Sara Gomez manager of the store. John and Sara, along with other officers of the club, held a store organizational meeting the next day. All the members listed their particular talents that they thought would be most helpful to get the store set up and to continue its operation.

Professor Wilson, the club's adviser, agreed that their talents were diverse enough to operate the store well, but he pointed out that someone would have to keep accurate records of the business and to produce a balance sheet and income statement in proper form at the end of each year. The statements' form must follow precisely the format set up by the finance and auditing department of the state. Furthermore, Professor Wilson said that someone should analyze the statements each year and compare them with past years' statements to see how well the store is doing and what decisions should be made for the future. Not one of the students felt qualified to perform these duties.

195

A. PREPARING THE BALANCE SHEET

One of the two major statements in accounting is the *balance sheet.* It is a list of the assets, liabilities, and capital of a business as of a specific date, usually at the close of the last day of a month or a year. It is the formal statement presentation of the basic accounting equation

Assets = Liabilities + Capital,

where *assets* are the properties owned by the business (including not only real property but also cash, equipment, accounts receivable, inventory, etc.),

liabilities are the creditor's *rights* to the properties (or the amount owed by the business), and

capital is the owner's *rights* to these properties (or the amount of clear ownership of the business by the owner).

A balance sheet is like a snapshot. It is a picture of the financial condition of the business at a particular instant in time (usually the end of an accounting period). When something happens in the business, the picture changes, and the balance sheet no longer represents the *present* financial condition of the business.

The first step in preparing a balance sheet (or any other accounting statement) is the heading. Often this is written in three lines to answer three identification questions: (1) Who? the name of the company or organization. (2) What? the name of the statement, here the balance sheet. (3) When? the date of the statement or the period covered by it.

Next comes the statement body, which is broken into three main sections—Assets, Liabilities, and Capital—each clearly labeled. A subtotal must be computed for each section, and total assets must equal total liabilities plus capital.

The statement may be a simple one, as in Example 1. The owner

Example 1   Balance sheet, report form

```
              Merry Merchandising Company
                    Balance Sheet
                    April 30, 1977


                        ASSETS

Cash  . . . . . . . . . . . . . . .   $15,000.00
Total assets  . . . . . . . . . .     $15,000.00

                     LIABILITIES

Notes payable   . . . . . . . . . .   $ 5,000.00

                      CAPITAL

Charles Merry, capital  . . . . .     $10,000.00
Total liabilities and capital  . .    $15,000.00
```

Example 2   Balance sheet, account form

Merry Merchandising Company
Balance Sheet
April 30, 1977

ASSETS		LIABILITIES	
Cash	$15,000.00	Notes payable	$ 5,000.00
		CAPITAL	
		Charles Merry, capital . . .	$10,000.00
Total assets	$15,000.00	Total liabilities and capital	$15,000.00

of a newly organized company has invested $10,000 in the business by depositing that amount in a special checking account in the name of the business. He has also borrowed $5,000 from a local bank.

This balance sheet is written in *report form*, that is, assets, liabilities, and capital are listed vertically, one under the other. The *account form* (see Example 2) has two columns with all the assets listed on the left and all the liabilities plus the capital on the right. The account form more clearly shows the balancing theory in a balance sheet, but it is difficult to prepare on a standard typewriter. The report form is becoming the more popular because it can be typed more easily than the account form. Notice in both forms that when a total is written to which nothing will later be added or subtracted, the total is underlined twice. Notice also that in the account form, total assets and total liabilities and capital are always placed on the *same* line, even if it means leaving extra space between some lines on one side.

After a company has been in business for a period of time, it may have many assets and liabilities. In the Gem Furniture Co. statement (Example 3), assets are classified as current assets and plant assets. *Current assets* are cash and any other assets that can be turned into cash, sold, or used up within a year through normal business operations. *Plant assets* are tangible assets of a fixed and permanent nature, such as machinery. Other asset clarifications are *long-term investments* and *tangible assets*. Liabilities are divided into current and long-term, like assets. *Current liabilities* are debts that will be due within a year and that are to be paid out of current assets. You should use as many columns in a statement as you consider necessary for full understanding and clarity. Subtotals and totals belong in the right-hand columns; the more detailed financial information appears on the left.

If a business is organized as a corporation, the capital section of the balance sheet is called the *stockholders' equity* section. This section is divided into *paid-in capital* and *retained earnings* (see Example 4).

Example 3 Balance sheet, report form, with assets classified

Gem Furniture Co.
Balance Sheet
September 30, 1977

ASSETS

Current assets:			
Cash		$ 8,460	
Notes receivable		9,150	
Accounts receivable		7,615	
Interest receivable		80	
Merchandise inventory		60,130	
Store supplies		350	
Prepaid insurance		1,340	
Total current assets			$87,125
Plant assets:			
Store equipment	$5,380		
Less accumulated depreciation	3,160	$ 2,220	
Office equipment	$2,955		
Less accumulated depreciation	1,495	1,460	
Total plant assets			3,680
Total assets			$90,805

LIABILITIES

Current liabilities:		
Notes payable	$ 3,740	
Accounts payable	3,925	
Salaries payable	125	
Interest payable	60	
Unearned interest	30	
Total liabilities		$ 7,880

CAPITAL

R. B. Moore, capital	82,925
Total liabilities and capital	$90,805

Example 4   Balance sheet, report form, for a corporation

Gem Furniture Co., Inc.
Balance Sheet
September 30, 1977

ASSETS

Current assets:			
Cash		$ 8,460	
Notes receivable		9,150	
Accounts receivable		7,615	
Interest receivable		80	
Merchandise inventory		60,130	
Store supplies		350	
Prepaid insurance		1,340	
Total current assets			$87,125
Plant assets:			
Store equipment	$5,380		
Less accumulated depreciation	3,160	$ 2,220	
Office equipment	$2,955		
Less accumulated depreciation	1,495	1,460	
Total plant assets			3,680
Total assets			$90,805

LIABILITIES

Current liabilities:		
Notes payable	$ 3,740	
Accounts payable	3,925	
Salaries payable	125	
Interest payable	60	
Unearned interest	30	
Total liabilities		$ 7,880

STOCKHOLDERS' EQUITY

Paid-in capital:			
Preferred 6% stock, cumulative, $100 par (1,000 shares authorized, 200 shares issued)	$20,000		
Common stock, $10 par (10,000 shares authorized, 5,200 shares issued)	52,000		
Total paid-in capital		$72,000	
Retained earnings		10,925	
Total stockholders' equity			82,925
Total liabilities and stockholders' equity			$90,805

Projects 40 and 41 may be done now.

PROJECT 40   BALANCE SHEET

1. Prepare a *report form* balance sheet for Henry's TV Repair Shop as of June 30, 1977. Then do again in *account form*.

Accounts payable	$ 100.00	Notes payable	$ 400.00
Accounts receivable .	400.00	Office equipment .	1,200.00
Cash	2,720.00	Henry Theriault,	
Delivery equipment ..	1,000.00	capital	4,820.00

[Handwritten balance sheet]

Henry's TV Repair Shop
Balance Sheet
June 30, 1977

Assets

Cash	2720.00
Account Receivable	400.00
Delivery Eq	1000.00
Office Equip	1200.00
	5320.00

Liabilities

Notes Payable	400.00
Accounts Payable	100.00
	500.00

Capital

Henry Theriault, Capital	4820.00
Total liabilities & capital	5320.00

201

[Handwritten balance sheet for Wenny TO Repair Shop, Balance Sheet, June 30, 1927]

Assets

Cash	2720. —	Notes Payable	400.00	
Accounts Receivable	400. —	Account Payable	100.00	
Delivery Eq.	1000. —		500.00	
Office Eq	1200. —	*Capital*		
		Wenny Theriault, capital	4820.00	
	5320.00	Total liabilities + capital	5320.00	

2. **Prepare a balance sheet in *report form* for Fred's Fishing Shop as of September 30, 1977.**

Accounts receivable	$ 1,051.75	Prepaid insurance	$ 372.57
Accounts payable	2,586.43	Store equipment	3,510.00
Cash	3,625.81	Store supplies	257.30
Merchandise inventory	17,655.00	Wages payable	1,623.86
Office equipment	1,656.35	F. A. Troy, capital	23,918.49

[Handwritten: Fred's Fishing Shop, Balance Sheet, September 30, 1977]

Assets

Cash	3625.81
Account receivable	1051.75
Merchandise Inventory	17655.00
Office Eq	1656.35
Store Eq	3510.00
Store Supplies	257.30
Prepaid Insurance	372.57
	28128.78

Liabilities

Acct. Payable	2586.43
Wages Payable	1623.86
	4210.29

Capital

F. A. Troy, capital	23918.49
Total liab. + capital	28128.78

PROJECT 41   BALANCE SHEET

1. From the information presented below, prepare a balance sheet in *report form* for the Marsh Company as of December 31, 1977. Use the back of this page for your answers, then go on to Problem 2 on p. 205.

Cash	$ 5,327
Accounts receivable	9,210
Office supplies	320
Store supplies	170
Delivery equipment	14,150
Accumulated depreciation—D.E.	3,200
Store and office equipment	7,500
Accumulated depreciation—S. & O.E.	2,000
Accounts payable	7,890
Property taxes payable	370
Salaries payable	1,390
M.J. Marsh, capital	21,827

2.   Prepare a balance sheet in *report form* for the Dart Corporation as of December 31, 1977 from the information below.

Accounts payable	$ 19,000
Accounts receivable	12,000
Accumulated depreciation—B	45,000
Accumulated depreciation—D.E.	21,890
Building	100,000
Cash	34,720
Common stock ($50 par, 1,500 shares authorized, 1,206 shares issued)	60,300
Delivery equipment	43,500
Interest payable	200
Land	20,250
Mortgage note payable	43,900
Notes receivable	8,500
Retained earnings	27,580
Salaries payable	1,100

Example 5 Income statement for a service business

```
              ABC Television Repair Co.
                  Income Statement
          For the Month Ended August 31, 1977
```

Service income		$8,324.43
Operating expenses:		
Salary expense	$5,630.00	
Supplies expense	955.25	
Truck expense	144.50	
Depreciation expense—trucks . .	110.00	
Rent expense	100.00	
Depreciation expense—equipment .	50.00	
Insurance expense	35.66	
Miscellaneous expense	303.48	
Total operating expenses . . .		7,328.89
Net income		$ 995.54

B. INCOME STATEMENT FOR A SERVICE BUSINESS

The other important accounting statement is the *income statement.* In a service business, the income statement is a statement presentation (see Example 5) of the basic formula

Gross Income (or Profit) − Expenses = Net Income

A service business does not sell merchandise. It offers knowledge or services; some examples are architects, accountants, doctors, lawyers, painters, television repairshops, and laundromats. The total income received minus the total expenses (costs of doing the work) yields the net income for the particular accounting period. Notice that the dateline of the heading is "For the month ended . . ." or "For the year ended. . . ." This is because an income statement covers an entire accounting period. The balance sheet, on the other hand, shows the condition of the business at a particular instant in time.

C. INCOME STATEMENT FOR A MERCHANDISING BUSINESS

The income statement for a merchandising business is an extension of the form for a service business. Because the business sells a product, the cost of the product as well as income and operating expenses must be considered (see Example 6). The income statement is a statement presentation of the formula

Cost + Gross profit = Selling price, or

Gross profit = Selling price − Cost.

But since in a service business

Gross profit − Expenses = Net Income

by substitution

(Selling Price − Cost) − Expenses = Net Income.

Example 6 Income statement for a merchandising business

Gem Furniture Co.
Income Statement
For the Year Ended September 30, 1977

Revenue from sales:			
Sales		$103,400	
Less: Sales returns and allowances		1,950	
Net sales			$101,450
Cost of goods sold:			
Merchandise inventory, Oct. 1, 1976		$ 59,325	
Purchases	$59,800		
Less: Purchases discount	960		
Net purchases		58,840	
Merchandise available for sale		$118,165	
Less: Merchandise inventory, Sept. 30, 1977		60,130	
Cost of goods sold			58,035
Gross profit on sales			$ 43,415
Operating expenses:			
Selling expenses:			
Sales salaries	$12,735		
Advertising expense	4,065		
Insurance expense—selling	970		
Depreciation expense—			
store equipment	540		
Store supplies expense	595		
Miscellaneous selling expense	495		
Total selling expenses		$ 19,400	
General expenses:			
Office salaries	$ 5,290		
Rent expense	3,000		
Insurance expense—general	330		
Depreciation expense—			
office equipment	285		
Miscellaneous general expense	580		
Total general expenses		$ 9,485	
Total operating expenses			28,885
Net income from operations			$ 14,530
Other income:			
Interest income		$ 685	
Other expense:			
Interest expense		475	210
Net income			$ 14,740

The merchandising business not only sells goods; sometimes it must also accept returns of merchandise. These returns are subtracted from *gross sales* to give *net sales*. Net income from operations results from subtracting operating expenses from gross profit on sales, but this does not give the final net income figure. There may be certain income or expense items not connected with the normal operations of the business. These items must be listed in the last two sections of the statement—"other income," or "other expense."

D. COMPUTATION OF COST OF GOODS SOLD

The "cost of goods (or merchandise) sold" section of the income statement is a very important section. In its simplest form this section states (all figures are *at cost*):

Beginning inventory	(*goods on our shelves* at the beginning of the accounting period)
+ Purchases	(goods bought during the period)
= Goods available for sale	(all we *could have sold*, if we sold out)
− Ending inventory	(goods we *did not sell*—still on our shelves)
= Goods sold	(or, since all the above figures are at *cost*, Cost of goods sold)

This computation may be summarized as

$B + P - E = CGS.$

Within this framework, the cost for purchases may have to be computed. As used here, the purchases are *net* purchases, that is, gross purchases plus freight costs and minus discounts and returns.

Projects 42 and 43 may be done now.

George Wiener, M.D.
Income Statement
For Year Ended March 31, 1977

Professional fee earness $ 50,645

Operating Expenses

Insurance Expense $ 5,600
Miscellaneous Ex   130
Rent Ex   2400
Salaries Ex   6750
Supplies Ex   8590
Telephone Ex   357
Utilities Ex   495
                                              $ 18322

                                              $ 32323

Linder Specialty Shops
Income Statement
For Year Ended Jan. 1, 1977

Revenue for Sales
Sales   240,170

PROJECT 42   INCOME STATEMENT

Show your work for these problems below and on the back of this sheet.

1. Prepare an income statement for George Minor, M.D., as of March 31, 1977 (one-year period).

Insurance expense	$ 5,600
Miscellaneous expense	130
Professional fees (income)	50,645
Rent expense	2,400
Salaries expense	6,750
Supplies expense	2,590
Telephone expense	357
Utilities expense	495

2. Linda Tompkins, owner of Linda's Specialty Shops, had a merchandise inventory balance of $46,750 on January 1, 1977. At the end of 1977 she had the following balances in her accounts. Prepare an income statement for the current year.

Advertising expense	$ 1,520
Depreciation expense, office equipment	380
Depreciation expense, store equipment	860
Insurance expense	1,230
Interest expense	380
Merchandise inventory	55,290
Miscellaneous general expense	680
Miscellaneous selling expense	970
Office salary expense	17,150
Office supplies expense	250
Purchases	161,890
Rent expense	7,200
Sales	240,170
Sales salary expense	31,350
Store supplies expense	2,860
Taxes expense	910
Utilities expense	1,420

211

PROJECT 43   COST OF GOODS SOLD

1.   Present the "cost of goods sold" section of the income statement for Gentry Sales Co. from the information below.

Merchandise inventory, Oct. 1, 1976	$ 72,431.67
Merchandise inventory, Sept. 30, 1977	31,112.18
Purchases	95,300.50
Purchases discounts	180.00
Sales	122,440.60

2.   The general expenses of Office Machines, Ltd., were 17% of sales and 34% of the cost of goods sold. The selling expenses were 10% of sales. The merchandise inventory (M.I.) at the beginning of the year was $40,000, and decreased 25% during the year. Net income for the year was $115,000. Prepare an income statement for the year ended June 30, 1977. [Hint: Sketch out the basic income statement and then fill in the known percentages. Find the unknown percentages and dollar amounts. More space is provided at the top of the next page.]

213

3. Two or more items are omitted in each of the following tabulations of income statement data. Find the amounts of the missing items, identifying them by letter.

Sales	Sales Returns	Net Sales	Beginning Inventory	Net Purchases	Ending Inventory	Cost of Goods Sold	Gross Profit
$41,000	(a)	$38,000	$ 7,000	$35,000	(b)	$30,000	$ 8,000
(c)	$ 4,000	54,000	(d)	45,000	$25,000	35,000	19,000
73,000	5,000	68,000	20,000	(e)	15,000	(f)	11,000
50,000	3,000	(g)	12,000	40,000	(h)	38,000	(i)
80,000	(j)	80,000	(k)	65,000	12,000	(l)	12,000

E. ANALYZING THE STATEMENTS

All businesspeople need to know how to analyze financial statements. The statements contain valuable information if you know how to read them. Users of financial statements often can get a clearer picture of a business by studying the relationships between items.

HORIZONTAL ANALYSIS

Horizontal analysis is the analysis of percent increase or decrease in like items in similar statements for two or more accounting periods (see Example 7). The amount of increase or decrease in each item is listed, with the rate (percent) of increase or decrease. When two statements are compared, the number from the earlier statement is used as the base or denominator of the fraction.

Example

Using the statement in Example 7, compute the amount and rate of increase or decrease, thus verifying the figures in the last four columns.

Gross sales, 1976–1977

$1,750,000	1977
−1,000,000	1976
$ 750,000	increase

$$\frac{750,000}{1,000,000} = \frac{75}{100} \text{ or } 75\%$$

Gross sales, 1977–1978

$1,750,000	1977
−1,500,000	1978
$ 250,000	decrease

$$\frac{250,000}{1,750,000} = \frac{1}{7} = 14\frac{2}{7}\% \text{ or } 14\%$$

Computations for all the other lines in the statement can be done in the same way. Rates may be rounded to the nearest whole percent. The same types of comparisons can be made with balance sheet information as with income statement information (see Example 8).

Project 44 may be done now.

Example 7   Income statement, set up for horizontal analysis

UHLMAN COMPANY
Condensed Comparative Income Statement
For the Years Ended December 31, 1976, 1977, 1978

| | 1976 | 1977 | 1978 | Increase or Decrease* | | | | |
| | | | | 1976–1977 | | 1977–1978 | | |
				Amount	Percent	Amount	Percent
Gross sales	1,000,000	1,750,000	1,500,000	750,000	75	250,000*	14*
Sales returns	50,000	100,000	75,000	50,000	100	25,000*	25*
Net sales	950,000	1,650,000	1,425,000	700,000	74	225,000*	14*
Cost of goods sold	630,000	1,200,000	1,000,000	570,000	90	200,000*	17*
Gross profit on sales	320,000	450,000	425,000	130,000	41	25,000*	6*
Selling expenses	240,000	300,000	280,000	60,000	25	20,000*	7*
General expenses	100,000	110,000	100,000	10,000	10	10,000*	9*
Total expenses	340,000	410,000	380,000	70,000	21	30,000*	7*
Net profit or loss* from operations	20,000*	40,000	45,000	60,000	—	5,000	13
Other income	50,000	65,000	75,000	15,000	30	10,000	15
Other expenses	30,000	105,000	120,000	75,000	250	15,000	14
	10,000	20,000	20,000	10,000	100	—	—
Net income before income tax	20,000	85,000	100,000	65,000	325	15,000	18
Income taxes	5,000	25,000	30,000	20,000	400	5,000	20
Net income after income taxes	15,000	60,000	70,000	45,000	300	10,000	17

*Asterisks indicate decrease.

Example 8 Balance sheet, set up for horizontal analysis

UHLMAN COMPANY
Condensed Comparative Balance Sheet
December 31, 1976, 1977, 1978

	1976	1977	1978	Increase or Decrease* 1976–1977		Increase or Decrease* 1977–1978	
				Amount	Percent	Amount	Percent
ASSETS							
Current assets	673,500	955,500	855,000	282,000	42	100,500*	11*
Investments	250,000	400,000	500,000	150,000	60	100,000	25
Plant and equipment (net)	675,000	875,000	775,000	200,000	30	100,000*	11*
Intangibles	100,000	100,000	100,000	—	—	—	—
Deferred costs	61,500	60,500	48,000	1,000*	2*	12,500*	21*
Total assets	1,760,000	2,391,000	2,278,000	631,000	36	113,000*	5*
LIABILITIES							
Current liabilities	130,000	546,000	410,000	416,000	320	136,000*	25*
Long-term debt	300,000	400,000	400,000	100,000	33	—	—
Total liabilities	430,000	946,000	810,000	516,000	120	136,000*	14*
CAPITAL							
6% preferred stock	250,000	350,000	350,000	100,000	40	—	—
Common stock	750,000	750,000	750,000	—	—	—	—
Additional paid-in capital	100,000	100,000	100,000	—	—	—	—
Retained earnings	230,000	245,000	268,000	15,000	7	23,000	9
Total capital	1,330,000	1,445,000	1,468,000	115,000	9	23,000	2
Total liabilities and capital	1,760,000	2,391,000	2,278,000	631,000	36	113,000*	5*

*Asterisks indicate decrease.

PROJECT 44   HORIZONTAL ANALYSIS OF STATEMENTS

Analyze the following two statements by comparing the 1977 figures with those of 1976. Compute the amount and the percent of increase or decrease (denote by *), and enter the answers in the columns at the right.

1.

MASON SHOE CORPORATION
Comparative Balance Sheet
June 30, 1977 and 1976

	1976–77	1975–76	Increase or Decrease*	
			Amount	Percent
ASSETS				
Current assets:				
Cash	$ 310,000	$ 791,000		
Accounts receivable (net) .	780,000	570,000		
Inventories	1,360,000	1,100,000		
Prepaid expenses	91,000	75,000		
Total current assets . . .	$2,541,000	$2,536,000		
Fixed assets:				
Land	$1,200,000	$1,200,000		
Buildings (net)	1,939,000	1,021,000		
Machinery (net)	650,000	500,000		
Total fixed assets	$3,789,000	$2,721,000		
Total assets	$6,330,000	$5,257,000		
LIABILITIES				
AND STOCKHOLDERS' EQUITY				
Current liabilities:				
Accounts payable	$ 540,000	$ 475,000		
Salaries payable	365,000	340,000		
Taxes payable	250,000	453,000		
Total current liabilities.	$1,155,000	$1,268,000		
Stockholders' equity:				
Capital stock	$1,400,000	$1,400,000		
Retained earnings	3,775,000	2,589,000		
Total stockholders' equity	$5,175,000	$3,989,000		
Total liabilities and				
stockholders' equity	$6,330,000	$5,257,000		

*Asterisks indicate decrease.

2.

MASON SHOE CORPORATION
Comparative Income Statement
for the Years Ended June 30, 1977 and 1976

	1976–77	1975–76	Increase or Decrease*	
			Amount	Percent
Sales (net)	$10,500,000	$10,000,000		
Cost of goods sold	7,750,000	7,500,000		
Gross profit on sales	$ 2,750,000	$ 2,500,000		
Less: operating expenses . .	1,775,000	1,763,000		
Net income before taxes . . .	$ 975,000	$ 737,000		
Less: estimated income taxes	459,000	355,000		
Net income	$ 516,000	$ 382,000		

VERTICAL ANALYSIS   *Vertical analysis* is the analysis in percents of the relationship of the component parts *to the total* in *one* statement. Although the analysis is done within each individual statement, the significance of both the amounts and the percentages is enhanced by preparing comparative statements. On an income statement, it is customary to compare all amounts with net sales, which is considered to be 100%. All other items on the income statement are reported as a percentage of net sales (see Example 9). On the balance sheet, the percentage of each asset is based on the total assets, while the percentage of each liability, the total liabilities, and the proprietorship are based on the total liabilities and proprietorship (see Example 10).

Example 9   Income statement, set up for vertical analysis

National Table Company
Comparative Income Statement
For the Years Ended December 31, 1976 and 1977

	1977		1976	
	Amount	Percent of Net Sales	Amount	Percent of Net Sales
Sales	$800,000	102.2	$760,000	102.2
Sales returns	17,000	2.2	16,000	2.2
Net sales	$783,000	100.0	$744,000	100.0
Cost of goods sold	470,000	60.0	444,000	59.7
Gross profit on sales	$313,000	40.0	$300,000	40.3
Selling expense	$102,000	13.0	$101,000	13.6
General expense	58,000	7.4	57,000	7.7
Total operating expense . . .	$160,000	20.4	$158,000	21.2
Net operating income	$153,000	19.5	$142,000	19.1
Other income	9,000	1.1	8,000	1.1
	$162,000	20.7	$150,000	20.2
Other expense	12,000	1.5	14,000	1.9
Net income before income tax	$150,000	19.2	$136,000	18.3
Income taxes	72,500	9.3	65,220	8.8
Net income	$ 77,500	9.9	$ 70,780	9.5

Example 10 Balance sheet, set up for vertical analysis

National Table Company
Comparative Balance Sheet
December 31, 1976 and 1977

	1977		1976	
	Amount	Percent of Total	Amount	Percent of Total
ASSETS				
Current assets:				
Cash	$ 118,000	9.2	$ 92,000	7.2
Accounts receivable	224,000	17.4	212,000	16.5
Merchandise	264,000	20.5	260,000	20.2
Prepaid expense	16,000	1.3	14,000	1.1
Total current assets	$ 622,000	48.4	$ 578,000	45.0
Fixed assets:				
Land	$ 40,000	3.1	$ 40,000	3.1
Buildings	280,000	21.8	286,000	22.3
Equipment	156,000	12.1	176,000	13.7
Total fixed assets	$ 476,000	37.0	$ 502,000	39.1
Patents	$ 187,000	14.6	$ 204,000	15.9
Total assets	$1,285,000	100.0	$1,284,000	100.0
LIABILITIES AND CAPITAL				
Current liabilities:				
Notes payable	$ 100,000	7.8	$ 110,000	8.6
Accounts payable	170,000	13.2	279,000	21.7
Taxes payable	40,000	3.1	35,000	2.7
Total current liabilities	$ 310,000	24.1	$ 424,000	33.0
Long–term liability:				
Bonds payable	$ 200,000	15.6	$ 200,000	15.6
Total liabilities	$ 510,000	39.7	$ 624,000	48.6
Capital:				
Preferred stock	$ 250,000	19.5	$ 150,000	11.7
Common stock	300,000	23.3	300,000	23.4
Retained earnings	225,000	17.5	210,000	16.3
Total capital	$ 775,000	60.3	$ 660,000	51.4
Total liabilities and capital	$1,285,000	100.0	$1,284,000	100.0

Examples   Using the information for the National Table Company from Examples 9 and 10:

(a) Income statement,
Gross profit on sales

(b) Balance sheet,
Accounts receivable

$$\frac{\text{Gross profit}}{\text{Net sales}} = \frac{313,000}{783,000} = 40\%$$

$$\frac{\text{Accounts receivable}}{\text{Total assets}} = \frac{224,000}{1,285,000} = 17.4\%$$

Project 45 may be done now.

PROJECT 45   VERTICAL ANALYSIS OF STATEMENTS

Analyze the following two statements by comparing the figures for *each* year with the proper base for *that* year. Compute the percent and enter it in the appropriate column.

1.

PLEASANT VIEW HOMES, INC.
Comparative Balance Sheet
October 31, 1977 and 1976

	1977		1976	
	Amount	Percent	Amount	Percent
ASSETS				
Current assets	$794,200		519,800	
Long-term investments	573,600		552,500	
Plant assets (net)	1,495,200		1,184,700	
Intangible assets	138,100		73,400	
Total assets	$3,001,100		$2,330,400	
LIABILITIES				
Current liabilities	$807,300		$570,500	
Long-term liabilities	500,000		200,000	
Total liabilities	$1,307,300		$770,500	
CAPITAL				
Preferred 6% stock	$300,000		$300,000	
Common stock	525,000		525,000	
Retained earnings	868,800		734,900	
Total capital	$1,693,800		1,559,900	
Total liabilities and capital	$3,001,100		$2,330,400	

2.

PLEASANT VIEW HOMES, INC.
Comparative Income Statement
For the Years Ended October 31, 1977 and 1976

	1977		1976	
	Amount	Percent	Amount	Percent
Sales	$3,922,000		$2,641,000	
Sales returns and allowances	25,800		19,600	
Net sales	$3,896,200		$2,621,400	
Cost of goods sold	2,773,900		1,756,000	
Gross profit on sales . . .	$1,122,300		$ 865,400	
Selling expense	$ 432,700		$ 258,200	
General expense	225,700		183,400	
Total operating expense . .	$ 658,400		$ 441,600	
Net operating income	$ 463,900		$ 423,800	
Other income	————————		10,750	
	$ 463,900		$ 434,550	
Other expense	16,100		15,750	
Net income before income tax	$ 447,800		$ 418,800	
Estimated income tax	223,900		209,400	
Net income after income tax	$ 223,900		$ 209,400	

COMPARING BY RATIOS   A *ratio* is the relation of one amount to another. It is found by dividing one amount by the other. The more common ratios used to analyze financial statements are listed below. Business people must use their own experience in their fields of business or fall back on standard ratios published by trade associations to determine whether a particular ratio signifies good or poor management of their companies. Computations in the following section are based on the National Table Company income statement and balance sheet (Examples 9 and 10).

1. The *working capital ratio* is probably the best-known measure applied to financial statements. It is computed by dividing the amount of the current assets by the amount of the current liabilities. If the answer is 2, the current assets are said to be in a "2 to 1 ratio"; that is, in a ratio of \$2 of current assets to each \$1 of current liabilities.

$$\frac{\text{Total current assets}}{\text{Total current liabilities}} = \frac{622,000}{310,000} = \frac{311}{155} = 2.0 \text{ to } 1$$

2. The *acid-test ratio* has the same significance as the current ratio but is a more severe test of the concern's solvency. It is computed by adding the cash, the receivables, and the marketable securities (sometimes called *quick assets*), then dividing that total by the current liabilities.

$$\frac{118,000 + 224,000}{310,000} = \frac{342,000}{310,000} = \frac{171}{155} = 1.1 \text{ to } 1$$

3. The *inventory turnover* gives the number of times the average investment in merchandise is sold during a year. It is found by the formula

$$\frac{\text{Cost of goods sold}}{\text{Average inventory}} = \text{Inventory turnover.}$$

The average inventory for the National Table Company in 1977 was:

Beginning (ending—1976)	\$260,000
Ending	264,000
Total	2) \$524,000
Average	\$262,000

$$\frac{\text{Cost of goods sold}}{\text{Average inventory}} = \frac{470,000}{262,000} = \frac{235}{131} = 1.8$$

4. The *ratio of accounts receivable to net sales* is another valuable comparison.

$$\frac{\text{Accounts receivable}}{\text{Net sales}} = \frac{224,000}{783,000} = 0.286 \text{ to } 1$$

5. The *rate of return on proprietorship* (or capital or stockholders' equity) is a major guide to investors. It shows the profitability of the stockholders' investment. It is computed by the formula

$$\frac{\text{Net income}}{\text{Proprietorship}} = \text{rate of return on proprietorship.}$$

$$\frac{\text{Net income}}{\text{Proprietorship}} = \frac{77,500}{775,000} = 10\%$$

6. The *ratio of plant (or fixed) assets to long-term liabilities* gives a measure of the margin of safety of the note holders or bond holders. It also indicates the potential ability of the enterprise to borrow additional funds on a long-term basis.

$$\frac{\text{Plant or fixed assets}}{\text{Long-term liabilities}} = \frac{476,000}{200,000} = 2.38 \text{ to } 1$$

Project 46 may be done now.

PROJECT 46   ANALYSIS BY RATIOS

A.   Compute the following ratios for each year from the Mason Shoe Corporation statements (see Project 44).

	1976–77	1975–76

1.   Working capital ratio

2.   Acid test ratio

3.   Inventory turnover (beginning inventory for 1975–76 was $1,250,000)

4.   Accounts receivable to net sales

5.   Return on proprietorship

227

B.   Compute the following ratios for each year from the statements of Pleasant View Homes, Inc. (see Project 45).

	1977	1976

1.   Working capital ratio

2.   Accounts receivable to net sales

(accounts receivable: 1977 = $105,000,
1976 = $80,000)

3.   Return (after taxes) on proprietorship

4.   Plant assets to long-term liabilities

5.   Markup based on sales

TOYLAND
DELIVERY ENTRANCE

JUMP ROPES

DOLLS

MANAGER

9 RETAILING MATH: PART ONE – GENERAL

KEY POINTS TO LEARN FROM THIS CHAPTER

1. How to compute trade discounts by a series of trade discounts or by a single equivalent discount

2. How to compute cash discounts using different dating methods and credit terms

3. F.O.B. destination vs. F.O.B. shipping point

4. How to figure a sales commission

MINICASE

In recent years, more and more two-year college students have been signing up for vocational programs than ever before. One important and popular vocational field is retailing. Knowing some basic math for retailing often can help managers to make vital decisions. For example, a leading toy manufacturer offers the manager of a department store toyland the choice of buying toys at either a certain billed cost or a higher "cash discount" price. If the final (net) cost of the goods is the same, does it make any difference to the manager? Suppose the toyland manager has been paying bills within the 30 days allowed by manufacturers and wholesalers. Should all the bills be paid within the cash discount period, even if it is necessary to borrow the money from the bank?

231

A. TRADE DISCOUNT

Trade discounts (sometimes called *mercantile* or *functional discounts*) are reductions from the list or catalog price granted to certain classes of buyers without regard to the time of payment. They are also given for buying in quantity or buying seasonally. Trade discounts are a convenience for sellers because they can issue a single catalog every year or two to all classes of customers. Then all they have to do is issue different discount rate lists to different customers and revise them periodically. *Remember*: trade discounts are only a convenient way to vary the catalog or list price. They do not affect the time or method of payment.

The amount of a trade discount is computed by multiplying the catalog price by the discount rate. Then the net price (or selling price) paid by the purchaser is found by subtracting the discount amount from the catalog or list price.

Examples

A manufacturer offers merchandise with a catalog price of $150 to Thompson Variety, Inc., for $150 less a trade discount of 30%. Find the selling price (*net price*).

$150 × 0.30 = $45.00 $150.00 − 45.00 = 105.00   selling price

Using the above catalog price but with trade discounts of 30%, 10%, and 5%, find the selling price (net price).

30% $150 × 0.30 = $45.00 $150.00 − 45.00 = $105.00
10% $105 × 0.10 = $10.50 $105.00 − 10.50 = $94.50
5% $94.50 × 0.05 = $4.73 $94.50 − 4.73 = $89.77
                                         manufacturer's selling price

[*Short cut:* If you don't need to know the amount of discount, only the net price, subtract the discount from 100% before multiplying. (The one-cent difference in the third example is caused by rounding.)]

```
$150.                    $105.                    $94.50
×0.7  (100% − 30%)       ×0.9  (100% − 10%)       ×0.95 (100% − 5%)
$105.Ø                   $94.50                   47250
                                                  85050
                                                  89.7750, or $89.78
                                                          net price
```

B. SINGLE EQUIVALENT DISCOUNT

While often only one discount may be given to a buyer, sometimes a number of discounts are granted. They are called *chain discounts* or *series of discounts.* Note in the last example that each discount in the Series is deducted *from the preceding net amount.* The order in which the discounts are deducted does not affect the result; thus $150 less 5%, less 10%, less 30%, still produces a net price of $89.77 (or $89.78). But each discount must be found and subtracted separately. Remember: you *cannot add* the discounts and multiply only once. In our example, 30% + 10% + 5% would give 45%; multiplying by $150 and subtracting that product from $150 would give $82.50, not the correct answer.

Often it is easier to find the single discount percent that is equivalent to a series of discounts and then multiply this percent by the list price to get the amount of discount. To find the *single equivalent discount* percent, subtract each discount from 100%, *multiply* together the results of the subtractions, and then subtract this product from 1.00.

Example   Using information from the earlier example:

100%	100%	100%
−30%	−10%	−5%
70%	90%	95%

Discount = 1.00 − (0.7 × 0.9 × 0.95)
= 1.00 − 0.5985
= 0.4015, or 40.15%

Multiplying by 40.15% is the same as taking the three discounts 30%, 10%, and 5% in series.

$$
\begin{array}{r}
0.4015 \\
\times \$150 \\
\hline
200750 \\
4015 \\
\hline
\$60.2250 = \$60.23
\end{array}
\qquad
\begin{array}{r}
\$150.00 \\
-60.23 \\
\hline
\$89.77 \text{ manufacturer's selling} \\
\text{price to Thompson}
\end{array}
$$

[*Short cut*: Again, if you don't need to know the amount of discount, just multiply (0.7 × 0.9 × 0.95) by $150 to get the net price.

(0.7 × 0.9 × 0.95) × 150 = 0.5985 × $150 ≐ $89.7750, or $89.78

In retailing terminology, 0.5985, or 59.85%, is known as the *on percentage.*]

Projects 47 and 48 may be done now.

15, 10, 10

$1.00 - (.85 \times .9 \vee .9) = 3.15$

$100\% - (85\% \times 90\% \times 90\%)$

PROJECT 47   TRADE DISCOUNTS; SINGLE EQUIVALENT DISCOUNTS

A.   In the following situations, find (a) the total amount of the trade discounts, and (b) the net price.

1.   List price = $680; discount rates = 15%, 10%, 10%

2.   List price = $255; discount rates = 25%, 15%, 10%

3.   List price = $49.25; discount rates = 5%, 3%

4.   List price = $1,800; discount rates = 30%, 20%, 15%

Using the short-cut method, find the net price.

5.   List price = $255; discount rates = 5%, 10%, 20%

235

6. List price = $175; discount rates = 40%, 20%, 15%

B. For Problems 1–6, find the single equivalent discount rate, and multiply the rate by the list price to check the net price computed above (within 1 or 2 cents).

PROJECT 48   TRADE DISCOUNTS; SINGLE EQUIVALENT DISCOUNTS

Find (a) the single equivalent discount rate and (b) the net price.

1. $1,800 less 20%, 10%, and 30%

2. $20.95 less 20%, 10%, and 10%

3. $164 less 25% and 20%

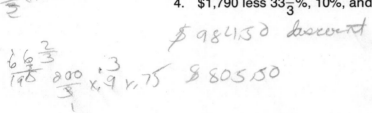

4. $1,790 less $33\frac{1}{3}$%, 10%, and 25%

5. $545 less $33\frac{1}{3}$% and 20%

237

Solve the following problems.

6.   Which is the better offer, and by what amount, on an invoice of $425: (a) 40%, 25%, and 5%, or (b) a single discount of 60%?

7.   Dean Co. offers merchandise at a list price of $7,500 less discounts of 25%, 10%, and 15%. Ryan & Sons offers the same merchandise at a list price of $7,250 less discounts of 20%, 15%, and 10%. Which is the better offer, and by what amount?

8.   Amy Horne buys a quantity of skis and equipment listed at $4,500 less 25% and 25% discounts. She sells this merchandise at the same list price, less 15%, 20%, and 5%. Does she gain or lose, and how much?

9. Swan Co. offers a retailer trade discounts of 33⅓%, 25%, 10%, and 3%. Monroe Co. offers the retailer trade discounts of 30%, 20%, and 20%. Which company offers the lower price on an article if the list price is the same at both companies?

C. CASH DISCOUNT AND DATING

A *cash discount* is a reduction in the net price allowed by a vendor (seller) for paying the invoice within a definite time period. The reason for a cash discount is to offer the retailer a premium for paying promptly. Here both parties benefit: the retailer (purchaser) pays a smaller amount, and the manufacturer or wholesaler (seller) gets the money sooner. This money pays for manufacturing or buying more goods, from which additional profit will result.

A common way of expressing a 2% cash discount is "2/10, n/30." This means that the purchaser may deduct 2% of the invoice price if the bill is paid within 10 days of the invoice date, and that the invoice is due in 30 days without discount. A penalty may be charged beyond 30 days.

More than one cash discount may be offered, such as 2/10, 1/30, n/60. This means that 2% of the invoice price may be deducted if payment is made within 10 days of the invoice date; 1% may be deducted if the amount is paid within 30 days *from the invoice date*; and the invoice is due in 60 days without the discount. Cash discounts are *not allowed* on returns of merchandise.

Example

On June 25, Jim Higgins buys $350 worth of merchandise for his hardware store. Credit terms are 3/5, 2/10, 1/15, n/30. He returns $25 worth of goods on July 2. If he pays the invoice on July 8, how much must he pay?

30	days in June	$350	original invoice
−25	June date	−25	goods returned
5	days left in June	$325	goods retained
+8	days in July	×0.01	
13	days invoice is outstanding	$3.25	discount

$325.00	goods retained
−3.25	
$321.75	cash paid

So he earns the 1% cash discount.

Promptness of payment of accounts as they come due is an important influence on credit ratings. Also, many companies show either a small profit or loss on their income statements, depending on whether they take advantage of all cash discounts. Even though it may be necessary to borrow money to accept the discount, it is usually worthwhile.

Example

An invoice for $500, with terms of 2/10, n/30, is to be paid within the discount period with funds borrowed at 8% for the remaining 20 days of the credit period. (It is necessary to borrow only $490 for 20 days because $490 will pay the invoice on the tenth day of the credit period.) (Computation on next page.)

$$\begin{array}{l} \$\ 500 \\ \underline{\times 0.02} \\ \$10.00 \end{array} \text{ cash discount}$$

$$I = \cancel{490}^{4.9} \times \frac{\cancel{8}^{4}}{\cancel{100}_{1}} \times \frac{\cancel{20}^{1}}{\cancel{360}_{\cancel{18}_{9}}} = \frac{19.6}{9} = \$2.18$$

$$\begin{array}{l} \$500 \\ \underline{-10} \\ \$490 \end{array} \text{ to be paid on invoice on tenth day}$$

$$\begin{array}{ll} \$10.00 & \text{discount earned} \\ \underline{2.18} & \text{interest on \$490} \\ \$\ 7.82 & \text{savings} \end{array}$$

The previous two examples in this section were concerned with invoices that have *ordinary dating*. Other, less common forms of dating are explained briefly below.

1. *End of Month (E.O.M.) Dating*. E.O.M. dating means that the discount days are counted from the end of the month following the date of the bill rather than from the date of the bill.

Example   An invoice dated July 3 is subject to terms of 2/10 E.O.M. When does the discount period expire?

Two percent can be deducted if the bill is paid within 10 days from the end of July (August 10).

2. *E.O.M. dating when bill is dated after the 25th of the month.* When an invoice is dated the 26th of the month or later, E.O.M. dating begins from the end of the following month.

Example   An invoice dated September 27 carries terms of 2/10 E.O.M. When does the discount period expire?

This invoice should be considered as dated October 1. Therefore, November 10 is the day the discount period expires.

3. *Receipt of Goods (R.O.G.) Dating*. R.O.G. dating means that the discount period is counted after receipt of the goods, not after the date of the bill. This dating method is used when the delivery time is longer than the cash discount period.

Example   An invoice is dated May 2 and carries terms of 2/10, *n*/30 R.O.G. The goods were received by the store on May 15. What is the last day of the discount period and of the credit period?

Discount period = May 25 (10 days from May 15)
   Credit period = June 14 (30 days from May 15)

Projects 49 and 50 may be done now.

PROJECT 49   CASH DISCOUNT

A. Find (a) the cash discount and (b) the net amount paid on each of the following invoices.

	Amount of Invoice	Terms	Date of Invoice	Date Paid
1.	$29.25	2/20, n/30	Aug. 3	Aug. 31
2.	$1,655	2/10, n/30	April 25	May 4
3.	$645	1/20, n/30	Sept. 13	Sept. 30
4.	$49.17	3/10, 2/20, n/30	Jan. 10	Jan. 16
5.	$4,191	3/30, n/60	June 15	July 6
6.	$5,452	5/10, 2/30, n/60	Oct. 19	Nov. 9

[Handwritten work:]

1. A — None   B $29.25
2. A — 33.10   B — 1621.90
3. A — 6.45   B — 638.55
4. A — 1.48   B — 47.69
5. A — 125.73   B — 4065.27
6. A — 109.04   B — 5342.96

241

	Amount of Invoice	Terms	Date of Invoice	Date Paid
7.	$95.00	$3/20, n/60$	Nov. 25	Dec. 21
8.	$4,595	$6/10, 3/30, n/90$	May 15	June 5
9.	$42.15	$3/10, 2/20, n/30$	June 30	July 7
10.	$2,254	$2/10, 1/30, n/60$	July 23	Aug. 4

B.   Solve the following problems.

1.   What is the amount of the check sent in payment of an invoice for $345.40 with terms $3/10, n/30$, dated May 16, and paid May 22?

2.   An invoice for $744 was issued on Aug. 12 with credit terms of $3/10, 2/20, n/30$. What amount should the buyer pay if he makes the payment in full on: (a) August 17? (b) August 24? (c) September 7?

PROJECT 50   CASH DISCOUNT AND DATING

A.   Compute the last date for taking the cash discount on each of the following.

	Date of Invoice	Terms
1.	Aug. 21	$1/20, n/90$
2.	September 14	3/20, E.O.M.
3.	November 5	2/10, E.O.M.
4.	July 27	3/10, E.O.M.
5.	May 3 (goods received on May 16)	$3/10, n/30$, R.O.G.
6.	June 27	1/10, E.O.M.
7.	October 14	2/10, E.O.M.

B.   Find (a) the cash discount and (b) the net amount paid on each of the following invoices.

	Amount of Invoice	Terms	Date of Invoice	Date Paid
1.	$77.35	3/10, E.O.M.	May 27	June 9

243

	Amount of Invoice	Terms	Date of Invoice	Date Paid
2.	$75.93	4/30, R.O.G. (goods received on July 27)	June 5	Aug. 15
3.	$925	4/10, 2/30, $n/60$	March 30	April 10
4.	$179.25	5/10, E.O.M.	October 27	December 9

C. Solve the following problems.

1. A purchaser receiving an invoice of $1500 with terms 3/10, $n/30$ borrowed money at 9% to take advantage of the 3% discount. How much was saved?

2. A store in Mobile, Alabama, sent a $755 order on August 15 to a New York manufacturer. The goods were shipped on August 26 and billed on that day. The store received the invoice on August 30 and the goods on September 14. Terms were 2/10, R.O.G. (a) When must the bill be paid to earn the discount? (b) How much must be paid on that date?

D. TRANSPORTATION CHARGES

Free on board (F.O.B.) *destination* means that the seller will pay the freight costs to the destination, usually the buyer's place of business. This means that the buyer pays no freight charges. Also, the legal title to the goods is not passed until the goods reach their destination. [Hint: Make the B stand for both Board and Buyer—free "for the buyer" to the destination.] Often, instead of the word "destination," an actual location will be stated, such as, F.O.B. store, F.O.B. factory, F.O.B. Detroit, etc. If the location named is not the buyer's place of business, then the buyer must pay the freight charge from the location named to his or her place of business.

When the buyer must pay the freight from the seller's place of business (really, all the freight cost), the term used is F.O.B. shipping point. Add "for the buyer," and the meaning is more easily remembered: free *for the buyer* to the shipping point, which is really not very far. Although the buyer is then responsible for the freight charges, it is often difficult to pay them, so the seller pays these charges and adds this amount to the invoice. *No* cash discount is allowed on the freight charge because the seller earns no profit on the freight. The freight must be subtracted from the invoice total to compute the cash discount.

Example

Virginia Brown buys $500 of merchandise with terms 1/10, n/30, F.O.B. shipping point. The freight charge is $15.

$500 merchandise
+15 freight
$515 total invoice

If she pays within 10 days:

$515
−15
500
×0.01
$5.00 cash discount

$515 total invoice
−5 discount
$510 cash paid

Summary Example

On May 5 Sally Howe buys merchandise with a list price of $2,600 and trade discounts 20% and 25% on account subject to the following terms: 1/10, n/30, F.O.B. shipping point. The seller pays the $30 transportation and bills Sally Howe. Sally returns $50 of merchandise on May 10 and receives credit. (a) What is the single equivalent discount? (b) What is the net price of the merchandise? (c) What is the total of the invoice? (d) What is the last day of the credit period and the balance owed on that day? (e) What is the last day of the discount period and the amount Sally Howe must pay to meet her obligation?

(a) Single equivalent discount $= 1 - (0.8)(0.75) = 1 - 0.6 = 0.4$, or 40%

(b) $2,600 list price
×0.4 discount rate
$1,040.0 discount

$2,600
−1,040
$1,560 net price

(c) $1,560   net price
     +30   transportation
    $1,590   invoice total

(d) May 31   30   days credit period $1,590   invoice total
      -5   -26   days in May   -50   return
      26   June 4 due date $1,540   balance owed

(e) May 5 $1,560   net price
     +10   -50   return
    May 15   last day of discount period $1,510
                                          ×0.01
                                          $15.10   cash discount

$1,510.00   amount owed on merchandise
  -15.10   cash discount
  +30.00   transportation
$1,524.90   cash paid

E. Sales Commissions

A sales commission or a commission on sales is an allowance made to an employee (department store clerk, a house-to-house sales representative, an automobile sales representative, a representative of a manufacturer or wholesaler, etc.) for selling the product of the company. This type of commission is usually in the form of a given percent of the value of the goods or services the employee has sold. Goods returned or orders canceled are generally deducted, so commissions are paid on actual sales only. Other types of commissions are paid to commission merchants, brokers, or agents.

Salespeople may receive the commission as their only compensation. Or they may receive a salary plus a commission on all sales over a certain figure. Or they may receive a commission on a sliding scale.

Examples

1. Harry Holt received a regular monthly salary of $500 plus 4% commission on all sales over $50,000 each month. What were his gross earnings in the month when his sales amounted to $76,500?

$ 76,500 $ 500   salary
-50,000   +1,060   commission
$ 26,500   excess sales $1,560   gross earnings
  ×0.04
$1,060.00 commission

2. David Perkins receives 2% commission on the first $10,000 of goods sold each month, 3% on the next $15,000, and 4% on any goods sold in excess of $25,000. What was his commission the month his sales amounted to $37,000?

$10,000 × 0.02 = $ 200
$15,000 × 0.03 =   450
($37,000 − $25,000) × 0.04 =   480
                                  $1,130   total commission

Project 51 may be done now.

PROJECT 51   TRANSPORTATION CHARGES: SALES COMMISSIONS; SUMMARY PROBLEMS

A.   The following invoices were paid by M. G. Gilks within the discount period. Find the amount he paid in full settlement of each invoice, assuming he returned any defective merchandise prior to payment.

1.   Merchandise $800
     Merchandise returned   75
     Transportation   25
     Terms
        1/10, n/30, F.O.B. shipping point

2.   Merchandise $1,500
     Merchandise returned   50
     Transportation   —
     Terms
        2/10, n/30, F.O.B. destination

B.   Solve the following problems.

1.   A Chicago firm received an invoice from a Portland manufacturer for $2,645, dated March 19; the terms were 3/10, R.O.G. The goods were 14 days in transit. (a) When must the bill be paid to earn the discount? (b) How much must be paid on that date?

2.   An invoice for $615.75 dated July 20 has terms 2/10, 1/15, n/30. Find the amount of payment if the bill is paid on: (a) July 24, (b) August 1, or (c) August 14.

3. M. Waring, an appliance retailer, received an invoice dated April 12, 1977, that gives the following information:

Item 1: 2 portable TV's: list price, $150 each, less trade discounts of 5% and 15%

Item 2: 12 hair dryers: list price $30 each, less trade discounts of 10% and 8%

Freight charges: $25.20; F.O.B. shipping point

Credit terms: 2/10, E.O.M.

Determine (a) the last date on which the cash discount may be taken, and (b) the total amount the retailer must pay on that date.

4. The three sales representatives of the D. L. Swanson Company are paid $500 per month plus a commission of 2% on sales between $10,000 and $20,000 and an additional 3% on sales over $20,000. From the information below, compute the gross earnings of each of the three.

	Sales
Black	$21,500
Horne	16,000
Mauch	31,100

5. Tom McHenry, a wholesaler, sold merchandise having a list price of $825 and a trade discount of 25%. He prepared the invoice on April 19 and included a freight charge of $19.25. The terms were 2/10, n/20, F.O.B. shipping point. How much should the customer pay if the bill is paid on (a) April 27? (b) May 2?

SALE!

LOOK AT
THE
SAVINGS

10 RETAILING MATH: PART TWO–MARKUP

KEY POINTS TO LEARN FROM THIS CHAPTER

1. **Defining markup**

2. **How to convert a markup on retail to a markup on cost**

3. **How to convert a markup on cost to a markup on retail**

4. **Ways of finding the cost**

5. **Ways of finding the selling price**

MINICASE

Linda Simmons, a student in Retailing I at Pear Valley Community College, wonders why her instructor is making retailing math an important part of the course, along with store organization, management, and advertising. He has allocated substantial time to the calculation of markup on retail and markup on cost.

Many of Linda's friends have recently purchased pocket calculators to help them in the course. Jane Smythe, Linda's closest friend, has volunteered to have her father sell Linda a calculator *at cost*. He normally sells it at retail for $85, after a 30% markup on cost.

Linda's father has also offered to sell her a calculator *at cost*. It normally also sells at retail for $85, after a 25% markup on retail.

Linda doesn't know where to buy her calculator. She guesses that her friend's offer is better, but she feels she had better compute the cost of each calculator. (See next page for her computations.)

Her Friend's Offer	*Her Father's Offer*
$C + M = R$	$C + M = R$
$100\%(C) + 30\%(C) = 85$	$C = R - M$
$130\%(C) = 85$	$C = 100\%(R) - 25\%(R)$
$\dfrac{1.3C}{1.3} = \dfrac{85.0}{1.3}$	$C = 75\%(R)$
	$C = 0.75(85)$
$C = \$65.38$	$C = \$63.75$

Linda can now see a study of markup is important. There can be a big difference between markup on retail and markup on cost.

A. DEFINITION OF MARKUP

Markup can be either a general or a specific term for the difference between the cost and the retail price of merchandise. It may affect a single item or all of the merchandise in a department or a store. Although markup sometimes has a precise definition, different from gross profit, margin, and markon, this book considers all of these as having the same meaning. The basic definition—difference between cost and retail price of merchandise—comes from the equation:

Cost + Gross profit = Selling price
Gross profit = Selling price − Cost

Alternatively:

Markup = Selling price (*or* Retail) − Cost

Example

What is the markup on an item costing 68¢ that we plan to sell for $1.00?

Markup = Retail − Cost
Markup = $1.00 − 0.68 = $0.32

B. MARKUP AS A PERCENTAGE

Although the markup may be expressed in dollars, more often it is expressed as a percentage of either the cost or the retail price of the product. Markup as a percentage is a convenient and helpful tool for comparison and control in a retail business. While percent based on cost is the older method, it is used less often now. Markup percentage based on retail is growing in popularity because the retail figures are easier to obtain, and each year more and more accounting ratios that have net sales for a base are being used.

The markup percentage is computed by dividing the *amount* of markup by the *base* (either cost or retail).

$$\text{Markup percentage of cost} = \frac{\text{Markup}}{\text{Cost}}$$

$$\text{Markup percentage of retail} = \frac{\text{Markup}}{\text{Retail}}$$

Example   Using information in the previous example:

$$\text{Markup} = \$0.32 \qquad \text{Retail} = \$1.00 \qquad \text{Cost} = \$0.68$$

$$\text{Markup percentage of cost} = \frac{0.32}{0.68}$$

$$= \frac{32}{68}$$

$$= \frac{8}{17} = 47.1\%$$

$$\text{Markup percentage of retail} = \frac{0.32}{1.00}$$

$$= 32\%$$

Notice that markup percentages on cost are always higher than markup percentages on retail. When someone says a markup is a certain percentage, you must always ask whether this percentage is based on cost or on retail price.

The opposite (complement) of the markup, or the *cost percentage*, is computed easily from the markup percentage on the retail price. This figure gives the cost as a percentage of the retail.

Example   Letting the retail price equal 100% and using the figures of the previous example:

Cost + Markup = Retail
Cost = Retail − Markup
Cost = 100% − 32% = 68%

$$\textit{Proof:} \quad \frac{\text{Cost}}{\text{Retail}} = \frac{0.68}{1.00} = 68\%$$

Therefore, 68¢ of every dollar received from customers goes for the cost of the product.

Project 52 may be done now.

C. CONVERTING MARKUPS   Very often retailers need to have markups expressed as a percentage of retail for planning and control purposes. They will also need these same markups expressed as a percentage of cost to help them price their merchandise. So a method for easily converting these markup percentages from one base to the other is very useful.

To find markup on cost:

$$\text{Markup percentage on cost} = \frac{\text{Markup percentage on retail}}{\text{Cost percentage of retail (\textit{or} complement of the markup)}}$$

For example, what is the percentage markup on the basis of cost when the percentage is 25% of the selling price?

$$\text{Markup percentage on cost} = \frac{25\%}{100\% - 25\%} = \frac{0.25}{0.75} = \frac{1}{3} = 33\tfrac{1}{3}\%$$

To find markup on retail:

$$\text{Markup percentage on retail} = \frac{\text{Markup percentage on cost}}{\text{Retail percentage of cost}}$$

For example, what is the percentage markup on the basis of retail price when the percentage is 25% of cost?

Cost + Markup = Retail
       (let cost = 100%, the base)
  100% + 25% = Retail
      125% = Retail

$$\text{Markup percentage on retail} = \frac{25\%}{100\% + 25\%} = \frac{0.25}{1.25} = \frac{1}{5} = 20\%$$

Notice that in both formulas the *known* percentage is divided by the percentage representing the *new base* (cost percentage when finding markup percentage on cost and retail percentage when finding markup percentage on retail).

Project 53 may be done now.

PROJECT 52   MARKUP

In each of the following problems, find (a) the markup, (b) the markup percentage of cost, (c) the markup percentage of retail, and (d) the complement of the markup.

1. Cost = $18.00; Retail = $22.50

2. Cost = $15.00; Retail = $21.00

3. Cost = $24.00; Retail = $36.00

4. Cost = $280.00; Retail = $350.00

5. Cost = $128.00; Retail = $166.40

6. Cost = $350.00; Retail = $420.00

255

7. Cost = $4.20; Retail = $6.30

8. Cost = $290.00; Retail = $406.00

9. Cost = $212.00; Retail = $254.40

10. Cost = $4.60; Retail = $7.67

11. Cost = $40.00; Retail = $58.50

12. Cost = $112.00; Retail = $149.95

PROJECT 53   CONVERTING MARKUPS

Find the markup percentage on cost in each of the following problems. Round all answers to three decimal places.

1. Markup percentage on retail is 40%.

2. Markup percentage on retail is 70%.

3. Markup percentage on retail is 28%.

4. Markup percentage on retail is 35%.

5. Markup percentage on retail is 76%.

6. Markup percentage on retail is 64%.

Find the markup percentage on retail in each of the following problems. Round all answers to three decimal places.

7. Markup percentage on cost is $66\frac{2}{3}\%$

8. Markup percentage on cost is 150%.

9. Markup percentage on cost is 15%.

10. Markup percentage on cost is 27%.

11. Markup percentage on cost is 43%.

12. Markup percentage on cost is 300%.

Solve the following problems. (Round to three places.)

13.   If the markup percentage on the sale of a radio is 45% of the selling price, what is the percentage based on the cost?

14.   When the markup percentage is 60% of the cost on a bag of potatoes, what is the percentage based on the selling price?

D. FINDING THE SELLING PRICE USING THE MARKUP PERCENTAGE ON COST

In the remaining sections of this chapter, we use the formula Cost + Markup = Retail. In the problems, two of the three terms are known and given as facts, and the third term must be found by applying principles of algebra (see Chapter 4). In each section the businessperson must compute an important figure to help operate the business wisely.

If cost and markup percentages are known, and the markup is *based on cost*, multiply the percentage by the cost and add this to the cost.

Example

Men's ties cost $2.45 each and are to be marked up 60% of cost. Find the selling price.

$$Cost + Markup = Retail$$

$$2.45 + (0.6 \times 2.45) = Retail$$

$$2.45 + 1.47 = Retail$$

$$\$3.92 = Retail$$

E. FINDING THE COST USING THE MARKUP PERCENTAGE ON COST

If the selling price (retail) and the markup percent are known, and the markup is *based on cost*, let the cost equal 100%. Add the markup percentage to the 100%, then divide both sides of the equation by the total percentage.

Example

A store wants to sell costume jewelry at $1.77 each retail. The buyer must obtain a markup of 65% of cost. How much can she afford to pay?

$$Cost + Markup = Retail$$

$$100\%(C) + 65\%(C) = 1.77$$

$$165\%(C) = 1.77$$

$$\frac{\cancel{1.65}\ (C)}{\cancel{1.65}} = \frac{1.77}{1.65}$$

$$C = \$1.07$$

Project 54 may be done now.

F. FINDING THE COST AND THE SELLING PRICE WHEN MARKUP ON COST IS KNOWN

If the amount of markup and the markup percentage on cost are known, the cost may be found by stating the known facts in the form of an equation and then solving for the cost (this is really the formula Rate × Base = Percentage):

Markup percentage on cost × Cost = Markup

Example   An item at the Household Furniture Company had a markup of $60, which was 75% of cost. Find the cost and the retail price.

Markup percentage on cost $\times$ Cost $=$ Markup

$$\frac{.75 \times \text{Cost}}{.75} = \frac{\$60}{0.75}$$

$$\text{Cost} = \$80$$

To find the retail price, substitute the known facts in the formula.

Cost + Markup = Retail

$$80 + 60 = \text{Retail}$$

$$\$140 = \text{Retail}$$

Project 55 may be done now.

PROJECT 54 SELLING PRICE AND COST (MARKUP ON COST)

A. Find the selling price (retail) at the following markups based on cost.

1. Cost = $280; Markup = 25%

2. Cost = $128.00; Markup = 30%

3. Cost = $7.75; Markup = 28%

4. Cost = $5.20; Markup = 50%

5. Cost = $627.45; Markup = 38%

B. Find the cost at the following markups based on cost.

1. Retail = $19.20; Markup = 60%

2. Retail = $198.50; Markup = 25%

3. Retail = $210; Markup = 32%

4. Retail = $12.65; Markup = 15%

5. Retail = $272.80; Markup = 24%

C. Solve the following problems.

1. C. Swartz planned to sell a portable radio for $56. Her markup is $166\frac{2}{3}\%$ of cost. Find cost.

2. Ms. Swartz also has a portable TV that cost her $210. Her markup is 20% of cost. Find retail, the dollar markup, and the percentage markup on retail.

3. An owner of a men's store wants to buy a lot of 100 suits on which he must obtain an average markup of 42% on cost. After examining them, he finds that he can sell 75 of them at $120.00 and the rest at $99.00. What price can he afford to pay for this lot of suits?

PROJECT 55 MARKUP ON COST;
REVIEW PROBLEMS

A. In each of the following problems, find (a) the cost and (b) the retail (the selling price) if the given markup is based on cost.

1. Markup = \$87.50; Rate of markup = 25%

2. Markup = \$115.50; Rate of markup = 42%

3. Markup = \$14.00; Rate of markup = $16\frac{2}{3}\%$

4. Markup = \$135.00; Rate of markup = 150%

B. Solve the following problems.

1. Jim's College Book Store obtains a markup of \$5.83 per book on a certain biology textbook, where the markup on cost is 26.5%. Find the cost and the retail per book.

2. Jefferson's Colonial Furniture Store had a total markup for last year of $33,600. Hans Jefferson figured the rate of markup on all pieces of furniture to be 40% of cost. What was (a) the total cost of the furniture and (b) the total selling price?

3. Find the markup on retail when the markup on cost is 19%

4. Find the markup on cost when the markup on retail is 24%.

5. Ladies' coats sell with a gross profit of $26.48, which is 48.15% of cost. Find the cost and the selling price of the coats.

6. The retail price of a small television set is $98.99. The markup is 40% of the cost. What is the cost?

G. FINDING THE SELLING PRICE USING THE MARKUP PERCENTAGE ON RETAIL

If the cost and markup percentage on retail are known, then to find the selling price, let retail equal 100%. Rearrange the formula so that Cost = Retail − Markup. Substitute in the formula and solve. Notice why we do this: since the markup is based *on retail*, we cannot find the selling price by multiplying the rate times the cost. The rate could be multiplied only by the retail price, which here is an unknown.

Example

A child's toy is sold by the manufacturer at $1.80. The markup that a retailer needs to realize a fair profit is 40% on retail. At what retail price should the toy be sold to obtain the desired markup?

Cost + Markup = Retail

Cost = Retail − Markup

$1.80 = 100\%(R) - 40\%(R)$

$1.80 = 60\%(R)$

$$\frac{\overset{3}{\cancel{1.80}}}{\underset{1}{\cancel{0.6}}} = \frac{0.\cancel{6}(R)}{0.\cancel{6}}$$

$\$3.00 = R$

H. FINDING THE COST USING THE MARKUP PERCENTAGE ON RETAIL

If a retailer knows the retail price that must be charged to be competitive and also knows the markup percentage *on retail* needed to cover selling expenses and a normal profit, the maximum amount (the cost) he or she can afford to pay the manufacturer or wholesaler can be calculated.

Subtract the markup percentage from retail (100%) to get the percentage that cost is *of retail*. Multiply the cost rate by the retail price.

Example

A retail buyer estimates that a particular dress will sell for $35. He needs a markup of 38% on retail. What is the maximum amount he can pay for the dress?

Cost + Markup = Retail

Cost = Retail − Markup

$Cost = 100\%(R) - 38\%(R)$

$Cost = 62\%(R)$

$Cost = 0.62(\$35) = \$21.70$

Project 56 may be done now.

I. FINDING THE COST AND THE SELLING PRICE WHEN MARKUP ON RETAIL IS KNOWN

If the amount of markup and the markup percentage on retail price are known, the selling price (retail) may be found by stating the known facts in the form of an equation and solving for the selling price (this is really the formula Rate × Base = Percentage):

Markup percentage on retail $\times$ Retail = Markup

Example On an item in Horace's Hobby Shop, the markup percentage on retail is $37\frac{1}{2}\%$ and the dollar markup is \$15. Find the cost and the retail.

Markup percentage on retail $\times$ Retail = Markup

$$37\frac{1}{2}\% \times \text{Retail} = \$15$$

$$\left(\frac{\cancel{8}}{\cancel{3}}\right)\frac{\cancel{3}}{\cancel{8}} \times \text{Retail} = \overset{5}{\cancel{15}}\left(\frac{8}{3}\right)$$

$$\text{Retail} = \$40$$

To find the cost, substitute the known facts in the standard formula.

Cost + Markup = Retail

$$\text{Cost} + 15 = 40$$

$$\text{Cost} + \cancel{15} - \cancel{15} = 40 - 15$$

$$\text{Cost} = \$25$$

Project 57 may be done now.

PROJECT 56   SELLING PRICE AND COST
(MARKUP ON RETAIL)

A.   Find the selling price (retail) at the following markups based on retail.

1.   Cost $= \$222.00$; Markup $= 66\frac{2}{3}\%$

2.   Cost $= \$50.00$; Markup $= 60\%$

3.   Cost $= \$6.50$; Markup $= 35\%$

4.   Cost $= \$1,280$; Markup $= 45\%$

5.   Cost = $2,680; Markup = 13.8%

B.   Find the cost at the following markups based on retail.

1.   Retail = $20.00; Markup = 25%

2.   Retail = $38.60; Markup = 38%

3.   Retail = $328.42; Markup = 45%

4.   Retail = $36.00; Markup = 30%

5. Retail = $132.26; Markup = 55%

C. Solve the following problems.

1. Frank's Furniture buys a desk for $182.00 and wants a markup of 30% of retail. What price must be put on the desk?

2. A dress sells for $13.95 and carries a markup of 31% retail. Find the cost.

3. The local shoe store sells a pair of shoes for $25.50 after a markup of 38% of retail. Find the cost, the dollar markup, and percentage of markup on cost.

PROJECT 57   MARKUP ON RETAIL; REVIEW PROBLEMS

A. In each of the following problems find (a) the selling price and (b) the cost if the given markup is based on retail.

1. Markup = $42.00; Rate of markup = 15%

2. Markup = $12.71; Rate of markup = 25%

3. Markup = $313.45; Rate of markup = $12\frac{1}{2}$%

4. Markup = $35.00; Rate of markup = 7%

B. Solve the following problems.

1. Princess Clothing had a total markup of $50,400 on all merchandise sold last month. The markup percentage on retail price was 40%. What was (a) the total amount of the sales and (b) the cost of the sales?

275

2. If a coffee maker sells for $18.00 and the markup on retail is 45%, find the cost.

3. If a pair of men's shoes sell for $39.90 and the markup on retail is 27%, find the cost.

4. Jones TV Center realizes a markup of $8.40 on a portable radio set. Jones's markup is 35% of retail. What did the set cost? What is the selling price?

5. The markup percentage on a bag of apples is 30% of the cost. What is the markup percentage based on retail?

6. The markup on the sale of a textbook is $4.90, which is 35% of the selling price. What is (a) the selling price and (b) the cost?

11 INVENTORY: RETAIL

KEY POINTS TO LEARN FROM THIS CHAPTER

1. **How to estimate inventory by the retail inventory method**

2. **How to estimate inventory by the gross profit method**

3. **Ways of determining how much merchandise to buy for next month**

4. **How to tell whether merchandise is selling as fast as it should**

Thursday, November 22, 1973
SHOPLIFTING 'TAX' HITS EACH FAMILY

New York (UPI)—Shoplifting imposes a "hidden tax" of $150 a year on the average American family, a new study indicates.

The study, made by the Mass Retailing Institute of New York, disclosed that last year 148,525 persons were arrested in 1,188 stores (one-sixth of the nation's total) on shoplifting charges. Another 3,000 store employees were arrested for theft.

The reported loss in discount stores alone amounted to $845 million or 2.56 per cent of sales. Retailing experts say this is much more than the stores can absorb, and so is reflected in higher retail prices.*

MINICASE

Gerry Manyak recently read the above article in his local newspaper. He had recently become manager of The Boston Store, a local department store, and was interested in improving management and control of the store. He wondered how much his store was losing to theft. His accountant explained that the retail inventory method is a useful tool to compare the actual inventory he should have on hand according to the accounting records. The accountant said that merchandise would have to be recorded at both cost and retail. If this was done, the retail inventory method could produce the amount of merchandise the store should have on hand. Gerry ordered the accountant to start immediately to collect these figures. Then, if theft was going on, he could implement stricter security measures.

*Reprinted by permission of United Press International.

279

A. RETAIL INVENTORY METHOD

The retail inventory method is a way to determine the total cost and the total retail value of unsold merchandise. Widely used in retail stores, it provides a check on inventory shortages when used with a physical count of goods. It also gives a reliable estimate of inventory for preparing interim statements without having to count the goods.

This method assumes that the inventory is made up of items that have a fairly similar percentage relationship of cost to selling price. Although the markup rate probably is not exactly the same on all items, it is assumed that the cost percentages are fairly close. If a store has more than one department with clearly different cost percentages, then the retail method should be applied to each department individually.

Recall from Chapter 8 the computation of the merchandise-available-for-sale section of the income statement. Basically, merchandise available is computed by adding the inventory at the beginning of a fiscal period to the goods purchased during the period. Merchandise available is computed at both cost and retail price. The sales for the period are subtracted from the merchandise available *at retail* to find those goods not sold, the *inventory* at *retail*. This inventory figure at *retail* must be converted to a cost basis. The cost of the available goods and the retail price of the same goods are then compared to develop a cost percentage. This cost percentage is multipiled by the ending inventory at retail to get the ending inventory at *cost*.

Example

	Cost	Retail
Merchandise inventory, January 1	$22,600	$39,000
Purchases in January (net)	40,400	61,000
Merchandise available for sale (during January)*	$63,000	$100,000
Less sales for January (net)		75,000
Merchandise inventory, January 31 at retail price		$25,000

*Ratio of cost to retail price:

$$\frac{\text{Cost}}{\text{Retail}} = \frac{63,000}{100,000} = 63\%$$

Therefore, 63¢ of every dollar collected from customers covers the cost of the product; 37¢ is the gross profit.

To convert inventory at retail to inventory at cost:

63% × $25,000 = $15,750   inventory *at cost*

There are some other items to consider when computing inventory at cost using the retail inventory method:

1. *Additional markups:* Increases in price above the original retail price. The additional markups are added to the retail purchase figure in determining merchandise available for sale.

2. *Additional markup cancellations:* Decreases in retail price from a point above original retail to (or in the direction of) original retail. These cancellations are subtracted from the retail purchase figure in determining merchandise available for sale. Rebates (allowances) from the manufacturer and returns of purchases also are subtracted.

3. *Markdowns:* Retail price reductions caused by reductions in value of the goods. One common reason for cutting the price is the slow sale of certain articles. Markdowns *are added to sales* to obtain total retail deductions. Notice they *do not* reduce merchandise available for sale. Other decreases that are added to sales are shortages and discounts to employees.

4. *Markdown cancellations:* Increases in price caused by marking goods back to (or in the direction of) the original retail price. They reduce the total markdowns to a net figure.

Example

		Cost	*Retail*
Merchandise Inventory—March 1, 1977		$16,000	$25,000
Purchases	$52,000		
+ Transportation	+ 500		
	$52,500		
− Returns	− 2,500	50,000	74,000
Markups	$1,200		
− Markup cancellations	− 200		1,000
Merchandise available for sale		$66,000	$100,000
Sales	$73,200		
− Sales returns	− 3,200		
Net sales			$ 70,000
Markdowns	$5,000		
− Markdown cancellations	− 600		4,400
Discounts to employees			900
Shortages			700
Total retail deductions			$ 76,000
Merchandise inventory at retail—Feb. 28, 1978			$ 24,000
($100,000 − $76,000)			

$$\frac{\text{Cost}}{\text{Retail}} = \frac{66,000}{100,000} = 66\%$$

Ending inventory at cost = $24,000 × 0.66 = $15,840

Projects 58 and 59 may be done now.

PROJECT 58   RETAIL INVENTORY

1.   From the following information, determine the estimated inventory cost on March 31.

		Cost	Retail
Mar. 1	Merchandise inventory	$200,000	$260,000
Mar. 1–31	Purchases (net)	450,000	740,000
Mar. 1–31	Sales (net)		340,000

2.   Estimate the cost of the ending inventory (by the retail method) of Samson & Sons based on the following information:

	Cost	Retail
Merchandise inventory, June 1	$180,000	$288,000
Purchases	148,800	212,000
Purchases returns and allowances	3,800	——
Sales	——	173,000
Sales returns	——	3,000

283

3. Calculate the inventory at retail and at cost on May 31, 1978, for the Sloan Plumbing Supply Co.

	Cost	Retail
Merchandise inventory, June 1, 1977	$116,600	$165,400
Purchases	135,000	199,000
Transportation	1,400	——
Purchases returns	5,000	7,000
Markups	——	2,600
Markdowns	——	1,800
Sales	——	163,800

4. The records of the girls' clothing department of the Coach Department Store show the following information:

	Cost	Retail
Merchandise inventory, August 1	$30,000	$43,000
Purchases	46,000	55,000
Purchases returns	1,000	1,500
Additional markups	——	5,500
Additional markup cancellations	——	2,000
Sales	——	76,000

Calculate the cost of the August 31 inventory by the retail method.

PROJECT 59   RETAIL INVENTORY

1. Estimate the ending inventory at retail and at cost for the month of December for Mod Fashions, Inc.

	Cost	Retail
Net sales	——	$80,000
Inventory, December 1	$8,000	9,700
Estimated shortages, 2% of sales	——	1,000
Markdowns	——	2,200
Additional markups	——	7,000
Transportation in	1,000	——
Purchases returns	3,500	——
Purchases	70,500	84,000
Markdown cancellations	——	600
Markup cancellations	——	700

2. Calculate by the retail inventory method the ending inventory at retail and at cost for Shannon's Shirt Shop.

	Cost	Retail
Sales	——	$60,800
Merchandise inventory, June 1	$12,600	18,000
Sales returns	——	800
Markdowns	——	3,600
Additional markups	——	4,700
Transportation in	4,000	——
Discounts to employees	——	400
Purchases	54,400	86,800
Purchases returns & allow.	3,200	3,200
Markdown cancellations	——	600
Additional markup cancellations	——	300
Estimated shortages,	——	600

B. GROSS PROFIT METHOD

Another way to estimate the present or ending inventory of a retail business is the *gross profit method.* It is very helpful in preparing interim statements or in estimating the cost of merchandise lost by fire or theft. In the case of fire or theft, complete records of the business must also be produced.

An estimate of the average *rate* of gross profit is essential for this method. This estimated rate may be based on the actual rate for the preceding year adjusted for any recent changes in markup. This method is based on the cost-of-goods-sold section of the income statement. First find the merchandise available for sale. Then convert the sales figure (always at *retail*) to cost of goods sold (really, sales at *cost*) by multiplying the net sales by the gross profit rate and then subtracting the result from the net sales. Subtract the cost of goods sold from the merchandise available (goods that could have been sold) to get the estimated ending inventory at cost (goods not sold).

Example

Merchandise inventory (at cost), January 1		$ 38,000
Purchases for six months, at cost (net)		+221,000
Merchandise available for sale, at cost		$259,000
Sales for six months (net)	$320,000	
Less estimated gross profit ($320,000 × 30%)	−96,000	
Estimated cost of goods sold		−224,000
Estimated merchandise inventory (at cost), June 30		$ 35,000

Project 60 may be done now.

C. DETERMINING STOCK SHORTAGES

Shortages in merchandise inventory can be computed only by comparing the book inventory with the physical inventory. The *book inventory* provides a guide to intelligent retailing between physical inventories. It is the amount of goods on hand, in dollars and cents, as determined from records, rather than from an actual count. If the inventory is to be computed at cost, the method is the same as that explained in the gross profit method.

Beginning inventory
+Purchases
−Cost of goods sold
Estimated present inventory, at cost

A shortage is the difference between the book and the physical inventory, the book inventory being the larger. It may be calculated at cost, at retail, or in terms of units.

If the inventory is to be computed at retail, simply add the beginning inventory at retail and purchases at retail, and then subtract sales.

Example   **1.** Find the present book inventory at retail.

Opening inventory at retail		$19,000
Purchases at retail		30,000
Merchandise available for sale		$49,000
Net sales	$31,000	
Net markdowns	2,000	
Discounts to employees	1,500	
Total retail deductions		34,500
Present book inventory at retail		$14,500

2. If a physical count shows inventory of $13,900 at retail, what is the amount of the retail shortage in dollars and as a percent?

$14,500   book inventory
−13,900   physical inventory
$ 600   shortage

$$\frac{600}{31000} = 1.9\% \text{ of } net \text{ } sales$$

D. MEASURING STOCK TURNOVER

The retailer must keep a close watch on *stock turnover*, or *stock-turn* (the ratio between cost of sales and average inventory). A low turnover rate can point to problems in the business, because heavy stocks add to costs and lower the return on investment in merchandise. See Chapter 8 for an example of stock-turn.

Project 61 may be done now.

PROJECT 60   GROSS PROFIT METHOD; RETAIL INVENTORY METHOD

1. Sean's Shoes, Inc., suffered a fire on April 15, 1977 that completely destroyed its merchandise inventory. Its records show the following: inventory on January 1, 1977, $48,000; sales for the period, $420,000; purchases during the period, $292,000. During the past three fiscal years it has had a gross profit on sales of 30%. Calculate the amount of inventory destroyed on April 15, 1977.

2. Estimate the cost of the merchandise destroyed in a fire at Kathy's Dress Shop on August 3, 1977. The following data were obtained from the store's records:

Merchandise inventory, July 1	$31,200
Purchases, July 1–Aug. 3	18,400
Purchases returns and allowances	2,400
Sales	30,000
Sales returns and allowances	2,400
Estimated gross profit rate	40%

289

3. Penny's Pet Shop was burglarized on the night of January 25, 1977. For insurance purposes, estimate the cost of the inventory stolen. On the morning of January 26, Mr. Warren took an inventory and found that he had $24,500 of merchandise on hand. The following facts were gathered from the store records.

Inventory (beginning)	$120,000	Sales	$92,000
Purchases	100,000	Sales returns	5,000
Purchase returns	2,000	Sales Discounts	3,000
Purchase discounts	4,000		
Estimated gross profit rate	20%		

4. From the records of Phil's Pharmacy, calculate the inventory on July 31 at retail and at estimated cost. Records show the following: inventory July 1, at retail $120,000, at cost $85,000; purchases in July, at retail $522,000, at cost $305,500, transportation, $6,000, additional markups, $15,000; markup cancellations, $7,000; sales $545,000; markdowns, $5,000.

PROJECT 61   STOCK SHORTAGES; STOCK-TURN

1. The June 1 physical inventory at cost at Benny's Bicycle Center was $75,000. Purchases at cost during June were $30,000, and net sales were $45,000. Last year's markup on sales during the May–June season was 30%. Find the book inventory at cost on June 30.

2. The August 31 physical inventory at cost at Mireku's Grocery Store was $98,550. Purchases during September and October at cost were $23,745, transportation charges were $457.50, net sales during the two months were $75,900, and the estimated markup on sales was 26%. Find the book inventory at cost on November 1.

3. Find the rate of stock-turn when the average inventory at cost is $40,000 and the cost of goods sold is $255,000.

291

4. For Don's Discount Store, find (a) the closing book inventory at retail and (b) the shortage percentage.

Net sales	$481,500
Net purchases at retail	459,000
Beginning inventory at retail	229,500
Net markdowns	42,750
Discounts to employees	4,500
Physical inventory at retail	156,600

5. The net sales for a year are $540,000. The book inventory at retail at the end of the year is $192,000, and the physical inventory at retail is $168,000. What was the shortage as a percentage of net sales?

6. Find the rate of stock-turn when the average inventory at cost is $60,000, and net sales are $400,000. The gross margin as a percentage of sales is 30%.

E. PLANNED PURCHASES OPEN-TO-BUY

Proper planning of merchandise purchasing is vital to the successful operation of a business. The decision to buy is based on carefully made estimates and is really the final step in the planning process. Planned purchases may be computed by:

Estimate of planned sales
+ Estimate of planned reductions (markdowns, shortages, employee and other discounts)
+ Estimate of ending inventory at retail
− Estimate of beginning inventory at retail

Planned purchases at retail

Example

$30,000	planned sales
+2,400	planned reductions
+70,000	inventory at retail at end of April
−80,000	inventory at retail on hand on April 1
$22,400	planned purchases at retail for the month of April

Since the figure $22,400 is at retail value, it must be converted to a cost figure to determine the amount the retailer may spend. This is done by taking the cost complement of the markup percentage (100% − the markup percentage) and multiplying by the retail figure. For example, if the markup percentage is 30%,

Cost complement = 100% − 30% = 70%

Planned purchases at cost = 0.7 × $22,400 = $15,680

Planned purchases refers only to the merchandise to be received and *available for sale* during a particular month. Very often orders must be placed many months in advance. These advance orders are counted only as a part of the purchases of the month in which they will be available for sale. The need to place orders in advance increases the importance of the planned purchases concept, to avoid overpurchasing.

An important principle of good store management is to maintain some *open-to-buy* allowances at all times. Some reasons for this are: (1) new products coming on the market, (2) special price concessions and discounts offered without notice during the month, and (3) the need to be able to purchase merchandise to maintain complete assortments on all lines carried. Open-to-buy merely means not spending the full amount of your planned purchases budget at the beginning of the month. Once a week, or whenever the information is wanted, facts showing purchase commitments to date and the unspent balance of the planned purchases are gathered. This balance represents the current open-to-buy.

Example

Using $22,400 as the planned purchases at retail (from the previous example), reduce it by the merchandise received this month and the merchandise on order that is scheduled to be received this month.

$22,400	planned purchases at retail for April
−12,000	merchandise received April 1–20
−3,200	merchandise on order to be received during April
$ 7,200	open-to-buy at retail on April 21

Open-to-buy *at cost,* which is the amount left to spend on merchandise this month, can be computed by multiplying the retail figure by the complement of the markup percentage (100% − markup). For example (using the information above),

Open-to-buy at cost = $7,200 × 0.7 = $5,040.

Project 62 may be done now.

PROJECT 62   PLANNED PURCHASES; OPEN-TO-BUY

1. In the girls' slacks department, the following estimates have been made for the month of July: sales, $52,500; retail reductions, $4,500; beginning inventory at retail, $210,000; ending inventory at retail, $225,000; markup, 35% of retail. Calculate planned purchases at retail and at cost.

2. For the month of March, the men's shoe department has set up the following plans.

Beginning of inventory at retail	$21,480	Planned sales	$5,370
Ending inventory at retail	20,880	Markdowns	280
Merchandise received by March 19	2,590.50	Shortages	53.50
Merchandise on order	621	Employee discounts	27
		Markup, 40% of retail	

Find the planned purchases and the open-to-buy as of March 19 first at retail and then at cost.

3. Find the planned purchases for April and the open-to-buy as of April 13, first at retail and then at cost, for the men's shoe department mentioned in Problem 2.

Planned sales	$5,220	Ending inventory at retail	$18,396
Markdowns	400	Merchandise received	
Shortages	52	as of April 13	1,984
Employee discounts	26	Merchandise on order	1,054.50

4. Calculate the open-to-buy as of October 10 for Sandy's Sewing Shop based on the information below.

Planned sales for October	$11,200	Merchandise on order	$ 2,000
Inventory, October 1	20,000	Planned reductions	800
Merchandise received, October 10	6,000	Planned inventory, October 31	22,000
Markup, 30% of retail			

LIKE NEW!
FOR SALE
BY OWNER!

12 DEPRECIAT METHODS

1. **The meaning of depreciation**

2. **Four methods of estimating depreciation**

3. **Uses of and ways of computing accelerated depreciation**

MINICASE Larry Cooper bought a new dump truck for his business—the paving of driveways and parking lots. He paid $15,000 for it three months ago. Today a local truck dealer told him that it would be worth only $13,000 on a trade-in for a larger truck. Larry complained that $2,000 was too much *depreciation* for three months. Later Larry's friend, Bill, an accountant, explained that although the truck's *market value* was now only $13,000 because it had become a used truck, it had not depreciated in the business sense of the word.

A. DEFINING DEPRECIATION

Businesses are concerned not with the decrease in market value (the value at which a property can be sold) but with the *usefulness value.* This value is the cost of long-lived property less the *estimated* loss of usefulness by wear, rust, age, and obsolescence. A company buys the asset to use, not to resell. Obsolescence is the decline in value caused by a fast-changing technology, and often it results in an asset's having little usefulness value, even though it has many years of life left in it.

The *book value* of the asset—its value on the company's books—is determined by subtracting from the original cost of the asset the total depreciation computed since purchase. The first step in determining how much an asset has depreciated is to estimate its useful life. The next step is to estimate the *scrap value* of that asset at the end of its life.

B. METHODS OF DEPRECIATION

There are four basic methods for estimating the depreciation of an asset in any particular business year.

STRAIGHT-LINE METHOD

The *straight-line method* of estimating depreciation is the oldest and easiest to use. It applies the same amount of decline in value against the cost each year. It is computed by subtracting the scrap value (often called the *residual* or *trade-in value*) from the original cost and dividing that number by the life of the asset, usually expressed in years. Consider a $10,000 machine with an expected life of five years and a scrap value of $1,000:

$$\text{Depreciation} = \frac{\text{Cost} - \text{Scrap value}}{\text{Life}} = \frac{\$10,000 - \$1,000}{5 \text{ years}}$$
$$= \$1,800 \text{ per year}$$

Each year the value of the machine will decline $1,800, until at the end of the fifth year, the book value will be $1,000 ($10,000 − $9,000), the same as the scrap value.

UNITS-OF-PRODUCTION METHOD

The *units-of-production* (sometimes called *service hours*) *method* is a variation of the straight-line method. It shows more accurately the decrease in value caused by wear on an asset that is used at irregular intervals. Some machines and other assets are used a great deal and then sit idle for months; the method of depreciation should reflect this usage.

The only difference between this method and the straight-line method is the denominator of the fraction, the *life.* The life is expressed in either the estimated number of units the machine can produce or the number of hours it can operate effectively during its lifetime. The formula gives a rate of depreciation that must be multiplied by the actual number of units produced or the actual hours operated in any one year.

Example

Suppose the same $10,000 machine with a scrap value of $1,000 has an expected life of 18,000 units. Assume also that the machine produced 3,000 units this year. How much depreciation should be allowed?

$$\text{Depreciation} = \frac{\text{Cost} - \text{Scrap value}}{\text{Life (in hours or units)}}$$

$$= \frac{\$10,000 - \$1,000}{18,000 \text{ units}} = \frac{\$9,000}{18,000} = \$0.50 \text{ per unit}$$

Depreciation for this year $= \$0.50 \times 3,000 = \$1,500$

DECLINING-BALANCE METHOD

The first of two accelerated methods is the *declining-balance method.* Here the depreciation is large in the early years of the asset's life and grows smaller in the later years. Many businesses prefer accelerated depreciation because of its income tax advantages, especially when fast-changing technology may force a business to trade in an asset before its useful life to the company is over.

The maximum rate allowable for income tax purposes is twice the straight-line rate. With certain types of assets, it is less than twice. The straight-line rate is computed by placing 1 over the life. For example, for the above machine with a five-year life:

$$\frac{1}{5} = 5\overline{)1.00}^{\,0.20} = 20\%$$

Declining balance rate $= 20\% \times 2 = 40\%$

This rate is then multiplied by the book value at the end of the previous year. The book value grows smaller each year, hence the name *declining balance.*

Example

For the same $10,000 machine with an expected life of five years and a scrap value of $1,000, apply the declining-balance method at twice the straight-line rate.

First year:

$10,000	cost	$10,000
−0	total depreciation to date	×0.4
$10,000	book value	$ 4,000.0
−4,000	depreciation for first year	Depreciation of
$ 6,000	book value at end of first year	first year

Second year:

$ 6,000	book value at end of first year	$6,000
−2,400	depreciation for second year	×0.4
$ 3,600	book value at end of second year	$2,400.0
		Depreciation of
$10,000	cost	second year
−6,400	total depreciation for first 2 years	
$ 3,600	book value at end of second year	

Year	Cost	Total Depreciation at Beginning of Year	Book Value at Beginning of Year	Rate	This Year's Depreciation	Book Value at End of Year
1	$10,000	——	$10,000	40%	$4,000	$6,000
2	10,000	$4,000	6,000	40%	2,400	3,600
3	10,000	6,400	3,600	40%	1,440	2,160
4	10,000	7,840	2,160	40%	864	1,296
5	10,000	8,704	1,296	40%	?	?

Notice that this method *does not* use the asset's scrap value, except as the bottom for the last year's book value. If scrap value has been estimated for an asset, then the book value for the last year cannot fall below the scrap value. In this case the last year's depreciation is computed by subtracting from $1,296 (book value at the end of the fourth year), the scrap value of $1,000. This gives a depreciation of $296 in the last year. If the scrap value were estimated to be zero rather than $1,000, the depreciation would be computed by multiplying 40% by $1,296, giving $518.40 as the depreciation and $777.60 as the final book value.

SUM-OF-THE-YEARS-DIGITS METHOD

The *sum-of-the-years-digits method* is the other accelerated method of depreciation. Its results and advantages are similar to those of the declining-balance method. The digits of the years of the asset's life, listed in reverse order, are used as the numerators in fractions in which the denominator is the sum of the digits. Each fraction gives the rate for the corresponding year. Multiply the fraction by the cost less the scrap value. Consider again the same $10,000 machine used in the previous examples.

Year	Digits	Rate	Cost Less Scrap Value ($10,000 − 1,000)	Each Year's Depreciation	Total Depreciation at End of Year	Book Value at End of Year (Cost − Total Depreciation)
1	5	$\frac{5}{15}$	$9,000	$3,000	$3,000	$7,000
2	4	$\frac{4}{15}$	9,000	2,400	5,400	4,600
3	3	$\frac{3}{15}$	9,000	1,800	7,200	2,800
4	2	$\frac{2}{15}$	9,000	1,200	8,400	1,600
5	1	$\frac{1}{15}$	9,000	600	9,000	1,000
	15	$\frac{15}{15}$		$9,000		

Notice that the *scrap value* is used with this accelerated method. Notice also that the book value is found by subtracting the total depreciation from the *cost.* If the life is long, a time-saving way to find the total of the digits (the denominator) is to use the formula

$$S = N\left(\frac{N+1}{2}\right), \qquad \text{where } S \text{ is the sum of the digits and } N \text{ is the number of years of life.}$$

For example, with a five-year life:

$$S = 5\left(\frac{5+1}{2}\right) = 5\left(\frac{6}{2}\right) = 5(3) = 15$$

Project 63 may be done now.

PROJECT 63   DEPRECIATION

A.   Record in the columns at the right the first year's depreciation of each of the following assets.

	Cost	Life	Scrap Value	Straight-Line	Declining-Balance (S.L. × 2)	Sum-of-the-Years-Digits
1.	$12,000	9 years	$3,360	_____	_____	_____
2.	2,445	5 years	245	_____	_____	_____
3.	4,700	35 years	500	_____	_____	_____
4.	13,500	15 years	no scrap	_____	_____	_____
5.	9,000	9 years	900	_____	_____	_____
6.	7,200	10 years	1,600	_____	_____	_____
7.	11,500	50 years	1,500	_____	_____	_____
8.	32,600	40 years	4,600	_____	_____	_____

B. Find the depreciation for the year and for the method indicated in the problems in Part A.

	Year	Method	Problem	Depreciation
1.	third	Declining-balance	5	————
2.	fourth	Sum-of-the-years-digits	6	————
3.	fifth	Declining-balance	2	————
4.	second	Straight-line	8	————

C. Monson Manufacturing Co. depreciates all its machines according to the units-of-production method. Find this year's depreciation on each of the machines listed below.

	Cost	Estimated Life	Scrap Value	Units Produced, or Hours Operated This Year	Depreciation
1.	$30,000	30,000 units	$1,200	5,400 units	_____
2.	18,100	90,000 units	3,100	12,960 units	_____
3.	2,100	62,000 hours	550	7,910 hours	_____
4.	22,200	8,000 hours	2,800	5,200 hours	_____
5.	6,200	20,000 units	700	4,900 units	_____

C. PARTIAL YEAR OF DEPRECIATION

In all the previous examples it is assumed that the asset was purchased at the beginning of the business year. In reality, most assets are purchased at some time during the year.

Example

A company, using the straight-line method to estimate depreciation allowances, purchased a machine on March 1 (2 months after the beginning of the year). This means that the company owned the machine for only 10 months of the year. Therefore, the depreciation for the first year is only $\frac{10}{12}$ of the 12-month amount. (See Part B—Straight-Line Method.)

$$\frac{10}{\cancel{12}}_{1} \times \cancel{1,800}^{150} = \$1,500$$

This problem does not arise with the units-of-production method because the rate is multiplied by the number of units produced or the number of hours the machine has run, no matter how many months the company has owned the machine.

Example

In another company, which used the declining-balance method, the machine was purchased on April 1 (3 months after the beginning of the year). The company owned the machine for only 9 months of the year; therefore, the depreciation for the first year is only $\frac{9}{12}$ of the 12-month amount (see Part B). The method for the following years would be the same as shown earlier, but the amounts in the depreciation schedule would change because the book values at the end of each year would be different.

$$\frac{9}{12} \times \$4,000 = \$3,000$$

$$\begin{array}{rl} \$10,000 & \text{cost} \\ -3,000 & \text{depreciation} \\ \hline \$\ 7,000 & \text{book value at end of first year} \end{array}$$

Then 40% would be multiplied by $7,000 to get the second year's depreciation.

Year	Cost	Total Depreciation at Beginning of Year	Book Value at Beginning of Year	Rate	This Year's Depreciation	Book Value at End of Year
1	$10,000	——	$10,000	40%	$3,000	$7,000
2	10,000	$3,000	7,000	40%	2,800	4,200
3	10,000	5,800	4,200	40%	1,680	2,520
4	10,000	7,480	2,520	40%	1,008	1,512
5	10,000	8,488	1,512	40%	?	?

Example

In a company preferring the sum-of-the-years-digits method, the same machine was purchased on April 1 (3 months after the beginning of the year). The company owned the machine for only

9 months of the year; therefore, the depreciation for the first year is only $\frac{9}{12}$ of the 12-month amount (see Part B). Because the total depreciation must come to exactly $\frac{15}{15}$ of the cost less the scrap value, each following year's depreciation must include the last $\frac{3}{12}$ of the previous 12-month depreciation figure plus $\frac{9}{12}$ of the current 12-month depreciation figure.

First year:

$$\frac{9}{\cancel{12}} \times \$\cancel{3,000}^{250} = \$2,250 \quad \begin{array}{l} \text{depreciation for first business year} \\ \text{(9 months only)} \end{array}$$

Second Year:

$$\frac{3}{\cancel{12}} \times \$\cancel{3,000}^{250} = \$\ \ 750 \quad \text{3 months}$$

$$\frac{9}{\cancel{12}} \times \$\cancel{2,400}^{200} = \underline{\ 1,800\ } \quad \text{9 months}$$
$$\phantom{\frac{9}{12} \times \$2,400 =} \$2,550 \quad \text{depreciation for second business year}$$

Project 64 may be done now.

PROJECT 64   DEPRECIATION

A.   Find the depreciation and the book value of the following assets by the method indicated and for the year shown. Declining-balance method is at twice the straight-line rate.

	Cost	Scrap Value	Life	Year of Depreciation	Method	Depreciation	Book Value
1.	$275	$25	8 yrs.	4th	St.-line	_____	_____
2.	750	50	8 yrs.	2nd	Dec.-bal.	_____	_____
3.	3,650	450	12 yrs.	9 mos.	Sum-y.-d.	_____	_____
4.	3,650	450	12 yrs.	1 yr., 9 mos.	Sum-y.-d.	_____	_____
5.	1,800	160	10 yrs.	2 yrs., 8 mos.	Dec.-bal.	_____	_____
6.	920	140	20 yrs.	4th	Sum-y.-d.	_____	_____
7.	27,900	——	25 yrs.	15th	St.-line	_____	_____
8.	55,000	5,000	25 yrs.	4th	Dec.-bal.	_____	_____

B. Solve the following problems.

1. Factory equipment with a cost of $74,000 and an estimated scrap value of $4,000 is expected to have a useful operating life of 350,000 hours. During April the motor was operated 1,700 hours. Determine the depreciation for the month.

2. Tom's Trucking Co. purchased a truck for $37,000. It has an estimated useful life of six years and an estimated scrap value of $1,000. Determine (a) the annual depreciation by the straight-line method, (b) the amount of depreciation for the second year by the sum-of-the-years-digits method, and (c) the amount of depreciation for the first year by the declining-balance method (at twice the straight-line rate).

3.   Don's Distributors bought a piece of equipment for $19,980. It has an estimated scrap value of $2,340 and an estimated life of 6 years. It was placed in service on May 7 of this business year, which ends on December 31. Determine the depreciation for the current year and for the following year (a) by the declining-balance method at twice the straight-line rate, and (b) by the sum-of-the-years-digits method.

13 STOCKS AND BONDS

KEY POINTS TO LEARN FROM THIS CHAPTER

1. The difference between stocks and bonds
2. How to compute dividends
3. What is cumulative preferred stock?
4. What is participating preferred stock?
5. The meanings of discounts and premiums on securities
6. How to compute rate of return on securities

MINICASE

Alice Henderson graduated from college about a year and a half ago. She found a good job at an advertising agency. She was encouraged by the payroll department to declare zero exemptions on her federal income tax because of the unusual effect of tax withholding tables on the income of unmarried people. In April of this year, Alice found that too much had been withheld from her salary, causing a $398 refund. Having already established a savings account and an insurance program, she decided to buy some stocks or bonds.

Alice talked with her father and a stockbroker (a person who is paid a commission for acting as an agent in the buying and selling of stocks and bonds) about whether she should buy common stock, preferred stock, or corporation bonds. As a starter, they recommended she buy 10 shares of Great Mid-West Airlines for $355. Commissions and other expenses amounted to $43.

After she purchased the stock, she became interested in reading the financial pages of her local newspaper. This was a new and exciting interest for her. Alice was determined to learn the meaning of terms such as *stock, common, preferred, premium, discount, cumulative, participating, bond, face value, amortization,* and *yield.* She wondered when she would get her first dividend check and how large it would be.

315

A. BASIC DIFFERENCES BETWEEN STOCKS AND BONDS

A business firm needs funds to purchase the fixed assets and to provide the working capital required to operate the business. There are two main sources of long-term funds, *bonds* and *stocks.* These are securities that a corporation sells to investors in order to raise money. Investors who purchase these securities from a company can sell them to other investors, usually through a stockbroker.

CORPORATION BONDS

When a corporation issues bonds, it borrows money from investors who purchase the bonds. A corporation *bond* is an IOU of a corporation in which the corporation promises to pay to the purchaser of each bond a fixed amount of interest each year and a stated amount of money at a specified maturity date in the future. The *face value* of a bond is the value of the bond that appears on the face of the bond and is the amount the issuing corporation promises to pay at maturity. Most bonds are issued with a face value of $1,000, although some bonds are issued in smaller or larger denominations.

Bondholders are creditors of the corporation. They are not entitled to vote. The corporation must pay the interest each year and the face value at maturity, regardless of the financial condition of the corporation. Interest must be paid before any dividends on the corporation's stock are paid and, in the event of liquidation of the firm, the corporation must pay the face value of the bonds to the bondholders before the stockholders receive anything.

CORPORATION STOCK

Corporation *stock* represents the ownership of the business. The charter of a corporation states how many shares of stock the company is authorized to issue. Sometimes the corporation has more shares than it has actually sold to investors so that if the need arises the corporation can sell additional shares to raise money. A stockholder receives from the corporation a *stock certificate* that states the number of shares he or she owns and is evidence of ownership.

The dollar value assigned to a share of stock by the corporation's charter, called the *par value,* is the amount that appears on the front of the stock certificate. The total dollar amount (*total par value*) at which the stock is carried on the corporation's balance sheet can be found by multiplying the number of shares outstanding by the par value per share. In some cases, companies issue no-par stock but give a stated value per share on the balance sheet. The par value of common stock usually has little significance to the investor.

If a corporation sells stock and receives more than par value, the difference is known as the *premium;* if the corporation sells the stock for less than par value, the difference is referred to as the *discount.* If a company sells 1,000 shares of common stock with a par value of $10 per share and receives $13,000 from investors, the total premium is $3,000 and the premium per share is $3.00.

$$\begin{array}{ll} \$13,000 & \text{total selling price} \\ -10,000 & \text{total par value} \\ \hline \$\ 3,000 & \text{total premium} \end{array} \qquad \frac{\$3,000 \text{ total premium}}{1,000 \text{ shares}} = \$3.00 \text{ premium per share}$$

The stockholders are the owners of the business. Therefore, the corporation does not have to pay dividends on stock and does not promise to pay a certain amount in the future because there is no maturity date.

There are two classes of stock, *preferred* and *common.* All business corporations have common stock outstanding, and some also have preferred stock outstanding.

Preferred stock is a class of stock that takes preference over common stock in the payment of dividends and in event of liquidation of the firm. Bond interest *must* be paid. The dividend on preferred stock is normally a fixed amount, but it is paid only if the board of directors decides to declare a dividend. However, dividends on common stock, also declared by the board of directors, cannot be paid until all the dividends to which the preferred stockholders are entitled have been paid. If the firm is liquidated, the preferred stockholders have a claim on the firm's assets after bondholders but before common stockholders. Normally, preferred stock does not carry the right to vote on corporation matters. Usually, preferred stock is *cumulative.* This means that if preferred dividends have not been paid in past years, all the omitted dividends and the current dividend on the preferred must be paid to the preferred stockholders before any dividends may be paid on the company's common stock. Occasionally, preferred stock is *participating.* Such an agreement means that preferred stock is entitled to a stated dividend plus an additional dividend on a specified basis when dividends are paid on the common stock.

Common stock is a class of stock that represents the residual ownership of the corporation. Dividends on common stock are paid at the discretion of the board of directors but cannot be paid until the appropriate amount of preferred dividends has been paid. There is no minimum or maximum dividend payment on shares of common stock. After preferred dividends have been paid, the directors determine what the common dividend, if any, will be, depending upon the corporation's earnings and cash position. If the firm is liquidated, the common stockholders share in whatever assets are remaining after all the claims are satisfied, including the claims of bondholders and preferred stockholders. Common stockholders have the right to vote on important matters pertaining to the corporation. Each stockholder has as many votes as the number of shares he or she owns.

B. INCOME FROM STOCKS AND BONDS

One of the primary reasons an investor buys bonds or shares of stock is the expectation of receiving periodic cash payments on the securities. In fact, before making an intelligent decision regarding the purchase of securities, an investor needs to know the amount of the income payments and when they will be received. The cash payments that an investor receives from the corporation by owning a bond are referred to as *interest;* the cash payments received because of stock ownership are known as *dividends.*

BOND INTEREST

Bond prices are quoted as a percentage of face value. A price of 98 for a bond with a face value of $1,000 means the bond is selling for $980. For the same bond, a quote of 105 is equivalent to a market price of $1,050. A quote of 98 for a $500 face value bond means a price of $490 (98% $\times$ $500). To find out how to compute the amount of interest on a bond, let us look at an 8% $1,000 bond of the Charles Corp. that matures in 10 years and is quoted at 96. In this case, each bond can be purchased for $960, and the corporation promises to pay the bondholder $1,000 ten years from today when the bond matures. In addition, Charles Corp. will pay $80 of interest each year for the next 10 years to the bondholder. The 8% interest rate is called the *coupon rate* or the *nominal yield.* This rate is stated on each bond. The amount of annual interest is found by multiplying the coupon rate or nominal yield times the face value of the bond (8% $\times$ $1,000), regardless of the market price of the bond.

Bond interest is normally paid semiannually; therefore, a Charles Corp. bondholder would receive $40 every six months ($\frac{1}{2} \times$ $80). He or she would receive the semiannual interest payment in one of two ways: either Charles Corp. will mail a check for the $40, or, the bond itself will have coupons physically attached to it. The bondholder merely clips the appropriate coupon every six months on the specified payment date and presents it to a bank for payment of the $40.

At the time of purchase an adjustment usually has to be made to the total purchase cost of a bond to reflect "accrued interest." For example, if interest is paid semiannually, an investor who buys a bond two months after the last interest payment date is entitled to only four months' interest. The seller is entitled to interest for two months. The corporation, however, will on the next payment date send a check for the full amount of semiannual interest to the buyer of the bond. If interest is received by presenting a coupon for payment, the buyer will get all the semiannual interest because he or she will have the bond on the next payment date four months hence. In order to even out this inequity, the usual procedure is for the buyer to pay the seller the quoted bond price plus the accrued interest since the preceding interest payment date. The amount of accrued interest is computed for the time period from and including the last payment date of to but not including the settlement date. The settlement date is normally five business days after the purchase date, and it is the day the seller's bond certificate is supposed to be delivered to the purchaser's broker.

Example An 8% bond, face value $1,000, with interest payment dates on April 1 and October 1 is bought on Monday, May 25, for 103 plus accrued interest. The settlement date is Monday, June 1. Thus, the accrual time period is from and including April 1 to and including May 31, or two months. What is the total cost of the bond, disregarding brokerage commissions?

$$\$1,000 \times \frac{8}{100} \times \frac{2}{12} = \frac{40}{3} = \$13.33 \quad \text{accrued interest for two months}$$

$$
\begin{array}{ll}
\$1,000 & \text{face value} \\
\underline{\times 1.03} & \text{103\% of face value} \\
\$1,030.00 & \text{bond price} \\
\underline{+13.33} & \text{accrued interest} \\
\$1,043.33 & \text{total cost of bond}
\end{array}
$$

DIVIDENDS ON STOCK   Dividends on stock are never guaranteed; they are paid only if declared by the corporation's board of directors. When dividends are paid, the corporation mails the dividend checks to its stockholders. Although some companies pay dividends semiannually or annually, the usual practice is to pay dividends quarterly.

Dividends on preferred stock are stated as a percentage of par value or as a dollar amount. For example, the annual dividend on a 5% preferred stock is $5 per share if par value is $100, but $2.50 if par value is $50. A $4 preferred means that the annual dividend per share is $4. To find the total amount of the regular annual dividends that all the preferred stockholders are supposed to receive, the number of preferred shares outstanding is multiplied by the annual dollar dividend per share. If the total dividend declared by the directors is not large enough to pay this amount, the preferred stockholders get all of the declared dividends. Consequently, the preferred stockholders would get less than the specified annual dividend and the common stockholders would receive nothing. On the other hand, if the amount declared exceeds the dividends to which preferred stockholders are entitled, the common stockholders get the excess. Of course, if there is no preferred stock outstanding, the full amount of the declared dividend would be paid to the common stockholders.

Example   The Thomasbury Corporation earned $50,000 last year. During the year, its board of directors declared and paid dividends of $40,000, retaining $10,000 to reinvest in the business. Thomasbury had outstanding 6,000 shares of $50 par 8% preferred stock and 10,000 shares of common stock, $10 par value. What were the total amounts of dividends paid to preferred and common stockholders, and how much was paid per share?

Preferred Stock

$50	par value per share
×0.08	stated dividend percentage
$4.00	preferred dividends per share
×6,000	preferred shares outstanding
$24,000	total preferred dividend

Common Stock

40,000	total dividends paid
−24,000	total preferred dividend
$16,000	total common dividend

$$\frac{\$16,000}{10,000} = \$1.60 \quad \text{dividend per share of common}$$

Project 65 may be done now.

PROJECT 65   BOND INTEREST; STOCK DIVIDENDS

1. Compute the premium or the discount for the following situations.

Number of Shares of Stock Sold by Company	Par Value Per Share	Selling Price Per Share	Premium		Discount	
			Total	Per Share	Total	Per Share
14,000	$ 50	$ 52				
2,000	100	96				
7,500	25	30				
900	200	220				
4,000	10	5				

2. Compute the market price and amounts of annual and semiannual interest for the following bonds.

Face Value of Bond	Price Quote	Coupon Rate or Nominal Yield	Price of Bond	Amount of Interest	
				Annual	Semiannual
$ 500	120	10%			
1,000	95	$7\frac{1}{2}\%$			
1,000	110	9			
500	80	7			

3. A 8% $1,000 face value bond is bought on Monday, July 25 for 110 plus accrued interest. Interest payment dates are April 1 and October 1. The settlement date is Monday, August 1. How much accrued interest must the buyer pay to the seller, and what is the total cost of the bond?

321

4. Ricky Tiant is considering the purchase of 500 shares of Appleton Corporation's 8% preferred stock, $50 par. How much is the stated annual dividend per share? How much in annual dividends would Ricky receive if he bought the stock?

5. Find the total amount of the premium or the discount and place the amount in the proper column for the following.

Number of Bonds	Face Value of Each Bond	Total Face Value of All Bonds	Quote Price	Total Market Price of All Bonds	Total Premium	Total Discount
500	500	_____	104	_____	_____	_____
700	500	_____	92	_____	_____	_____
400	100	_____	98	_____	_____	_____
1,000	1,000	_____	105	_____	_____	_____
80	100	_____	106	_____	_____	_____
250	100	_____	96	_____	_____	_____
4,000	1,000	_____	102	_____	_____	_____

DIVIDENDS ON
CUMULATIVE AND
PARTICIPATING
PREFERRED STOCK

If the preferred stock is cumulative and if preferred dividends have not been paid in past years, the preferred stockholders are entitled to all the dividends in arrears plus the current dividend before the common stockholders receive any dividends.

Example

1. Assume the same facts as in the previous example, except that $10,000 of preferred dividends were in arrears.

$24,000   current year's preferred dividend
+10,000   preferred dividends in arrears
$34,000   total preferred dividend

$$\frac{\$34,000}{6,000 \text{ shares}} = \$5.67 \quad \text{preferred dividend per share}$$

$40,000   total dividend paid
−34,000   total preferred dividend
$ 6,000   total common dividend

$$\frac{\$6,000}{10,000 \text{ shares}} = \$0.60 \quad \text{common dividend per share}$$

2. Assume the same facts as in the earlier example, except that preferred dividends for one year were in arrears.

$24,000   current year's preferred dividend
+24,000   one year of preferred dividends in arrears
$48,000   total dividend to which preferred entitled
−40,000   total preferred dividends paid
$ 8,000   total preferred dividends in arrears at beginning
           of following year

$$\frac{\$40,000}{6,000 \text{ shares}} = \$6.67 \quad \text{preferred dividend per share; no}$$
common dividend can be paid

A participating preferred stock is entitled to its stated dividend rate and to additional dividends in the manner specified in the stock agreement when common dividends are paid.

Example

The board of directors of Kitchens, Inc., declared a $150,000 dividend. The total regular, stated preferred dividend is $20,000. After common stockholders receive a dividend of $2 per share, the agreement provides that preferred stock will share with the common in the excess dividends in proportion to the total par values of the two classes of stock. There are 10,000 preferred shares, par value $40 per share, and 50,000 common shares, par value $40 per share. What were the total dividend amounts paid to each class of stock? (See next page for computations.)

```
    50,000  shares of common
      ×$2  rate
  $100,000  total common dividend at $2 rate
   +20,000  total regular preferred dividend
  $120,000  total regular dividend on stock

  $150,000  total dividend declared
  −120,000  total regular dividend on stock
  $ 30,000  total participation dividend
```

10,000 shares $\times$ \$40 $=$ \$ 400,000   total preferred par value
50,000 shares $\times$ \$40 $=$ \$2,000,000   total common par value
$\qquad\qquad\qquad\qquad$ \$2,400,000   total par value of stock

$\dfrac{\$400,000}{\$2,400,000} = \dfrac{1}{6}$ preferred fraction of participation dividend

$\dfrac{\$2,000,000}{2,400,000} = \dfrac{5}{6}$ common fraction of participation dividend

$\dfrac{1}{6} \times \$30,000 = \$\ 5,000$ preferred portion of participation dividend

$\dfrac{5}{6} \times \$30,000 = \underline{25,000}$ common portion of participation dividend
$\qquad\qquad\qquad\qquad\ \ \$30,000$

Common:$\qquad\qquad\qquad$ \$100,000 $+$ \$25,000 $=$ \$125,000
Preferred:$\qquad\qquad\quad$ \$ 20,000 $+$ \$ 5,000 $=$ $\underline{25,000}$
Total dividend declared:$\qquad\qquad\qquad\quad$ \$150,000

Project 66 may be done now.

PROJECT 66   DIVIDENDS ON PREFERRED STOCK

1. Century Seats, Inc., during the period 1976 to 1979 had outstanding 10,000 shares of $100 par 6% preferred stock and 50,000 shares of $25 par common stock. The preferred is noncumulative and nonparticipating. Compute the total dividends and the dividends per share for each class of stock for each year.

Year	Total Dividends Declared and Paid	Preferred Dividends		Common Dividends	
		Total	Per Share	Total	Per Share
1976	$ 90,000	_____	_____	_____	_____
1977	42,500	_____	_____	_____	_____
1978	65,000	_____	_____	_____	_____
1979	200,000	_____	_____	_____	_____

2. Using the facts in Problem 1, compute the dividends if the preferred stock is cumulative and if $40,000 of preferred dividends were in arrears at the beginning of 1976.

Year	Total Dividends Declared and Paid	Preferred Dividends		Common Dividends	
		Total	Per Share	Total	Per Share
1976	$ 90,000	————	————	————	————
1977	42,500	————	————	————	————
1978	65,000	————	————	————	————
1979	200,000	————	————	————	————

3. Using the facts in Problem 1, compute the dividends if the preferred stock is cumulative and participating. Assume that preferred dividends in arrears at the beginning of 1976 amount to $120,000. Also assume that preferred stock participates with common in excess dividends in proportion to the total par values of the two classes of stock after the common stockholders receive a dividend of $1.50 per share.

Year	Total Dividends Declared and Paid	Preferred Dividends		Common Dividends	
		Total	Per Share	Total	Per Share
1976	$90,000	_____	_____	_____	_____
1977	42,500	_____	_____	_____	_____
1978	65,000	_____	_____	_____	_____
1979	200,000	_____	_____	_____	_____

C. RATE OF RETURN ON STOCKS AND BONDS

Knowledge of the expected annual income from a security, whether in the form of interest or dividends, is not the only information needed to make a wise investment decision. The expected annual income from an investment must be related to the investment's cost. Annual income of $1,000 from an investment that costs $10,000 would be preferred over the same $1,000 a year from an investment that costs $20,000, assuming no other significant differences between the two investments. The *rate of return* or the *yield* on a security shows in percentage terms the relationship between the annual dollar return from a security and its market price or purchase price.

RATE OF RETURN ON CORPORATION BONDS

The *current yield* on a bond is the annual interest expressed as a percentage of the market price or purchase price:

$$\text{Current yield on bond} = \frac{\text{Annual interest}}{\text{Market price or purchase price}}$$

Thus, the current yield on a 6% $1,000 face value bond selling at 100 is 6% $\left(\dfrac{\$60}{\$1,000}\right)$. If the bond is quoted at 90, the current yield would be 6.67% $\left(\dfrac{\$60}{\$900}\right)$; at a quote of 120, the current yield would be 5.00% $\left(\dfrac{\$60}{\$1,200}\right)$.

In order for a purchase and sale to occur, buyer and seller must agree on price. They compare the bond's nominal yield with the *market rate of interest* to determine a mutually agreeable price. The market rate of interest is the prevailing yield on comparable bonds of other companies at the time of the transaction. In the earlier example, the company, when it first sold the bonds to investors, had to promise to pay interest of $60 a year (a nominal yield of 6%) to get investors to pay about $1,000 for a bond. This means that the market rate of interest at the time the bonds were issued was about 6%. The issuing company would like to have received more than $1,000 for a bond, but investors would not pay more. They knew that they could get a return of 6% on other comparable bonds. After the bonds were issued by the company, buying and selling investors will agree on a price of $1,000 if the market rate at that time is the same as it was when the bonds were first sold by the company. But the market rate changes due to changes in the economy. If the prevailing market rate of interest drops to less than 6%, sellers will demand and buyers will be willing to pay more than $1,000 for a bond paying interest of $60 a year. On the other hand, buyers and sellers will agree on a price of less than $1,000 if the market rate increases to more than 6%.

From the previous discussion, it is apparent that bond prices fluctuate as the market rate of interest changes. If an investor pays more than face value for a bond, the difference is called a *premium;* if a bond is purchased for less than face value, the difference is called a *discount.*

Examples

1. A 7% $1,000 face value bond of Standard Toys, Inc., was purchased for 104. Find the premium.

```
$1,000   face value
 ×1.04   104% of face value
$1,040   purchase price
−1,000   face value
$   40   premium
```

2. A 6% $1,000 face value bond of Standard Toys, Inc., was purchased for 97. Find the discount.

```
$1,000   face value
 ×0.97   97% of face value
$ 970    purchase price
```

```
$1,000   face value
 −970    purchase price
$   30   discount
```

The premium paid on a bond bought for more than face value is spread evenly over the life of the bond just as the cost of a fixed asset is spread over its life by the straight-line method of depreciation. This process is called *amortization of bond premium.* To find the periodic amortization amount, the premium is divided by the remaining life of the bond, which is the number of years or months from the bond purchase date to the bond maturity date. The *bond-carrying* value on a particular date is the cost of the bond minus the sum of all the periodic amortization amounts from the bond purchase date to the date for which the carrying value is being computed. Consequently, the bond-carrying value for a bond bought at a premium gradually declines over the life of the bond and on the maturity date equals the face value.

Examples

1. A premium of $40 is paid for a 10-year 7% $1,000 bond purchased on the issue date, March 1, 1977. Find the bond-carrying value at the end of 1977 and at the end of 1978.

$$\frac{\$40}{10 \text{ years}} = \$4 \quad \text{premium amortization per year}$$

$$\frac{10}{12} \times \$4 = \frac{10}{3} = \$3.33 \quad \text{total premium amortization by year-end} \\ 1977 \text{ (March 1 to December 31)}$$

$1,040 − $3.33 = $1,036.67   bond-carrying value at year-end 1977

$4   premium amortization for full year 1978

$1,036.67 − $4 = $1,032.67   bond-carrying value at year-end 1978

2. Assume the same situation as in Example 1, except that the bond was purchased on May 1, 1977, two months after the date of issue. Again, find the bond carrying value at the end of 1977 and at the end of 1978.

10 years $-$ 2 months $=$ 9 years, 10 months
$$= 9(12) + 10$$
$$= 118 \quad \text{months remaining life of bond}$$

$\dfrac{\$40}{118 \text{ months}} = \$0.34$ premium amortization per month

8 months $\times$ \$0.34 $=$ \$2.72   total premium amortization by year-end 1977 (May 1 to December 31)

\$1,040 $-$ \$2.72 $=$ \$1,037.28   bond-carrying value at year-end 1977

12 months $\times$ \$0.34 $=$ \$4.08   premium amortization for full year 1978

\$1,037.28 $-$ \$4.08 $=$ \$1,033.20   bond carrying value at year-end 1978

When a bond is purchased for less than face value, the bond-carrying value is computed by adjusting for the *accumulation of bond discount.* The procedure for treating bond discount accumulation is mathematically identical to that of bond premium amortization. In the case of a discount, however, the discount accumulation amounts are added to the purchase price of the bond. Therefore, the carrying value gradually increases over time and equals face value at maturity.

An investor who buys a bond and plans to hold it until the maturity date is interested in a rate of return measure called *yield to maturity.* This yield relates in percentage terms the annual total dollar return to the average principal invested in the bond. The total annual return is made up of two components: the annual interest and the annual premium amortization if the bond was purchased at a premium or the annual discount accumulation if the bond was purchased at a discount. The principal invested during the life of the bond is calculated by taking an average of the bond purchase price and the face value expected at maturity. Although bond tables that enable an investor to determine the exact yield to maturity are available, fairly accurate results can be achieved by either of two formulas:

Yield to maturity for bond purchased at a premium

$$= \frac{\text{Annual interest} - \text{Annual premium amortization}}{\text{Average principal invested}}$$

Yield to maturity for bond purchased at a discount

$$= \frac{\text{Annual interest} + \text{Annual discount accumulation}}{\text{Average principal invested}}$$

Example   Assume that an investor paid $5,300 for a 6% $5,000 face value bond that matures in 10 years. Compute the yield to maturity.

$5,300   purchase price
−5,000   face value
$ 300   premium

$$\frac{\$300}{10 \text{ years}} = \$30 \quad \text{annual premium amortization}$$

$$\$5,000 \times \frac{6}{100} = \$300 \quad \text{annual interest}$$

$$\frac{\$5,300 + \$5,000}{2} = \frac{\$10,300}{2} = \$5,150 \quad \begin{array}{l}\text{average principal}\\ \text{invested}\end{array}$$

$$\frac{\$300 - \$30}{\$5,150} = \frac{\$270}{\$5,150} = 5.24\% \quad \text{yield to maturity}$$

The investor paid $300 more for the bond than she expects to get back at maturity. Therefore, the yield to maturity (5.24%) is less than the nominal yield (6%) stated on the bond. The yield to maturity of a bond bought at a discount would be greater than the bond's nominal yield. This occurs because the investor receives annual interest based on the nominal yield and also expects to receive at maturity the bond's face value that is more than her cost.

RATE OF RETURN
ON STOCK

One way to determine the rate of return on stock is to compute the current yield:

$$\text{Current yield on stock} = \frac{\text{Annual dividends}}{\text{Market price or purchase price}}$$

The current yield expresses the relationship between annual dividend income and the market price or purchase price of the stock.

Example   Harry Hanson bought 200 shares of Massachusetts Steam 8% $100 par value preferred for $120 a share. What is the current yield?

$100 par × 8% = $8   annual dividend per share

$$\frac{\$8}{\$120} = 6.67\% \quad \text{current yield}$$

The current yield on stock is a rate of return measure that focuses only on annual dividend income. It does not take into consideration another important aspect of the return on stock, that is, the gain or loss incurred when stock is sold. Although the yield to maturity formulas previously discussed can be adapted to solve this problem, it is beyond the scope of this text to do so.

Project 67 may be done now.

PROJECT 67   RATE OF RETURN PROBLEMS

1.   The TV Electronics Corporation issued (sold to investors) 1,000 twenty-year bonds with a face value of $1,000 per bond and with a coupon rate or nominal yield of 6%. The bonds were issued on April 1, 1977, at 103. Interest is payable semiannually on April 1 and October 1. (a) What is the total amount of interest the company is required to pay on October 1, 1977? (b) What will be the premium amortization amounts on all the bonds during 1977 and during 1978? (c) What will be the total bond carrying values on December 31, 1977, and on December 31, 1978? (d) What is the current yield? (e) What is the yield to maturity?

2. On January 1, 1978, Bill Smith paid $920 for a 8% $1,000 face value bond that matures in 10 years. Interest is payable semiannually on January 1 and July 1. (a) How much interest will he receive on July 1, 1978? (b) What will be the discount accumulation amounts during 1978 and during 1979? (c) What will be the bond-carrying values on December 31, 1978, and on December 31, 1979? (d) What is the current yield? (e) What is the yield to maturity?

3. Tom Lanza recently bought 20 shares of the common stock of School Books, Inc., for $50 a share. The company is expected to pay a quarterly dividend of $0.75 a share. What is the current yield on the stock?

4. Using the facts in Problem 3, what would be the current yield if Tom had purchased the stock for $60 a share?

5. Al Fuller just bought 200 shares of Texas Tea, Inc., 6% preferred stock, $100 par, for $120 a share. What is the current yield on the stock?

6. Using the facts in Problem 5, what would be the current yield if Al had acquired the stock for $100 a share?